Professor Fred C. Pampel teaches in the sociology department of the University of Iowa.

Professor John B. Williamson teaches in the sociology department of Boston College.

The Arnold and Caroline Rose Monograph Series
of the American Sociological Association

Age, class, politics, and the welfare state

For other titles in this series, turn to p. 200.

Age, class, politics, and the welfare state

Fred C. Pampel
The University of Iowa

John B. Williamson
Boston College

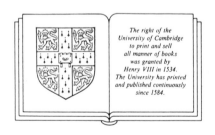

*The right of the
University of Cambridge
to print and sell
all manner of books
was granted by
Henry VIII in 1534.
The University has printed
and published continuously
since 1584.*

Cambridge University Press

Cambridge
New York   Port Chester   Melbourne   Sydney

Published by the Press Syndicate of the University of Cambridge
The Pitt Building, Trumpington Street, Cambridge CB2 1RP
40 East 20th Street, New York, NY 10011, USA
10 Stanford Road, Oakleigh, Melbourne 3166, Australia

First published 1989

Printed in the United States of America

Library of Congress Cataloging-in-Publication Data
Pampel, Fred C.
Age, class, politics, and the welfare state
/ Fred C. Pampel, John B. Williamson.
p. cm. – (The Arnold and Caroline Rose monograph series of
the American Sociological Association)
Bibliography: p.
Includes index.
ISBN 0-521-37223-2
1. Public welfare. 2. Welfare state. 3. Social conflict.
4. Aged – Political activity. I. Williamson, John B. II. Title.
III. Series.
HV37.P28 1989
361 – dc19   88–27028
                                                          CIP

British Library Cataloguing in Publication Data
Pampel, Fred C.
Age, class, politics, and the welfare state
– (The Arnold and Caroline Rose monograph series of the American
Sociological Association)
1. Social equality
I. Title II. Williamson, John B. III.
Series
305

ISBN 0-521-37223-2 hard covers

For Jane, Seth, Sarah, and Steven
F.C.P.

For J.W.W. and M.E.W.
J.B.W.

Contents

Tables

Preface

Current orthodoxy views expansion of the welfare state as the result of conflict between labor (i.e., unions) and capital and the political parties that represent each class. Theorists differ on whether worker or capital interests drive the growth of welfare spending, whether benefits improve the conditions of the poor or the environment for capital accumulation, and whether class-based parties differ in their ability to implement redistributive programs. Still, the unquestioned acceptance of capital and labor as the major actors in the welfare state characterizes the field today. The neo-Marxist, class-based approaches to government, politics, and stratification have replaced the more nonideological, apolitical, and technocratic views common during the 1950s and correctly emphasize conflict, politics, and the power resources of social factions. At the same time, the current literature has come to incorporate politics and the state as crucial components of the welfare state. Whatever the conceptualization of the stratification system and the division of interests within the welfare state, the mechanisms by which classes, groups, and actors influence public policy must include politics and the state. Current efforts by neo-Marxists and others in this regard have improved on earlier technological and class-based functionalist theories that emphasize the automatic response of societies and governments to technological and demographic change or to crises of capital accumulation.

The conventional views, however, may fail to deal with groups crucial to the growth of the welfare state that do not fit the division between labor and capital. The growth of middle-class occupations (i.e., contradictory class locations), the political fragmentation and economic embourgeoisement of workers, and the emergence of collective action by ascriptive groups create conceptual problems for traditional class-based theories. In our view, these problems are particularly acute in the lack of attention paid to the role of the aged in the welfare state. Since the welfare state is understood in terms of conflict between labor and capital, the aged are treated as an afterthought, either as passive beneficiaries or as victims (depending on the theory) of class conflict. Given the huge size of the programs for the aged and the obvious interest of older persons in the level of pension and medical benefits, the aged might profitably be seen as representative of the growing importance of middle-class and ascriptive groups that transcend traditional class boundaries. Other middle-class groups, as well as ethnic, racial, linguistic, and sex-based ascriptive groups, are equally important in understanding the structure of stratification, but in the arena of the welfare state, where programs traditionally deal with problems faced during the latter part of the life cycle, the aged become particularly important. Similarly, political theories of the welfare state are weakened by their neglect of the political aspects of ascriptive movements, middle-class power, and the influence of the aged on policy. Po itics is clearly important to the welfare state, but not only in the form of conflict between class-based parties representing labor and capital. The diversity of interest groups, parties, and state bureaucracies in the political process must be considered as well.

These notions about the political importance of ascriptive, middle-class groups – particularly the aged – for the growth of the welfare state in political democracies drew us into this broader study. First, we suspected that the aged, acting as an interest group in democratic societies, may politically influence spending, particularly pension expenditures, but also spending for health care, disability, and other programs. The aged and age structure may, in fact, be the most important influences on the growth of the modern welfare state. Second, perhaps the role played by the aged, pensions, and health care in the growth of welfare spending limits the redistributive consequences of social welfare spending. As a heterogeneous group, the aged display nearly as much dispersion of income as the nonaged and, in high-income nations, come primarily from middle-income groups. Pension and medical benefits may thus do little to redistribute income to the lower class but may transfer income within classes and across generations. Third, if the aged influence social welfare spending by more than mere numbers, and have some political importance, democratic politics and nonclass interest groups may be central to the growth of the welfare state and social equality. Public policy may reflect more than the conflict between classes and class-based political parties; it also may reflect age, ethnic, sex, and other ascriptive divisions that cut across class boundaries.

This book represents our attempt to develop and test these ideas, as well as the alternative views so much more common in the literature. To do so, we analyze the cross-national patterns and trends in welfare spending and social equality, and consider the causal roles of democratic politics, age structure, class power, and a variety of other characteristics of nations and states. We find support for our original speculations, but also find that much else is involved in the growth of the welfare state. Distinguishing among the many different types of welfare spending and the groups to which they are targeted shows the complexity of the processes we study. In what follows, we lay out our understanding of the welfare state, indicating where our guiding theses receive support, where they need qualification, and where they must be supplemented by other perspectives. Still, the evidence to follow in support of our arguments warrants some reassessment of current understandings of the welfare state.

Our approach to the causes and consequences of the social welfare state is decidedly theoretical, comparative, and empirical. There may be thousands of empirical studies and millions of tabular figures on the welfare state, but there are lamentably few efforts to make theoretical sense of these varied and overwhelming empirical results. We attempt to organize, compare, and evaluate competing theories of the structure of the welfare state and its connection to other aspects of the stratification system. Testing these theories requires comparative data and analysis. Since nations vary in economic, demographic, political, social, and welfare policies, they are the logical unit for the study of welfare spending. Without a comparative framework and data, our understanding of public welfare policy in the United States or any other single nation must be limited. Even with comparative data, however, previous studies have been hampered by reliance on single cross sections of nations, failure to analyze diverse groups of nations separately, or avoidance of multivariate analysis and generalization altogether. We explicitly attempt to test causal propositions and establish empirical generalizations using multivariate techniques for data from advanced industrial democracies from 1950 to 1980 and from developing nations for a shorter time span, 1965 to 1975. In short, we hope to offer a useful classification and explication of the theories, along with thorough and systematic analysis of comparative data.

We were not able to study as many components of the welfare state as we would have liked. A wide variety of government programs and expenditures are often included in studies of public policy, and scholars often focus on the form of benefits and the right to coverage, along with the resources spent. We limit our own study to levels of spending for those social welfare or social security programs designed to protect households from loss of income and earnings. Other types of government spending and variations in the form of benefit entitlements require different data, models, and theories. Similarly, we were able to study only some of the consequences of the welfare state: those relating to social equality. The importance of these consequences is obvious, but there are others that might also be studied. The effects of welfare spending on economic growth, productivity, and public attitudes, for instance, are beyond the scope of this study.

Nonetheless, even with these limitations, our interests in the social welfare state, its causes, and its consequences for social equality reflect the concern of many others. The welfare state is the subject of hundreds of empirical studies, political tracts, and theoretical expositions. In response to problems of the welfare state experienced by many of the world's high-income democracies, a renewed interest in theories of the state and social welfare has emerged in the last few years. This provides a fruitful environment for a new approach to the topics, an empirical evaluation of current theories, and our study of the influence of age structure, interests, and democratic politics. We present yet another study of the welfare state, but one that we hope can add substantially to the already large literature on the topic.

We acknowledge with gratitude the comments colleagues have offered on all or part of the manuscript and the assistance of graduate students in gathering the data. We have benefited from the criticisms and suggestions of Jill Quadagno, Robin Stryker, Rosemary Gartner, James Price, Ed Lawler, Charles Mueller, Charles Derber, Kenneth Branco, Paul Schervish, Erich Weede, Vijayan Pillai, Ken Bollen, and Catherine Zimmer. The critical but encouraging comments of two reviewers and the editor of the Rose Monograph Series, Ernest Campbell, all of whom devoted considerable care and effort to the full manuscript, were particularly helpful. Finally, we have benefited over the years from the research assistance of Sookja Park, Soon-Heung Kim, Catherine Zimmer, Anna Petronzio, Debra Kattler, Emily Kearns, Larry Zaborski, and Xiaoxi Tong. We thank all these colleagues. The research has been funded by the National Institute on Aging, Grant No. AG01580. Both The University of Iowa and Boston College have greatly aided the completion of the manuscript by releasing us from teaching duties. Finally, we would like to thank our families, not for allowing us unlimited time in which to devote ourselves single-mindedly to the book, but for offering the joyful alternative to work that has kept this book in perspective.

Parts of Chapter 3 appeared in the *American Journal of Sociology* (Fred C. Pampel and John B. Williamson. 1988. "Welfare Spending in Advanced Industrial Democracies, 1950–1980." 93:1424–56) and parts of Chapter 6 appeared in *Demography* (Fred C. Pampel and Vijayan K. Pillai. 1986. "Patterns and Determinants of Infant Mortality in Developed Nations, 1950–1975." 23:525–42). We acknowledge the University of Chicago Press and the Population Association of America for permission to use this material.

1. The welfare state: some neglected considerations

The social welfare state has come to play a crucial – perhaps dominant – role in the study of stratification. Social welfare spending is meant to reshape and limit market-based inequality and increasingly mediates how economic structures translate into social equality. The importance of the welfare state is shown not only by the huge amounts of income transferred by governments, or by the heated political debate over its effectiveness, but also by the large number of studies on the topic that exist in the social scientific literature. The fiscal problems experienced by many of the world's high-income democracies have renewed the interest of scholars in the welfare state, led to new theories of its causes and consequences, and placed researchers in the midst of political debates. All this effort and interest has not led to consensus; the politics and ideologies of the welfare state have become more contentious, and the social scientific literature has become increasingly disorganized and fragmented. Behind the bewildering array of arguments, findings, and conclusions, however, lies a set of three interrelated debates that together help to define the approaches taken to understanding the welfare state.

One debate concerns the relative influences of economic-demographic development and class structure as sources of the growth of welfare spending and as bases of group interests and mobilization. On one side, early theories of the welfare state focused on the standardizing effects of spreading industrial technology (Kerr et al., 1964). One effect is the growth of the social welfare state, which deals with the needs of groups less easily employed in industrial societies – the less educated, the aged, and victims of declining occupations and industries – when family supports are not available (Wilensky, 1975). These theories stem from a functionalist tradition and are subject to criticisms applied to functionalist theories in general (e.g., overemphasis on equilibrium, naively optimistic predictions). Other arguments also focus on the crucial role of technology in the welfare state, but without the functionalist assumptions. According to Lenski (1966), industrial technology leads to an educated labor force that controls valuable, specialized knowledge and demands political power. The resulting growth of political democracy allows the masses to combine politically

1

against the elite in competition for resources and leads to higher welfare spending. Despite their differences, however, industrialism theory and Lenski's ecological-evolutionary theory represent similar responses to the question of what determines social welfare expenditures. Both place crucial importance on technology and economic structures and on concomitant changes in population structure.

In contrast, theories from a Marxist tradition, in which class structure and class struggle play a pivotal role, reemerged during the 1960s and 1970s. These theories agree on the failure of other theories to address the class structure of society, but versions differ on just what class characteristics explain the rise in social welfare expenditure. Some see welfare as the result of the concentration of monopoly capital (O'Connor, 1973), others as the result of the strength of the working class and leftist government control (Stephens, 1979; Korpi, 1983). Either way, the structure of classes in a society and the distribution of economic and political power among them, rather than demographic structures and levels of resources, determine levels of social welfare spending and equality.

The debate over these views of the welfare state stems from long-standing theoretical traditions going back to Durkheim and Marx. In more recent times, the debate has taken an empirical turn in dozens of cross-national studies. This work first supported the industrialism arguments but more recently has provided evidence for class theories, which have emerged as the current orthodoxy. Yet, for reasons to be discussed later, support for any of the theories is limited. The existing empirical studies neglect important explanations and variables, suffer from methodological problems, and, in general, fail to test adequately the theories they claim to test. Further study of the issues – with more careful specification of all relevant theories and improved data, measures, and analytic techniques – is needed.

The second debate centers on the redistributive consequences of social welfare spending for social equality and quality of life among low-status groups in societies. Scholars on one side of the issue state that the effects are positive – equality and quality of life improve due to the welfare state. They claim that welfare does much of what it is intended to do: benefit those with the least income and economic power in society, such as the unemployed, poor, aged, and working class. Accordingly, advocates of this view, primarily from the center and left, support high taxation and government spending. The left views continued growth of the welfare state as the progression of capitalism toward socialism and equality (Stephens, 1979). Cuts in social welfare spending represent attempts by capital to regain lost wealth from the working class and reduce equality (Piven and Cloward, 1982). Others, who reject the class struggle assumptions and the goal of socialism, likewise support welfare expenditures because they contribute to the functioning and integration of society and improve the quality of life of its most deprived members (Wilensky, 1975).

On the other side of the issue, many suggest that the welfare state does little to redistribute income or help those in need. Instead, welfare spending dampens short-run discontent among the working class and poor without improving the long-term life chances of these groups. The welfare state may benefit monopoly capital, which requires government spending for continued capital accumulation, or the welfare state may benefit a variety of government bureaucracies, professionals, and other middle-income groups. Even if benefits go to the needy, they fail to redistribute income to the extent that they are based on regressive tax policies. Advocates of these arguments form an unexpected coalition of the right and far left. One group sees the reduction of social welfare as increasing class consciousness and the social protest needed for change; the other group sees the result as increasing incentives for upward mobility of individuals. Despite different political orientations and strategies for improving the position of the poor, these diverse groups share the view that welfare spending maintains or increases inequality.

This debate over the efficacy of the welfare state and the causes of inequality has engendered much political conflict. Even had the empirical literature offered clear support for one side or the other, opinions may have changed little because of the strong political beliefs involved. As it stands, the evidence is mixed: Some studies, mostly based on cross-national comparisons, emphasize the meliorative effects of economic development, whereas other studies, mostly based on survey data for the United States, favor the egalitarian impact of welfare spending. Both types of studies, however, often suffer from the same methodological problems as the studies of the causes of social welfare spending, and lack systematic specification and testing of the theories. The question warrants more empirical study.

The third debate is over the ability of democratic politics and political parties to play an important role – independent of economic and class structures – in determining levels of social welfare spending and social equality. One view claims that democratic politics and political parties have little independent influence on government policies or inequality beyond the influence of productive, economic, or population structures. Political action reduces to industrial structure or class relations. The versions of how this occurs vary: The state may be an instrument of the dominant class (Miliband, 1969), may be relatively constrained by the economic or political configuration of the class structure (Poulantzas, 1973), or may more or less automatically respond to the needs of industry and groups in distress (Kerr et al., 1964; Wilensky, 1975). Yet, all versions locate the crucial causal dominance in the technological, economic, and productive relations in society rather than in the political arena.

Another view attributes more importance to political democracy and parties and considerable autonomy to the state. The state is not reducible to structural factors, and can independently influence class and economic relations. State policy may generally favor the dominant class, but under certain conditions the working class may be able to wrest political control of the government from capital – even though it lacks economic power. Alternatively, it may be that smaller, more numerous and diverse interest groups obtain and manipulate political power to their benefit (Olson, 1982); in fact, the state itself may become an autonomous actor influencing welfare spending (Skocpol, 1985a). For a variety of reasons, then, the state may act against the economic interests of the dominant capitalist class, and political parties and democratic politics may play a crucial role in explaining social welfare and equality.

Much of the empirical work of this topic has been devoted to proving that a connection exists between democratic political procedures (simple democracy) or leftist control of the government (social democracy) and inequality. The consensus is that the former has little influence, whereas the latter proves crucially important. However, the connection between politics and the potential for social change in the structure of inequality may be more complex than is recognized by these studies. Structurally deterministic views of politics agree that income redistribution is not possible in the absence of further technological development or change in productive relations and that neither change is likely to occur through short-term political activity or partisan policies alone. Yet, some determinists see technological change and the welfare spending it spawns as conducive to greater equality, whereas others claim just the opposite. For those advocating autonomy, democratic political procedures may favor numerically large but economically less powerful groups, and public policies may reduce inequality through higher taxes and redistributive policies. By the same token, however, democratic politics may retard change: The demands of mass constituencies may just as likely favor middle-income groups and maintain the existing structure of inequality. The complexity and diversity of the debate over the role of politics in the welfare state and social equality suggest that, to test the arguments adequately, empirical studies need to do more than search for simple relationships.

In summary, debates over the structural causes of the growth of welfare spending, the redistributive consequences of public programs, and the underlying importance of democratic political procedures and parties address major questions confronting stratification research and topics of political debate. Further, cross-classification of the positions taken in the debates defines the major theoretical approaches to the welfare state (as we discuss in more detail in Chapter 2). Theories that make similar predictions concerning the role of class or industrialism variables in determining social welfare expenditures make different predictions concerning the consequences of social welfare spending and the role of politics. A full understanding of the welfare state and a complete test of the theories require that all three issues be studied together.

Some neglected considerations

Despite its huge size, the literature has failed to deal adequately with some crucial components of the welfare state. Certain changes in the nature of the welfare state – the growth of the aged population and their influence, the limited efficacy of public spending, and the rise of interest group politics – suggest that reconsideration of the debates and theoretical approaches is necessary. With the perspective of recent trends, it may be that dominant views (1) underemphasize the importance of the aged and middle-class groups, (2) overstate the effectiveness of social welfare spending relative to changes in the structure of the economy and wages in reducing social inequality, and (3) overemphasize class-based politics at the expense of interest group democratic politics.

Role of the aged. Although explanations of the welfare state commonly focus on labor, technology, monopoly capital, and the political parties that represent these groups and forces, they seldom attend to the influence of the aged population or age structure on welfare spending. Since the aged do not have clear ties to labor or capital and represent, at least in industrial societies, a diverse constituency centered in the middle of the stratification system, it is not clear how the aged population fits class-based concepts and theories of the welfare state. Indeed, the neglect of the aged as a group with resources and capacities that can influence public policy reflects a broader failure of the welfare state literature to deal with middle-class groups.

If for no other reason, the aged may be important for the sheer size of the programs that benefit them. Benefits paid for retirement, old age, survivors, disability, and medical care comprise the major source expenditures of the welfare state. In the advanced industrial democracies in 1980, over 60 percent of all social welfare expenditures went for two programs – pensions and medical care (International Labour Office, 1985). In the United States from 1960 to 1978, federal budget expenditures for the aged rose from 13 to 24 percent; as a percentage of the gross national product (GNP), such expenditures rose from 2.5 to 5.3, an increase of 112 percent (Clark and Menefee, 1981; Torrey, 1982). Moreover, by adding the substantial tax subsidies that go primarily to the wealthy and middle-class aged, federal support for the aged more than doubles (Nelson, 1983).

Programs for the nonaged, such as public assistance and unemployment, are tiny compared to programs for the aged. The size of the benefits paid to the aged places them at the center of the debate over the welfare state.

In addition, a number of characteristics may make the aged effective participants in the politics of the welfare state. First, unlike nearly all other groups faced with the decision to work or not to work, the aged are urged not to work. Employers encourage (or require) older workers to retire, institutionalized norms ease the change in status, and governments pay for leisure time. What is more, the shift from work to leisure and the government benefits that go with it are legitimately accepted as deserved. Coughlin (1979), in his study of public opinion in several nations, found stronger support for public pensions than for other social welfare programs. In the United States, public support for pensions is so strong that many desire tax increases rather than cuts in benefits (Tomasson, 1984). Issues of distributional justice are seldom raised over the benefits of the aged, even though current beneficiaries at all income levels receive more than they have invested in and earned from the system (Burkhauser and Warlick, 1981). This contrasts with the circumstances of the unemployed, disabled, and family dependents, all of whom suffer a stigma from loss of work and benefit payments.

Second, the ascriptive characteristics of the aged make them special. Unlike other recipients of social welfare programs, the aged occupy a status identified by biological, age-related characteristics. These characteristics make for relatively easy group consciousness, recognition of group membership, and organization into interest groups (Cutler, 1977, 1981). The emergence of age-segregated housing and communities may further contribute to organization of the aged. Many have noted the resurgence of ethnic, racial, and gender movements, all based on solidarity among ascriptively defined groups (Nielsen, 1985). The aged may be part of this resurgence, and their influence on public policy may increase as a result (Fox, 1981).

Third, as an ascriptive characteristic, old age is unique in that nonaged persons expect eventually to pass through this stage. Many may identify their own interests with those of the aged, which may prevent a backlash against increasing benefits for the aged. As Preston (1984) notes, this situation contrasts sharply with that of children. Since adults have already passed through childhood, they have less direct interest in increasing benefits for the young. Thus, the influence of the aged is increased by the tacit support of other age groups. They obtain special legitimacy that women, children, minorities, and disabled persons do not.

Fourth, the structure of the family in modern societies makes the aged an independent political force and social group. Davis and van den Oever (1981) argue that in societies where the family is the dominant institution, family solidarity prevents the aged from emerging as a separate interest group. Changes in the nature of the family – the geographic, residential, and social separation of age groups in the family – allow old age to become an independent force in modern societies (Foner, 1974).

Finally, several characteristics of the aged may make them particularly effective users of political power. They have among the highest voting rates of all age groups (Wolfinger and Rosenstone, 1980; Hudson and Strate, 1985), and the increasing education and political experience of recently aged cohorts make them more sophisticated politically than previous ones (Neugarten, 1974). Organizations for the aged have been able to recruit members through the use of selective incentives such as travel, insurance, and pharmaceutical discounts (Hudson, 1978) and use that base to represent well the interests of the aged in Washington (Cutler, 1981). Although the aged may not have a generalized ideology common to all, and although there is much diversity in their status and political beliefs, they appear able to unite with respect to specific issues concerning government benefits. In fact, diversity of background with strong representation of middle-class members provides a particularly strong position for collective action (Nielsen, 1987). Politicians from all parties must remain sensitive to a group like the aged.

As a result, the political influence and mobilization of the aged have grown over the years – at least in the United States (Pratt, 1976; Fox, 1981; Williamson et al., 1982). By the 1980s, interest groups of the aged included coalitions of over 300 organizations and over 20 million members, and supported the circulation of weekly cable programs and newspaper columns reaching additional millions (*Wall Street Journal,* 1985). Since these organizations have fought politically to maintain benefits, the elderly have been least affected by the budget cuts of the 1980s (Storey, 1983; Moon, 1986). The political role of the aged was demonstrated further in recent presidential elections, where major candidates vied over who would best protect the financial interests of the aged. Similar changes and patterns may be equally likely in other advanced industrial, democratic nations.

All these characteristics of the aged may affect welfare spending and equality. Benefits for already large programs for the aged have grown dramatically in recent years among advanced industrial nations, as they have been tied to inflation, allowed earlier retirement and receipt of benefits, and become available to more groups (Social Security Administration, 1984). As a result, funding problems have emerged in nearly all developed nations (Fischer, 1978). Future beneficiaries cannot be funded at the same rate as current beneficiaries without major tax increases (Rosa, 1982). Benefit and funding provision changes in recent years in the United States and other nations project a funding balance but assume the creation of a surplus in the next several decades to deal with the deficit that will occur with retirement of the baby boom generations (Storey, 1983). Some doubt that politicians, given the political climate and demands for spending, will allow the needed surplus to grow (Boskin, 1986).[1]

Despite large outlays, the success of the system in reducing inequality has been less than expected. A possible outcome of the political influence of the aged has been a middle-class bias in public pension and related programs. In the United States, initial backers of Social Security, hoping to gain middle-class political support, intentionally limited redistributive initiatives in the legislation (Cates, 1983). Such a strategy has been maintained to keep political support for the program strong (Cohen and Friedman, 1972), and the resulting redistributive impact on the poor has been small (Burkhauser and Warlick, 1981; Browne and Olson, 1983). Because of the need to appeal politically to the middle class, public policies for the aged have created two quite different worlds of aging for the poor and the nonpoor (Crystal, 1982).

The end result of programs for the aged has been to increase the mean level of income of the aged but to maintain relatively high levels of inequality within the aged population. Studies demonstrate that, controlling for household size, income levels of the aged approach those of the nonaged (Danziger et al., 1984; Smeeding and Torrey, 1986). Since recent cohorts in the United States receive benefits twice the size of their contributions and a typical rate of return (Burkhauser and Warlick, 1981), much improvement in the income of the aged in recent years is due to rising pension benefits. Despite higher mean income, however, the spread of income of the aged around the mean remains broad, with dispersion among the aged being larger than that between the aged and nonaged (Quinn, 1987). Little redistribution occurs across income groups when current benefits are compared to past contributions, even with progressive rates of return (Burkhauser and Warlick, 1981). Further, the cross-national figures of Smeeding and Torrey (1986) show that the ranking of levels of income inequality among the aged in six Western nations is closely related to the levels among the nonaged, and that in many nations the absolute level of income inequality among the aged is higher than that among the nonaged.

In summary, the aged may have emerged as a politically powerful group that can influence spending in ways that other welfare state recipients cannot. Their political influence may raise spending for certain programs but, at the same time, may maintain existing levels of inequality. Unfortunately, the influence of the aged on welfare spending has not been carefully studied. Many ignore the aged altogether, and others explicitly deny their importance – all without rigorous empirical evidence. Clearly, the field needs a thorough examination of the role of the aged in welfare state spending and social equality.

Structural sources of social inequality. If the level of welfare spending depends on both the demographic structure of society and the operation of democratic procedures it implies limits on the redistributive efficacy of spending. Programs in political democracies are most likely to be directed toward more powerful middle-income groups and to be based on contributions that preserve wage inequality. Means-tested programs for less powerful poor and unemployed persons are likely to comprise only a small part of total spending. As a result, huge government expenditures show little ability to reduce inequality substantially. As Page (1983:211) concludes in a thorough study of the effects of government spending in the United States: "Social welfare policies, though taking up a large part of the budget, have had surprisingly little redistributive effect. The bulk of money goes for Social Security and other retirement insurance plans that smooth out people's lifetime incomes but do not greatly increase equality across individuals. Much the same is true of the biggest health program, Medicare. Programs (like AFDC and Food Stamps) that are more sharply targeted for the poor are quite small by comparison and have been the first to lose out in budget cuts." Page notes in this context that government spending more likely transfers income within classes than across classes. Intraclass (or intergenerational) transfers involve life-cycle redistribution in which the relative income standing of individuals at particular ages remains unchanged. Interclass (or intergenerational) transfers shift upward the standing of the poor relative to the more well-off in the same age range. The bulk of transfer programs, being based on contributions and social insurance spending schemes, represent within-class redistribution and may do little to improve the relative income share of the poor (Page, 1983).[2] The redistributive limitations of welfare spending can be reduced with generous means-tested programs or flat-rate universal benefits, but many countries do not have such programs. Contribution-based benefit programs or low-benefit, flat-rate schemes are much more common (Myles, 1984).

LeGrand (1982) makes much the same point concerning the ability of public spending for social services such as health, education, housing, and transportation to achieve equality. In Britain, the growth of such services, either for free or at subsidized prices over the last several decades, may have exacerbated inequality. Because of their advantages in dealing with service agencies and their greater political influence, middle-income groups reap a disproportionate share of the services and appear better able to translate the services into better health, educational attainment, and home ownership (status differentials in mortality, for instance, have changed little since the founding of the National Health Service; LeGrand, 1982). In fact, among the groups likely to benefit most from public services are the professionals and administrative workers who staff hospitals and welfare agencies. Given the existence of structural inequality, public services reflect rather than surmount inequalities.

Although many factors are involved, political interests that divert government spending from the poor may be one source of the persistence of inequality. Stigler (1970:1) favors this view in his statement of Director's Law: "Public expenditures are made for the primary benefit of the middle-classes, and financed by taxes borne in considerable part by the poor and the rich." This implies that the failure of government programs to redistribute income results from voter coalitions among the large middle-income groups in high-income political democracies. Some make even stronger criticisms of the welfare state, namely, that public benefits for the poor create dependency and harm chances for mobility (Gilder, 1981; Murray, 1984). More likely, benefits in political democracies may seldom if ever reach the poor in sufficient amounts to change the level of income inequality; or, if they do reach the poor, may fail in the long run to change the shape of the distribution. The poor may be better able to compete economically and productively for growing numbers of jobs than they are able to compete politically for government transfers (Olson, 1982:175).

Similar processes may be at work in low- and middle-income nations, where the level of government spending and the ability to target benefits to the poor are lower than in high-income nations. In one of the rare studies of social security in the Third World, Midgley (1984) argues that programs are generally based on regressive taxation, and benefit more powerful civil servant elites and union members rather than the majority of citizens. The urban bias so common in most government programs in the Third World (Lipton, 1977) likewise is shown in the distribution of social welfare benefits, where the rural poor are especially unlikely to be covered by programs. Such programs are unable, especially with economic limitations on benefit levels and the sharp cleavages in power and influence, to change levels of inequality substantially (Midgely, 1984).

If not from government spending, improvements in social and economic inequality must come from structural changes in the economy, technology, and skill-based wage differentials (Lenski, 1966; Williamson and Lindert, 1980). Political forces may influence the level and type of welfare spending, but economic ones may ultimately determine the level of income inequality that precedes growth of the welfare state. Yet, a simple point concerning the distribution of a society's rewards – that, above a certain threshold of development, the more rewards available to a society, the more equally the rewards are distributed and the more go to low-status groups – has been subject to a long-standing and heated debate. Many now claim that social equality is spuriously associated with technological and economic advance and is more directly determined by other factors. Trade dependency, government redistributive efforts, social democratic or socialist governments, sexist family structures, and monopolization of capital are causally dominant and render any effect that development may have on social welfare and inequality nil. Indeed, comparative theoretical and empirical work in the 1970s can be seen as an attack on the role of economic growth.

Part of the problem with economic development arguments, and a basis for the attacks during the 1970s, rests with the excessively optimistic and exaggerated claims made by functionalists during the 1950s and 1960s. Scholars predicted the quick spread of the industrial mode of production, continued economic growth, and convergence toward Western models of social structure, politics, and psychological makeup (Kerr, 1983). They further predicted the end of class struggle, ideology, the working class, the power elite, poverty, and scarcity – all to be replaced by economic growth, pragmatic problem solving, technical planning, embourgeoisement, and equality.[3] These arguments have been harshly criticized for their naive functionalism and failed predictions. A crucial error was made either in misstating the current situation in the 1950s and early 1960s or in assuming that current trends would continue indefinitely.

In rejecting these arguments during the 1970s, however, critics tended to discount the benefits of economic growth altogether. Scholars in the 1970s argued that because of the international economic power of core nations, multinational corporations were able to withdraw the profits of economic growth and prevent improved redistribution of income in developing nations (e.g., Bornschier Chase-Dunn, and Rubinson, 1978). Others argued that developed nations also faced a permanent structural economic crisis, an irreversible decline in their standard of living, and an inevitable rise of inequality (Blumberg, 1980; Thurow, 1981).

Despite the critics, cross-sectional studies of the distribution of income have shown the clear existence of a curvilinear relationship (Kuznets, 1955, 1963; Jackman, 1975; Bollen and Jackman, 1985). As Lenski (1966) suggested, inequality rises initially with economic growth at the lowest levels, declines with continued growth, and then levels off at the highest income levels. Such a pattern fits the historical experience of the United States and Great Britain (Williamson and Lindert, 1980; Williamson, 1985) and is consistent with the recent experiences of Taiwan and other developing countries (Barrett and Whyte, 1982; Berger, 1986). The evidence is by no means complete, as other nations (e.g., Brazil, South Korea) have shown little improvement in their income distribution in recent decades, despite economic growth, and inequality in the most developed nations has been resistant to further change. Economic growth may not be sufficient for reduced inequality – it must be labor intensive so as to increase the wages of low-skilled workers and encourage structural differentiation (Berger,

1986) – but it still provides repeated examples of its benefits for reducing social inequality.

In the last several decades, then, the views of economic development and growth have come full circle. In rejecting the optimistic views offered during the 1950s and 1960s, advocates of the welfare state claimed that economic development concentrates wealth among the upper and middle classes, and that its benefits diffuse slowly (if at all) and trickle down to the poor. Continued inequality in the face of massive increases in government social welfare spending over the last two decades, however, suggests the need to reassess the benefits of structural change in the economy. A long, valuable tradition that considers the relationship between technology and social equality (e.g., Lenski, 1966) has been surprisingly quiescent in recent years and deserves reconsideration.

Interest group competition and class politics. A third theme or issue to which we give particular attention concerns the relative roles of interest groups and classes in the politics of the social welfare state. The literature on the welfare state focuses almost exclusively on class politics, neglecting the importance of political competition and collective action among a variety of increasingly powerful nonclass interest groups. Changing this focus does not mean reasserting traditional pluralist views. Earlier functionalist conceptions of pluralism postulated balanced competition and accommodation (i.e., equilibrium) among interest groups. These groups have the power to veto policies that they strongly oppose, that are particularly harmful to them, and that might disrupt the balance of power. The social policies that emerge from these pluralistic processes represent compromises among multiple groups. The state performs a regulatory role, setting and enforcing the rules for competition among the groups and preventing excessive advantages from accruing to particular groups.

More recent views of interest group competition reject the equilibrium view of traditional pluralism. The growth of the welfare state has seen the dispersion of benefits to a wide variety of groups that come to act in favor of continued or increased expenditures (politicization, in the terms of Griffin and Leicht, 1986). Like older pluralist views, more recent views of interest groups claim that they cannot be reduced to clearly organized classes. Unlike the older views, more recent views claim that group competition creates political divisiveness, loss of social control, and ungovernability rather than equilibrating cooperation among groups for the societal good. The collective actions and political demands of varied interest groups are often contradictory, narrow, and harmful to other groups. This pushes up government costs, encourages wasteful and duplicative spending, and replaces incentives for economic action with incentives for political action.

The ultimate result is to create difficulties in funding or controlling expenditures, subsidize powerful interests, and slow economic growth (Olson, 1982).[4]

There are several reasons to suppose that the importance of interest group competition has been increasing. First, traditional political divisions along class lines may have declined (noted by Lipset, 1981, in his updated discussion of the democratic class struggle). The growth of rightist parties in several nations, declining union membership and power, and the support of many working-class members for rightist parties contradict the expectations of class-based theories. Most claim that these changes result from the process of embourgeoisement, rising income, declining size of unionized industries, or the emergence of post-materialist values (Bell, 1973; Inglehart, 1977; Kelley, McAllister, and Mughan, 1985). As scarcity diminishes in advanced industrial nations, economic factors become less decisive sources of political conflict, and class-based voting declines (Inglehart, 1987). The growth of the ideologically and organizationally fragmented middle class thus blunts the division between labor and capital (Hicks and Swank, 1984). Political parties may still remain important as the organizational units of electoral support in the face of these changes; when judged on their ability to win elections, the major parties in advanced democracies are perhaps stronger than ever (Schlesinger, 1984). Yet, because of recent economic and social changes, parties appear increasingly less tied to traditional class constituencies and less able to maintain traditional loyalties.

Some argue even more strongly that class-based political parties have never effectively represented the sides in a democratic class struggle (Jackman, 1986). One reason is the inherent tendency of parties in democracies to move toward the center. Although philosophical differences exist among parties, they may not translate into clear, class-based policies and outcomes (Bollen and Jackman, 1985a). Party programs with concrete policy consequences risk offending established interests and large segments of voters who will strongly oppose the party and its actions. To attract large numbers of voters with divergent interests, all parties thus face pressures to move toward the center and downplay tangible policy outcomes (Downs, 1957). The pressure may be particularly acute for working-class parties whose strongest supporters – union members – are too few to gain political control of the government without alliances (Esping-Andersen, 1985a). Even if voters do elect a leftist party with a clear egalitarian program, few if any of the advanced industrial democracies have the majoritarian system that would allow the program to be directly implemented (Lijphart, 1984). Consensus, power sharing, and minority rights would disperse the power needed to translate majority votes into public policy without compromise (Jackman, 1986). As a result, compromising ideals in coalition governments is a necessary require-

ment for the rule of working-class and other parties (Przeworski, 1985). As Parkin (1971:103) states, "the history of European socialist parties is a chronicle of
gradual and continued dilution of these early radical aims."

A second indication of the importance of nonclass interest groups, particularly
in advanced industrial democracies, is the renewed collective political action of
racial, ethnic, religious, linguistic, gender, and age groups. Collective action on
the basis of ascriptive characteristics has increased, as shown by the resurgence
of ethnic and racial movements in Great Britain, Belgium, Canada, and the United
States, as well as by the growth of women's and aged persons' movements. This
has occurred despite functionalist and Marxist predictions that such movements
would decline. Nielsen (1985) argues that ethnic mobilization results from the
processes of economic, polity, and state modernization. Since modernization
incorporates culturally deprived groups into the advanced economy, extends political rights to them, and offers centralized state action in their support, it places
them in a position to compete more equally with dominant groups. Such competition increases ethnic group solidarity, collective action, and political activity.
Parkin (1979) criticizes Marxist and neo-Marxist theories for ignoring divisions
such as these, which cut across class divisions and blur class boundaries, and he
develops an alternative Weberian theory of inequality based on status as well as
class. Overall, then, ethnic- and ascriptive-based politics may increase in sa-
lience relative to class-based politics in modern democracies.

Third, besides encouraging the resurgence of ascriptive group solidarity and
collective action, economic change increases the heterogeneity of occupations,
industries, and economic groups – all of which produce social fractions within
broad classes (Hodson et al., 1988). Functionalists refer to this process as *differentiation*, but Marxists also refer to the *atomization* of interests of the capitalist
and working classes (Poulantzas, 1973). O'Connor (1973), for instance, claims
that the capitalist class tends to become more organized along interest group lines
over time. Associations of manufacturers, distributors, retailers, business clubs,
and industry groups demand special executive and legislative policies in their
favor. With such disparate demands, contradictory policies may emerge, planning becomes difficult, and capital accumulation suffers. Diverse businesses –
in the monopoly and competitive sectors, manufacturing and service industries,
or productive and information technologies – find it difficult to present a unified
front. Similar diversification of interests emerges among the working class. Form's
(1976, 1982, 1985) studies of blue-collar workers show internal class stratification, with divergence of interest among manual workers scattered among a variety of specialties. Combined with ascriptive characteristics, business and worker
differentiation creates a variety of smaller interest groups that transcend and fragment broad class categories. Hence, generalized class strategies of collective

action are increasingly replaced by specialist groups with more homogeneous interests and lower organizational costs for collective action (Nielsen, 1985).

Wright (1985) contrasts the clearly defined class positions of laborers and capitalists with those of workers in contradictory class locations, and Wright and Martin (1987) demonstrate the growth of the labor force in contradictory class locations. Middle-class positions cannot be subsumed under those of one of the other classes because the middle class has interests that are inherently contradictory to those of the other classes. In the area of welfare state politics, the structure of interests and the changes in class sizes suggest the growing importance of middle-class and mass constituencies (Hicks and Swank, 1984). Occupational change may thus blunt the conflict between labor and capital by increasing the importance and relevance to transfer policies of groups in contradictory class locations.

Finally, along with those for the growth of ascriptively based and middle-class groups and specialist strategies of collective action, another argument for the predominance of interest group competition comes from rational choice theory. Olson (1965) shows that individual commitment to collective action is irrational, since persons share the same benefits whether they are brought about by others or by their own action. Without some incentives, then, individuals will seldom act collectively. Smaller groups are better able to impose incentives on members, share larger benefits, and motivate collective action more effectively. Such groups are likely to be disproportionately influential in government policies, not only through elections but also through lobbying and pressure group tactics. Since associations for collective goods are difficult to establish, they tend to remain once established and to bring benefits not available to unorganized groups. Over time, other larger groups are able to exert the control needed for collective action, so group influences on the polity and economy accumulate. The longer the period of political freedom and stability, the greater the opportunity for the growth of group interests or distributional coalitions (Olson, 1982). In developed democracies, such conditions have existed at least since World War II, resulting in declining confidence in and identification with political parties and rising interest group action and financing (Berry, 1984).

Over recent decades, then, the politics of the welfare state have increasingly come to involve a large number of groups. Some are ascriptively based, some are organized interest groups, and some are unorganized but potentially effective voting blocs. The growing importance of these groups, with the concomitant decline in class-based party support, reflects a major component of state modernization: the extension of political rights to include the social right to share in the economic product (Gronbjerg, 1977; Zald, 1985). By guaranteeing extended social rights, the state incorporates a variety of new groups into the sphere of the government, encourages the growth of interest groups, and raises social welfare spending (Janowitz, 1976). Our goal, then, is to study the nature of the influence of democratic politics on welfare spending and equality, giving particular attention to changes in the role of class-based political parties, interest groups, and the extension of political rights.

Some definitions: social welfare spending and social equality

The processes we describe concerning the aged, inequality, and political conflict apply to some nations more than to others, and may fit the United States and other English-speaking nations with liberal, market-oriented cultures and traditions better than European nations with solidaristic and egalitarian values and institutions. The empirical question thus restated is: To what extent do our arguments fit the patterns of social welfare expenditure across a diverse sample of both high-income democracies and developing democracies and nondemocracies? We begin by defining and clarifying what we intend to study.

The social welfare state consists of the complex of government programs designed to guarantee or protect minimum standards of living of households against loss of income or earnings (Wilensky, 1975; International Labour Office, 1985). The minimum standard of living may be defined as an income floor appropriate for the size of the family or as adequate food, nutrition, housing, or medical care for all family members. Welfare payments may be in the form of cash or in-kind benefits, and they may be based on contributory insurance programs or direct assistance. The form of the spending is not as important as the fact that it protects against loss of income from such contingencies as unemployment, retirement and old age, sickness or injury, and family increase or breakup (Dixon, 1986; Rein and Rainwater, 1986). A popular view of welfare equates it with assistance for the poor, but such payments are only a small part of government transfers. The encompassing definition more accurately depicts the scope of welfare spending.[5] The International Labour Office (ILO) (1985) uses the term *social security spending* rather than *social welfare spending,* to make the connection between security and loss of income explicit. We rely here on the more commonly used term *social welfare,* but in so doing refer to the same programs defined by the ILO under the rubric social security.

This definition clearly delimits the types of spending we consider. It avoids excessively broad consideration of all government spending or even all civilian government spending. Measures so conceived mix a variety of diverse programs, from business subsidies to highway construction to regulatory control. The call for disaggregation of government spending into multiple components, each of which may then be modeled separately, has become strong in recent years (Shalev,

1983; Taylor, 1983; Rose, 1984a, 1986). We follow this approach by focusing explicitly on a subset of government spending.

Within the category of social welfare spending, we can still consider spending for specific programs such as pensions and old age, sickness and health care, work-related protection such as unemployment and occupational injury, and family allowances (Coughlin and Armour, 1983). Nations also differ in their reliance on contributory social insurance and noncontributory, means-tested public assistance programs. The former may favor the middle classes, which contribute most to the programs, whereas the latter are more directly targeted to the poor. Public assistance programs for the poor make up only a small part (usually less than 10 percent) of any nation's expenditures for social protection but warrant special attention by virtue of their redistributive goals. The determinants of different programs and the contribution each type of program makes to total spending deserve study.

By attempting to delimit and distinguish the types of government spending we study, our definition excludes expenditures for certain programs. First, it does not include education. Wilensky (1975) argues that educational expenditures are regressive, contribute to equality of opportunity rather than results, and are justified by meritocratic rather than egalitarian values. In contrast, welfare transfers are designed to be progressive in contributions and egalitarian in results. Educational spending and welfare spending are simply quite different responses to inequality and warrant separate study (Hewitt, 1977). Here we concentrate only on social welfare spending. Second, our definition does not include spending for the profitability of firms or the public production of schools, hospitals, roads, and housing. Friedland and Sanders (1985) note that such spending is also part of the modern state but differs from the more standard welfare support of households in its support of capital accumulation and production (see also Devine, 1985). Our definition refers specifically to household support programs; we leave to others the study of the determinants of the quite different forms of social capital spending. Third, although our definition includes various expenditures for housing, energy, and transportation that are parts of a bewildering array or programs and policies, such expenditures in miscellaneous and varied categories cannot be measured comparably across nations. However, it is unlikely that this gap biases the results because most welfare spending is included in the measurable categories and that which is not nonetheless correlates highly with measured welfare spending (Wilensky, 1975).

Finally, the definition includes only public or governmental programs and spending. Some nations rely more than others on private, market-based rather than public, non-market-based resources to deal with retirement and medical care. However, private pensions and medical insurance differ conceptually from public transfers. Private transfers are part of the economic process of wage bargaining between employees and employers, whereas our focus is on competition in the political arena for public resources. By dealing with public spending, we consider conditions under which governments control the transfer process, and social protection shifts form the province of market forces to that of nonmarket forces (Esping-Anderson, 1985b). Even so, Rein and Rainwater (1986) report figures for 10 nations in 1977 that suggest that inclusion of private benefits would not drastically change the cross-national pattern shown by public expenditures. Their figures show that an inverse relationship exists between private and public expenditures but that private expenditures comprise only a small part of the total package of social protection in most nations. As a result, the ranking of nations on public expenditures as a percentage of GNP is identical to the ranking for total (public plus private) expenditures as a percentage of GNP (see Table 1.4, Rein and Rainwater, 1986:17).

While accepting the definition of social welfare that we use, others suggest the need to study the presence of universalistic citizen rights to program benefits as necessary for a complete understanding of welfare state effort (Myles, 1984; Esping-Anderson, 1985b). Although they are not irrelevant to concerns with benefit rights, spending figures may be unable to capture national differences in coverage, guaranteed minimum benefits, and qualification tests. In fact, both spending levels and benefit rights can be viewed as distinct and consequential dimensions of welfare state effort (Jones, 1985), each worth study in its own right. For instance, without generous expenditures, welfare policies, whatever their structure, can do little to protect the population. In this book we focus on spending levels, but we recognize the additionally important task of studying the structural characteristics of these programs.

As defined, social welfare spending does not guarantee equality; it corresponds to effort or input rather than equality of result (Jackman, 1975). Since we conceptualize social welfare spending as redistributive effort and social equality as the structural result, the link between social welfare effort and its consequences becomes an empirical issue rather than a definitional one. Specifically, equality is defined as the degree to which access to and consumption of material goods are distributed in an egalitarian manner (Jackman, 1975). Generally, equality refers to the relative distribution of income shares rather than to levels.

Social equality also refers more broadly to the extent to which the distribution of material resources provides for basic human needs. Among others, human needs include health and adequate food, nutrition, shelter, and security to maintain health and well-being. A large number of indicators of quality of life have been developed (Estes, 1984), but one that proves particularly useful is infant mortality. Infant mortality reflects the consequences of the income distribution for the lives of members of a society, is highly responsive to the socioeconomic conditions of the poor, and is a critical part of the well-being of a society. Moreover, infant mortality summarizes a number of other components of the quality of life, such as nutrition, education, and sanitation, and is more reliably measured across divers nations – rich and poor, capitalist and socialist – than other measures of less clearly identifiable events or characteristics. Because infant mortality reflects the dispersion as well as the level of social resources, it fits our definition of social equality. Infant mortality has biological limits such that improvements cannot be monopolized by high-status groups. As the infant mortality rate reaches its lower limits, further benefits must go to high-risk, low-income groups.[6] Along with income inequality, then, the dispersion of nonmonetary resources and outcomes, as shown in infant mortality, can be studied as a component of social equality.

In summary, our study of the effects of social welfare considers social equality broadly conceived and includes commonly studied income inequality as well as another aspect of equality – infant mortality – involving the physical quality of life. In addition to providing a more comprehensive, multidimensional study of social equality, our strategy provides opportunities for testing arguments regarding the efficacy of the social welfare state. If social welfare spending does not redistribute income, it may still reduce infant mortality. Indeed, with this approach we may be better able to specify the scope of the arguments and the aspects of social equality to which they best apply.

Finally, a third topic to be studied is democratic politics, not as a factor to be explained but as a determinant of social welfare and inequality. Many other determinants of social welfare spending and inequality are, of course, to be studied. But democratic politics are central in the conception of the welfare state and warrant special consideration. Democracy has been defined as a political system that supplies regular constitutional opportunities for changing government officials and allows the largest possible part of the population to influence major decisions by choosing among political contenders (Lipset, 1964:7–8). Equally important, however, is the way activities of the population in a democracy are organized. For some theories, such activity operates through class-based political parties; for other theories, it operates through smaller interest groups and voting blocks. We address these differing views of democracy in more detail in the next chapter.

Overview

We propose to study the determinants of social welfare spending, the effects of social welfare spending net of other factors (such as economic development) on social equality, and the role of democratic politics in both processes. The next chapter presents a general theoretical scheme to distinguish among explanations of social welfare spending and social equality, and provides some organization to the diversity of ideas that have emerged. Given the questions, themes, research strategy, and theory, the following chapters can focus on the empirical analyses. These chapters can be divided into two groups: those examining the determinants of several types of social welfare spending and those examining the consequences for two forms of social equality of social welfare spending.

Chapters 3 and 4 examine the causes of social welfare spending in two groups of nations. Chapter 3 begins with an analysis of advanced industrial democracies from 1950 to 1980. Reliable, accurate data and measures for these nations make it possible to examine in detail the influence of working-class strength and democratic party politics, as well as more standard economic and demographic variables. Examining this limited set of nations allows more detailed analyses and complex models than would be possible for a group of developing nations. Chapter 4 turns to the causes of social welfare spending among middle- and low-income developing nations. Reliable, complete data for these nations are available only from 1965 to 1975, and measures of class strength and political parties are rare. Unlike advanced industrial democracies, however, these nations vary greatly in level of democracy and position in the world system. We can examine how a democratic political environment facilitates the influence of other variables on spending and how economic and trade dependency directly affect spending. Welfare spending in developing nations, however low, offers opportunities for study unavailable with advanced industrial democracies. Our efforts in both of these chapters show the need for contextual analysis of different groups of nations and offer diverse but complementary findings.

Chapter 5 examines income inequality, or the share of income going to various groups positioned along the income distribution continuum, with particular focus on the role of welfare spending relative to economic and demographic change. Chapter 6 examines an additional aspect of equality relating to the physical quality of life and health of a nation – infant mortality. Much variation in infant mortality exists across nations – as illustrated by the unexpectedly high rate in the United States – and it provides a useful indicator of equality among high-income, low-inequality nations. It also allows comparison of equality in Western nations with that in East European socialist nations, where measurement problems make the study of income inequality difficult. Finally, it allows the study of the influence of social welfare spending and economic dependency on infant mortality in developing nations, where problems of health, nutrition, and poverty are most pressing. The final chapter then returns to the original questions, themes, and theories considered in the first two chapters. We review and integrate the results in the empirical chapters to provide answers to our questions and evaluate the theories.

Notes

1. For a review of the debate over what should be done with the surplus being accumulated by the social security fund in the United States, see Gist (1988).
2. This raises the question of whether or not the aged would be poor were it not for government transfers. By bringing the aged out of poverty, transfers within classes might still be claimed to redistribute income to the poor. Some have argued this point by showing that the pretransfer income of the aged places dramatically more persons in poverty than the posttransfer income (Danziger and Gottschalk, 1986). Others (Duncan, Hill, and Rodgers, 1986) suggest that the improved status of the aged is due to the better financial condition of new cohorts entering old age. We address this issue in more detail later in our study.
3. Not all scholars were so positive. Olson (1963) argued that rapid growth is destabilizing and exacerbates inequality. Other empirically oriented economists (Kuznets, 1955, 1963) noted that inequality first increased and then declined in response to economic development.
4. McFarland (1987) distinguishes the traditional pluralism of Dahl (1956) and Lindblom (1977) from what he terms the *plural elitism* of Olson (1982) and Lowi (1979). Although this term may be less than ideal, the distinction between the two types of pluralism is a good one. The arguments of the latter two scholars, and those of public choice theorists (Mueller, 1979) and rent-seeking theorists (Buchanan and Tullock, 1980), lie closer to the arguments we present than does functionalist pluralism.
5. Janowitz (1976) makes a further distinction between the welfare state and welfare spending. In addition to high spending levels, the social welfare state is based on parliamentary democracy and legitimate acceptance of the role of government to intervene on behalf of individual rights. Hence, the term *welfare state* applies primarily to advanced industrial democracies. For our study of welfare spending in developing nations, where the welfare state is not fully institutionalized and democratic rights are limited, we refer more specifically to *welfare spending* rather than the welfare state.
6. We can assume that a differential in infant mortality exists between low- and high-status groups. As high-status groups, having eliminated most problems due to poor nutrition and medical care, reach minimum levels of infant mortality, further improvements that occur in the societal rate must be concentrated among less advantaged groups. To some degree, then, continued improvement in infant mortality must eventually reduce the differential, and therefore reflects improved equality.

2. Theoretical perspectives on the welfare state

The remarkable growth of explanations and studies of the welfare state has brought about some theoretical disorganization. Scholars often fail to distinguish adequately among the various explanations, use broad terms such as *pluralist* or *neo-Marxist* to cover quite different arguments, and gloss over the fact that different theories contain similar arguments. It is well worth the effort to systematize the different theories of the welfare state into a parsimonious yet meaningful scheme that can guide the specification and testing of the hypotheses to follow in the empirical chapters. We begin this effort by making a distinction between demand-based theories, which attend to the externally generated demands of groups and classes for spending, and state-based or supply theories, which consider the characteristics of states that autonomously determine the supply of spending. Concentrating initially on the demand theories, we review the three questions raised at the outset of the book but attach more distinct theoretical labels to the answers and systematically present the theories. We then turn to the state-based theories, laying out their basic arguments and predictions and contrasting them with those of the demand theories.

Demand theories

To review, theories of the welfare state address each of the three questions we discussed in the first chapter. First, does welfare spending respond primarily to class structure and class interests or to economic development and the size of ascriptive groups such as the aged? Second, does the welfare state redistribute income to groups most in need and reduce inequality, or does it maintain inequality and the power of dominant classes or interest groups? Third, do technological, economic, and class constraints limit the independent actions of democratic political institutions to affect welfare spending and social equality, or can democratic political processes and parties counteract economic pressures to raise or limit social welfare spending? Because these questions are presented as clear dichotomies, the answers to them are simplified, but they still allow us to compare and contrast the basic positions of existing theories. As a preview of the

22

Table 2.1. *Summary of theoretical predictions*

Theory	Class-based	Reduced inequality	Politics independent
Industrialism	No	Yes	No
Monopoly capitalism	Yes	No	No
Social democratic	Yes	Yes	Yes
Interest group politics	No	No	Yes

more detailed treatment to follow, we can briefly summarize the theories by connecting them to the preceding questions.

First, *industrialism theory* explains the welfare state as the necessary result of technological development (Kerr et al., 1964). This theory assumes that welfare spending helps maintain economic and social equilibrium in industrial societies. In functional terms, the welfare state benefits all members of society, but the needy who receive the benefits are rewarded most directly (Wilensky, 1975). Since it transfers income from the well-off to the poor, welfare spending leads to lower inequality. Overall, the theory predicts nonclass determinants of social welfare spending, reduction of inequality from welfare, and little influence of democratic politics on either. These arguments are summarized in Table 2.1, where the dichotomized answers of the industrialism theory to the three questions are listed in the first row.

Second, neo-Marxists, who disagree with the functionalist assumptions of industrialism theory, offer arguments that are similar in nature but different in their implications. Rejecting the view that industrial growth and welfare benefit all members of a society and reduce inequality, O'Connor (1973) argues that welfare functions to maintain the power of capital and reduce social protest. Although such arguments attribute little independence to the state, they have been extended to consider how a more autonomous state can mediate class struggle while maintaining conditions for capital accumulation (Poulantzas, 1978; Offe, 1984). The *monopoly capitalism theory,* then, predicts class determinants of social welfare spending, no effect of welfare on equality, and little influence of democratic politics on either (see Table 2.1).

Third, another neo-Marxist theory focuses on the strength of worker movements and the social democratic or socialist parties that represent them in the political class struggle. Like the monopoly capital theory, this theory emphasizes the importance of class; yet, it argues that the welfare state results from the political efforts of a strong working class rather than from monopoly capital. The political efforts of workers can lead to the election of leftist parties, which then implement welfare programs that redistribute income to workers and the poor. The *social democractic theory* predicts class determinants of social welfare spending, reduction of inequality from welfare, and important class-based political influences on both.

Fourth, an *interest group politics theory* claims that democratic political institutions combined with demographic and economic changes in group structures explain the growth of welfare spending. Unlike the functionalist views of the industrialism theory, it emphasizes the impact of political conflict and mobilization of interest groups in democracies. Unlike class theories, it recognizes the competition among a variety of ascriptive and economic groups that transcend and fragment the distinction between labor and capital. The state and democratic political processes have the potential to influence the economy, according to the theory, but since spending goes to groups with the most political power, the influence is seldom in the direction of greater equality.

This brief review fails to capture the complexities of the theories and provides only a preliminary overview of what is discussed in more detail in the next sections. However, it does illustrate several themes that run through the various theories. To some degree, each theory addresses common questions and offers a unique set of answers to the questions. This is apparent in Table 2.1, which shows, in simplified form, how the combination of predictions uniquely defines the theories. It also provides a strategy for testing the theories. For any single issue or question, the theories overlap; it is only when at least two of the questions are considered that the theories can be fully distinguished and tested.

Another way to compare the theories is to cross-classify the questions and answers. This is shown in Table 2.2. The rows in the table identify the different views of the role of class in social welfare spending; the columns classify the redistributive consequences that welfare spending may have; and the diagonals indicate which of the institutions – economic or political – dominate welfare spending and equality.[1] Each cell defines one of the four demand theories of the welfare state. Given the $2 \times 2 \times 2$ classification, there are eight potential cells but only four theories. This indicates overlap in the classification (or overidentification): Two of the dimensions are sufficient to identify each of the theories, and the third is redundant. However, considering all three dimensions shows precisely how each theory (1) shares some arguments with each of the other theories and (2) differs in important respects from each of the other theories. The monopoly capitalism and social democratic theories share assumptions about the dominance of class cleavages, and the industrialism and interest group theories share pluralist assumptions. Monopoly capitalism and interest group theories both argue that the welfare state maintains inequality, whereas the industrialism and

Table 2.2. *Typology of theories of social welfare spending, social equality, and the influence of political institutions*

	Maintain inequality[a]	Structural dynamics		Reduce inequality[a]
		Primarily economic (structuralist)	Political and economic (group agency)	
Organizational unit for mobilization of interests	Social classes	Monopoly capitalism theory	Social democratic theory	
	Social-demographic groups (strata)	Industrialism theory	Interest group politics theory	
	Reduce inequality[a]			Maintain inequality[a]

[a]Dimension refers to the diagonals of the table.

social democratic theories argue that it reduces inequality. The industrialism and monopoly capitalism theories, despite having widely divergent ideological bases, both focus on the response of state action to economic and productive relations, whereas the social democratic and interest group theories, also from widely different ideological perspectives, attribute the ability to political institutions and parties to act independently of economic structures. With this background and overview in mind, we can consider in more detail each of the theories.

Industrialism theory

First, we can consider the logic of industrialization or industrialism theory as applied to the welfare state and social equality. Advocates of the theory (Kerr et al., 1964; Form, 1979; Kerr, 1983) argue that the technological imperatives of industry shape the economic and social institutions of all industrialized nations. As a result, nations tend to converge, or become more similar, as they industrialize (Inkeles, 1981). Like other institutions, the state responds to exogenous technological imperatives and takes a specific form in all advanced industrial nations. The state performs a regulatory function to help organize and plan for technological development and to provide the stable environment needed for complex production procedures. Expansion of the state is closely tied to the direct requirements of the industrialization process and contributes to economic progress (Goldthorpe, 1969).

Implications for determination of social welfare spending follow from these general arguments. Industrialization involves dislocations and differentiation in family and work. Urbanization, divorce, geographical mobility, and smaller families reduce the functions of the family and the support it can provide during periods of financial need. At the same time, the demands of industry for young, recently educated, efficient workers create employment problems among the sick, the unemployed, single-parent families, and the aged. Since many vulnerable persons are unable to obtain traditional support from family members, the state, serving as a mechanism to meet the needs of the population, expands to provide social welfare support. The benevolence of the state, a more or less automatic response, stems ultimately from the needs of industrialization. Support for superfluous groups through welfare spending allows employment of a specialized, skilled labor force that contributes to economic growth in industrial societies.

An early statement of much the same argument comes from Wagner (1983 [1883]). His *law of increasing state activity* holds that the size of the public sector relative to the private sector rises with real per capita income. In part, public sector growth is a response to the expanded administrative needs of an increasingly complex industrial society (Larkey, Stolp, and Winer, 1981). Perhaps more importantly, the public sector grows because the demand of households for services and their willingness to pay taxes are income elastic (Cameron, 1978). The need of governments to meliorate the harmful effects of industrialization thus occurs simultaneously with increases in income, which enables funding of public programs.

Besides income, demographic changes in age structure are important for the growth of the welfare state. Because of the growth, in absolute and relative terms, of the aged and retired population in industrial societies and loss of traditional family support, much of the social welfare effort of governments is directed to the aged (Wilensky, 1975). Private pensions, if they exist, are seldom adequate, so the state responds to the financial plight of this population by providing public pensions. Again, the state is not an autonomous force in the growth of pensions but responds to substructural changes in the age structure, family, and labor force.

In addition to arguments about the aged, other aspects of population structure may be important in the determination of welfare spending, particularly in developing nations. Entwisle and Winegarden (1984) argue that as fertility and family size decline, parents recognize that there will be fewer children to support them in old age. Children, as they grow to adulthood, likewise recognize that they have fewer siblings with whom to share the burden of supporting their parents in old age. Pressure for governmental old-age pensions thus comes from nonaged family members and relates to the number of children relative to the number of parents they have to support. Like proponents of other industrialism arguments, Entwisle and Winegarden emphasize the response of governments to the needs of the population, but consider the effects of declining fertility during industrialization as well as those of the increasing aged population.

According to the industrialism arguments, technological and industrial development leads to reduced inequality, partly through the growth of social welfare and pension spending. Directly, the logic of industrialization leads to greater social equality through the growth of middle-level occupations, greater knowledge and skills of workers, higher educational levels, increasing worker control over crucial knowledge, and growth of high economic rewards (Kerr et al., 1964). Indirectly, industrial development leads to greater social equality through higher welfare spending. Groups in need receive the greatest share of welfare expenditures, and, on the whole, the effects of welfare spending are egalitarian (Wilensky, 1975).

Because of the common economic and demographic constraints, state actions in general and social welfare expenditures in particular tend to be similar among industrial nations (Pryor, 1968). A particularly important example of convergence relates to the comparison of capitalist and socialist nations. Given that both desire industrial development and face the homogenizing demands of advanced industrial technology, work, public policies, and inequality in the different societies have much in common (Parkin, 1971; Connor, 1979) despite vastly different political systems and forms of economic ownership. The systems are clearly not identical: The form of welfare spending may vary from cash transfers in capitalist societies to full employment and state-owned housing in socialist nations. Yet, the demands leading to the varying forms of social welfare are the same in both types of societies (Bell, 1973).

To sum up, we can describe the theory in terms of the three dimensions listed earlier. First, the theory recognizes but minimizes the importance of class divisions and gives primary attention to a variety of economic and demographic groups, with particular attention to the aged. A pluralist conception of group competition best fits this theory; consensus and cooperation, with regulation of competition by the state, is the norm among these multiple groups. Second, the theory argues that the welfare state is on the whole egalitarian in result. Wilensky's study offers a defense of the efficacy of the welfare state; others similarly see problems in the welfare state as due to failures of desire and implementation rather than problems inherent in such programs (Mishra, 1984). The welfare state benefits not only the needy but society overall through its contribution to industrial growth. Third, the theory sees the state as responsive to the needs of technology and industry and, as a result, responsive to the economic and demographic needs of the population. Although not denying the necessity of political democracy for long-term industrial development, the theory nonetheless attributes little independent influence to the political parties that occupy the government or to the institutional structures of the state. Since all political parties favor economic growth, all support the demands of industrial and technological development.

Critique. Critics of the industrialism theory focus on weaknesses in both the theoretical arguments and the quality of empirical evidence in support of them. Theoretically, the industrialism arguments fail to specify clearly the mechanisms by which problems or needs of the aged and other groups translate into higher social welfare expenditures. Entitlement provisions in welfare programs may automatically raise expenditures in response to more recipients; deprived groups or their professional and bureaucratic representatives may exert political pressure to raise spending; or leftist and working-class parties acting in the interest of the subordinate classes may intervene to raise spending. By emphasizing the automatic response of governments to the needs of the population, industrialism theory only vaguely identifies the causal linkages involved.

In addition, industrialism theory fails to predict or account for the financial problems and weakened political support for the welfare state apparent in many advanced industrial nations. Given that the welfare state responds to the needs of industries and groups adversely affected by industrialization, and contributes to economic growth and increased equality, there is little reason to expect the emergence of sustained political opposition to the welfare state in recent years. Because of the functionalist emphasis on equilibrium, and the assumed responsiveness of the welfare state and political institutions to the imperatives of industry, industrialism theory applies less well to the crisis of the welfare state in the 1970s and 1980s than it does to the consensus in the 1950s and 1960s. The theoretical assumptions formulated during optimistic earlier decades may not generalize well to other time periods and cast doubt on the general validity of the theory.

Empirically, support for the industrialism theory comes from a number of studies, most of which quantitatively analyze a large cross section of developed and developing nations. Cutright (1965) and Jackman (1975) examine the experience with social insurance programs, and Wilensky (1975) and Aaron (1967) look at the actual expenditures of nations for various programs. Most of these authors also study income inequality (Cutright, 1967; Jackman, 1975; Wilensky, 1975). Their results generally show a strong influence of economic development and percentage aged on various forms of social welfare effort and a strong influence of social welfare effort on income inequality. Political variables, except for some weak effects of political democracy, have little effect on any of the dependent variables. Such findings have been updated by Wilensky (1976, 1981), who adds corporatism to the determinants of social welfare spending, and by Entwisle and Winegarden (1984), who add fertility to the determinants of pension expenditures. Other more specialized studies of infant mortality (Shin, 1975), educational institutions (Inkeles and Sirowy, 1983), and female labor force participation (Wilensky, 1968) find strong effects of industrialization and modernization variables.

However, these quantitative studies may be methodologically flawed. Castles and McKinlay (1979) argue that because there is a bimodal distribution of nations on development, with a huge gap between advanced industrial nations and others, analysis of both clusters together merely shows that rich nations can afford to spend more on social welfare than nations with barely enough food to feed the population – a trivial conclusion. What is needed to support the industrialism theory is the demonstration of a relationship between development or percentage aged within as well as across these clusters.[2]

Neo-Marxist theories of advanced monopoly capitalism

The late 1960s and 1970s proved to be a period of theoretical innovation and resurgence for Marxist theory. The neo-Marxist theories, at least as they apply to the welfare state and social equality, differ in important respects from traditional Marxist theory and deal with a number of problems in the original formulations (Buroway, 1982). This theoretical revival has led to a variety of new ideas, each with its own variations on the standard arguments. What links them is their focus on class conflict and productive relations in societies and their view of the capitalist state. In this section, we focus on these neo-Marxist theories of monopoly capitalism (in the next section, we consider a group of fundamentally different neo-Marxist theories of working-class strength).

According to the monopoly capitalism theories, the state plays a more active – albeit not completely independent – role in advanced monopoly capitalism than it did in the theories of Marx. Traditional Marxist theory views the state as an instrument to be filled and controlled by representatives of the dominant class and to serve primarily as a means to repress protest among workers. In contrast, the work of O'Connor (1973), Offe (1984), and Poulantzas (1973, 1978) sees the state as crucial to capital reproduction. For O'Connor (1973), the state must perform two major but contradictory functions. The first is to assist in private capitial accumulation. In order to increase the productivity of labor and the profits of capital, the state subsidizes the costs of education, social insurance, research and development, and transportation and communications. The second function is to maintain social harmony or legitimacy through expenditures for nonproductive parts of the population (e.g., public assistance, food and housing subsidies). These expenditures control the surplus population politically and expand demand in domestic markets.[3] The purposes of these two types of expenditures are ultimately contradictory. With subsidies from the state, monopoly capital grows in the short run, but in the long run it necessarily overproduces, contracts, and lays off workers. Since the state receives few of the profits during periods of economic growth and must support surplus workers during periods of economic recession, public costs exceed revenues. Hence, the fiscal crisis of the state emerges. Offe (1984) makes the similar point that monopoly capitalism must preserve the commodification of labor for economic growth and at the same time decommodify labor to reduce the harmful effects of the private market. Both processes are necessary for the survival of monopoly capital but are inherently contradictory. Recurrent crises of fiscal policy, national planning, and population loyalty occur, making governance in capitalist democracies problematic (Offe, 1984). Given the structure of monopoly capitalism, then, advanced capitalist economies converge in both levels of state expenditures and the economic and social problems that result (Gough, 1979).

In part to deal with inevitable crises, capitalism may transcend the boundaries of individual nations. The need for capital accumulation leads to the search for foreign markets and cheap foreign labor. Through economic and trading ties, as well as political and military relations, low- and middle-income peripheral and semiperipheral nations are exploited by multinational corporations in the core nations. Just as in core nations, forms of foreign aid and welfare spending may emerge in noncore nations to maintain social harmony in the face of the harmful effects of capitalist production (O'Connor, 1973). Capitalism still creates, even among economically dependent nations, the same problems of unemployment, poverty, and social discontent and the same need for social welfare spending to maintain conditions for continued capital accumulation as in core nations.

The state in monopoly capitalism need not be directly manipulated and occupied by class-conscious capitalists (Block, 1977; Przeworski and Wallerstein, 1988). O'Connor (1973) sees the state as a partner in capital accumulation and Offe (1984) as the outcome of the contradictions of capital accumulation. Poulantzas (1973, 1978) further extends the concept of the relative autonomy of the state. He argues that the state must neutralize contradictions rooted in capitalist economies in order to reproduce the capitalist structure. The state functions to atomize working-class interests and organize unity within the capitalist class. This requires an autonomous state that transcends the short-term interests of a few capitalists in the longer-term interests of the class (see also Gough, 1979). Ultimately, the state may become the site of class struggle and mediate conflict between class power blocks (Poulantzas, 1978; Quadagno, 1984). Whatever the views, however, they are related by their assumption that the state is embedded in the capitalist system and must contribute to capital accumulation. The state may be relatively autonomous, but it cannot be emancipated completely from the constraints of the capitalist logic of accumulation (Gold et al., 1975; Przeworski, 1985:201).

Up to this point, the monopoly capitalism theories show some similarities to the functionalist, industrialism theories. Myles (1984) argues that both theories are structural-functionalist, since both see the welfare state as responding to functional imperatives: In one case, the imperatives are technological; in the other case, they relate to the needs of monopoly capitalism. In Stinchcombe's (1968:80) terminology, functional explanations treat the consequences of a social arrangement as the causes of that arrangement. Monopoly capitalism theory, by focusing on the beneficial consequences of welfare spending for capital accumulation, relies on a functional explanation. The explanation differs from that of functionalist theory in that there is no focus on general societal needs or equilibrium – only on the needs of the capitalist class – but the similarities of the two theories should not be overlooked (Stinchcombe, 1968).[4]

The theories more strongly diverge over the effectiveness of social welfare spending in reducing inequality. According to the monopoly capitalism theory, the welfare state reduces class tensions, but without threatening control of the capitalist market. Social insurance programs are most likely built up from the contributions of workers themselves and do little to transfer income from the rich to the poor (Stinchcombe, 1985). Other types of programs may place income in the hands of the needy, but they do not cover the loss in wages brought about by changes in the capitalist economy; whatever the benefit levels to the unemployed, retired, or single-parent families, they do not equal income from productive employment. If, as some claim (Szymanski, 1978), taxes to finance welfare programs are regressive, even meager benefits to the poor may do little more than return to the poor what they contribute to the government. Although offering some short-term benefits to the poor, public assistance programs more importantly dampen discontent and help maintain the environment for capital accumulation (Offe, 1972; O'Connor, 1973). Rather than a means to achieve equality, the welfare state is a means of social control employed to regulate and exploit the lower classes (Piven and Cloward, 1971). Although advocates of the theory are vague about whether they support dismantling of the welfare state (Mishra,

1984), they are critical of its intent, hold opinions similar to those of neoconservative critics of the welfare state (Skocpol, 1985a), and reject the welfare state as a source of equality for the poor and the working class.

Neo-Marxist arguments have also been extended and applied to the aged, but again differ from industrialism arguments. Piven and Cloward (1971) argue that Social Security in the United States was a response of the government to social protests such as the Townsend movements. Although the program offered meager benefits and covered modest numbers of workers, it quelled the protests and maintained conditions for the growth of capital. Similar points are made in more detail by Laura Olson (1982). Aged persons in modern capitalist societies become the least productive workers (as also argued by industrialism theory) and face loss of work. Public pensions mute the protests that result from forced retirement while raising the productivity of the work force. Private pensions, although benefiting retirees to some degree, have the more important characteristic of providing a source of capital for further investment. Pensions are thus a form of social control that reinforce existing inequalities.

In summary, there are many diverse neo-Marxist views of the state, yet they share a number of common attributes.[5] The welfare state is seen as a response to the contradictions of advanced monopoly capitalism and is largest where capitalist power is most concentrated. The welfare state relieves pressure from the contradictions in the short run, although this does little to change the nature of class relations, the power of capital, or the levels of social equality. The state may become relatively autonomous compared to traditional Marxian conceptions but is not a source of structural change for the good of the working class. This creates considerable ambivalence toward the welfare state among neo-Marxists. While arguing that the welfare state creates and exploits a permanent underclass (Offe, 1972), advocates of the theory likely oppose the logical goal of dismantling the welfare state (e.g., compare Piven and Cloward, 1971 and 1982). Still, this ambivalence distinguishes the theories from others that support the welfare state more unambiguously.

Critique. Monopoly capitalism theory avoids one problem of industrialism theory – it does not reify societal needs. It specifies which groups benefit from the structure and which do not, and recognizes conflicting interests among groups. Even so, monopoly capitalism theory and neo-Marxist theories are subject to other criticisms of functionalist arguments: They tend to be tautological and difficult to falsify. The theories assume that state policies benefit the capitalist class; empirical study then illustrates how events can be interpreted to fit the assumptions. When contrary evidence is indisputable, the arguments are reframed to maintain the original assumptions without allowing the assumptions to be falsified. As Cawson (1985:4–5) states, "neo-Marxism asserts a structurally guaranteed dominance for class interests of capital through the institution of the state. Evidence of state policies which favor noncapitalist interests is rendered by some theorists consistent with this assertion by the tortuous logic of the idea of the relative autonomy of the state." The theories thus lack specific, testable propositions and rely on abstract assertions that are plausible but difficult to prove false.

A related weakness of the neo-Marxist theories is that they devote little attention to explaining the diversity among similar capitalist nations. None of the theories attempts to make systematic comparisons across nations, and each assumes that its arguments apply to all advanced capitalist economies. Yet, enormous variation in welfare state policies exists among capitalist nations that is not adequately explained by the neo-Marixist theories. Even if all capitalist nations face the same accumulation demands, each nation may fulfill them differently.

Another criticism of the neo-Marxist theories is that they provide inadequate treatment of democratic politics. The argument that the state is autonomous co-exists with the argument that incumbents in the government make little difference in the level of social welfare spending. The argument of autonomy must be accepted to deal with many examples of policies implemented that were opposed by capitalists. Yet, the next logical step, that the state may act against the needs of capital, is not taken. Skocpol (1980) argues that neo-Marxist theories really do not take the state seriously, since they do not recognize the potential of the state, independent of class structure, to realign economic institutions and productive relations. Similarly, Stephens (1979) and Korpi (1983) criticize the theory for ignoring how public policies respond to democratic elections and philosophical differences between parties. The theory's excessive economic determinism fails to account for the different policies of nations like Sweden and the United States, which vary in the electoral power given to social democratic or labor parties.

Finally, although illustrative evidence exists for the monopoly capitalism theory, there is little systematic empirical support. Griffin's time-series studies of the United States (Griffin, Devine, and Wallace, 1983; Griffin and Leicht, 1986) show that measures of economic downturn, such as unemployment in competitive sector industries and industrial utilization, affect transfer payments net of government revenues, inflation, defense expenditures, and transfer payments lagged (see also Isaac and Kelly, 1981, Devine, 1983, 1985, for similar studies). Their model, however, explains short-term fluctuation in payments rather than long-term growth of, or cross-national differences in, the welfare state. Debate also exists over the validity of treating endogenous variables in the budget-making process – revenues and expenditures – as exogenous (Jennings, 1983; Jencks,

1985). Cross-national studies show less support for the theory. Stephens (1979) and Myles (1984) use a measure of monopolization (in part estimated from gross domestic product) but find that it has no effect on social welfare or pension spending. Hicks and Swank (1984) use a measure of assets of the world's largest industrial corporations in a nation divided by GNP and find positive effects on cash transfer payments. Although their measure is promising, its influence needs to be replicated before it offers firm support for the theory. Thus, systematic empirical evaluation of the theory remains to be done.

Working-class strength, social democracy theory

The third theory shares the assumption of the dominant role of class conflict in capitalist societies but differs from the monopoly capitalism theory in its view of the relative power of the subordinate class. Where monopoly capitalism theory sees welfare spending as a means for capital to maintain its dominant position (at least temporarily), the working-class strength theory sees welfare spending as a reflection of the political power gained by workers. Although markets may place workers under the control of capital, politics in democratic nations provides the resources for workers to counteract, through social welfare spending, the harmful effects of markets (Esping-Andersen, 1985a). Working-class political power rather than capitalist dominance of the economy thus becomes crucial for the growth of the welfare state.

The major point of the working-class strength or social democratic theory is well summarized by Shalev (1983:319): "the welfare state is a class issue . . . its principal proponents and defenders are movements of the working class." The welfare state is an outcome of democratic class struggle, and levels of expenditures reflect the balance of class forces in a society. The theory assumes, first of all, that the basic cleavage in society – between capital and the working class – is reflected in political behavior (Korpi, 1983). In developed nations, parties are based on the upper and lower classes, with low-income persons voting for the left and high-income persons voting for the right (Lipset, 1964). Workers and capitalists are not the only relevant groups, and alliances with other groups may be necessary for electoral victory (Esping-Andersen, 1985a, 1985b). Yet, the group most important to the growth of the welfare state, and the source of power of leftist parties, is the working class. Secondly, it assumes that the choices and actions of the government and the dominant party define the characteristics of the welfare state. Unlike other neo-Marxist theories, this theory proposes that the state autonomously and substantially affects economic relations, and is not necessarily dominated or constrained by capital. The power of the state may be wrested from the capitalist class by workers through democratic means. Then social democratic or socialist parties that represent the working class dominate the government, and spending for social welfare is high. When dominated by rightist parties that do not represent the working class, governments spend little for social welfare (Castles, 1982).

The degree of working-class power, represented by the size and centralization of reformist labor unions, then, determines whether or not leftist parties are elected and expand social welfare spending. In the economic sphere, since power depends on ownership of capital, labor occupies a subordinate position. However, labor can obtain power resources in the political sphere through organization of its relatively large numbers. Where unions are organized, strong, and large, they can translate these resources into political power that can compete with and win over market power in the class struggle for equality. Where union strength is fragmented and employers have more power, centrist and rightist parties are elected, governments are dominated by capital, and welfare spending is low. What, then, determines when unions will be centrally organized and able to obtain political power? The underlying causes of working-class strength depend on the unique historical circumstances of nations. Stephens (1979) emphasizes that small population size, late industrialization, and vulnerability to external economic forces lead to a strong working class, but beyond this, working-class organization is treated exogenously.

The social democratic arguments can be restated more broadly in terms of conflict over citizenship rights. Citizenship involves expansion of civil and political rights to include social rights to access to a tolerable standard of living (Marshall, 1964; Zald, 1985). Social democratic theorists emphasize political conflict over the desires of classes to tie income and services to either labor force participation or citizenship rights (Hasenfeld et al., 1987). The ability of the working class to rectify social inequalities through expansion of citizenship rights to economic well-being and social inclusion thus depends on union organizational resources, the political power of social democratic parties, and expanded welfare spending.

The social democratic theory explicitly applies to advanced industrial democracies. Political democracy and economic development are necessary but not sufficient conditions for growth of the welfare state. Economic development creates a large working class and the material basis for redistribution of income; political democracy allows a large, organized working class to gain political power. However, only when unions and leftist parties use these conditions to organize the working class can they gain power, implement policies favorable to the working class, and increase social welfare spending. Among the advanced industrial democracies, according to Korpi's (1983) classification, Sweden, Austria, and Norway have had the highest union mobilization and the most stable leftist control of government, and have the highest social welfare spending and equality. Other nations with high union mobilization and occasional leftist control (Denmark, New Zealand, the United Kingdom, and Belgium) also have high spending and equality. Nations with low mobilization and exclusion of leftist control, such as Canada, the United States, and Ireland, have low welfare spending and equality. Other nations fall between these extremes. Even though all industrial nations may face the same functional demands, these national differences in working-class strength and political party control determine how the demands are met and what role spending plays in the processes.

Although nearly all advocates of the social democratic arguments posit a direct, one-to-one relationship between the degree of leftist (or rightist) rule and the level or growth of welfare spending, some suggest that the relationship may be less simple. Hicks, Swank, and Ambuhl (1989) argue that the influence of leftist regimes varies, depending on the institutional strength of labor and the macroeconomic context. A strong union environment facilitates the realization of working-class demands in the form of leftist electoral programs, as it does the influence of status-based groups such as the aged. Hence, the influence of unions and leftist parties may occur only in combination rather than directly and additively.

The social democratic view of the consequences of social welfare spending on inequality follows straightforwardly from its view of the source and beneficiaries of welfare spending. Since welfare spending is supported by the disadvantaged working and lower classes who benefit from such expenditures, it must reduce inequality. One need only look at the lower income inequality and social democratic-controlled governments in Scandinavia, and compare them to the higher inequality and weaker labor parties in the United States, Canada, and Japan, to see the benefits of the welfare state (Stephens, 1979). It is also clear from these arguments that politics and political institutions independently influence economic relations and the structure of rewards in society through implementation of progressive taxation policies, income transfers, and reduction of poverty and income inequality. In this sense, the state is potentially autonomous of the capitalist class in capitalist societies. The state still responds to the structural characteristics of society, such as the organization of the working class, but is able to use political means to create economic and class change. As Stephens (1979) argues, there is a political, democratic road to socialism.

Myles (1984) applies the social democratic theory directly to pensions and the aged. Public pensions may benefit the working class in several ways so as to be consistent with the theory. Assuming that most workers receive little intrinsic satisfaction from their work, they would desire leisure if sufficient income were available to afford it (Barfield and Morgan, 1969; Bowen and Finegan, 1969).

Retirement is thus a desired status and a goal for which unions focus their collective bargaining efforts. This is consistent with the strong causal effect of pension benefits on the retirement decision found in studies of American men (Clark and Spengler, 1980). In addition, old-age pension contributions made by employers are a type of deferred wage. Other public pension contributions may come from general revenues and reflect transfers of income through taxes. In either case, public pensions – like private pensions – are a means for the working class to raise their wages (Myles, 1984). Public pensions offer the additional advantages of stability and security in benefits that are not available from private pension programs. Where private pensions may suffer from vesting or funding problems, government programs are guaranteed (Schulz, 1980). For these reasons, the growth of public pensions can be accounted for by the same factors explaining the growth of more general social welfare programs – namely, the strength of working-class and social democratic parties.

Critique. Critics of the social democratic theory point out that Marxist and neo-Marxist theories fail to deal with ethnic, racial, religious, and cultural cleavages that cut across class boundaries (Parkin, 1979). Class may be only a subsidiary influence on party choice, less important than language or religious differences (Lijphart, 1980; see also Kelley et al., 1985, for evidence on the decline of class voting in Great Britain). Even if class position dominates electoral choice, it is not clear that class-based policies can be directly implemented. Parkin's (1971) review of the evidence concludes that European socialist programs have not had clearly egalitarian results. To gain suppport, parties may need to move toward the center and avoid adopting strong positions that offend large parts of the electorate (Downs, 1957). For leftist parties, their unionized constituency in most countries is too small to gain control of the government without alliance with other groups; these alliances, however, may require a compromise of social democratic ideals (Przeworski, 1985). Even if labor gains control, implementation of a program may be difficult or impossible in the face of a powerful minority bloc opposed to the program. Hence, few differences may exist among parties in terms of the programs implemented or the effects of redistribution (Bollen and Jackman, 1985a). The class basis of political action and the egalitarian potential of class action may both be greatly exaggerated by the social democratic theory.

The emphasis of class theories on the political action of labor and capital to the exclusion of other groups active in the politics of the welfare state may, in particular, slight the aged. They may have interests that do not coincide with those of either the working or capitalist classes but that may still be a major source of political pressure for higher welfare spending. Pensions in particular may be less sensitive to class influence than other expenditures, since the connection between working-class interests and pensions – often seen as a middle-class program – is less clear than for unemployment or occupational injury benefits. In fact, interests of the working class and the aged may diverge over pensions. Generational conflict over the tax burden required to support generous pension systems may separate the working class and the aged. Although the social democratic theory is right to emphasize the role of politics, it may err in limiting its attention to class politics.

Despite these weaknesses, the empirical literature shows strong support for the theory. Of the studies of working-class power in the eighteen or so most developed democracies, "nearly all agree that the strength of parliamentary socialism is more important for welfare state development than other plausible influences" (Shalev, 1983:323). A list of studies that support the class arguments through various forms of cross-national, quantitative analyses includes Castles and McKinlay (1979), Castles (1982), Cameron (1978), DeViney (1983, 1984), Esping-Andersen (1981, 1985b), Friedland and Sanders (1986), Hewitt (1977), Hibbs (1978), Hicks and Swank (1984), Korpi (1983), Stephens (1979), Myles (1984), and Williamson and Weiss (1979). The studies differ in their measures of working-class strength: Some use leftist rule, some rightist rule, and others union density, union centralization, or strike activity. Yet, they all support a new orthodoxy that takes the validity of the class arguments as proven (Hollingsworth and Hanneman, 1982; Shalev, 1983).

A weakness of these studies, however, is that they rely on approximately eighteen nations at one time point. Although the theory clearly delineates the nations to which it applies, the empirical tests of the theory truncate variation in development and age structure with their sample and discredit industrialism variables through analysis of data in which such factors are nearly constant. Even if sufficient variation did exist, reliable multivariate analysis is difficult with only eighteen cases. Support for working-class variables is often obtained without adequate controls for industrialism variables, particularly percent aged. To test the class theory, researchers need to use multivariate techniques to examine the effects of all relevant variables on a sufficiently large sample with variation in both industrialism and class variables. Lacking these methodological requirements, all the aforementioned studies may be suspect.

Democracy and interest group politics

Just as the social democratic theory may be seen as a political version of Marxist theories, the interest group politics theory may be seen as a political version of industrialism theory. A brief statement of the theory comes from Janowitz (1976:75): "The growth of the welfare state since 1945 represents less and less the influence of conceptualized goals – including class goals – and more and more the influence of the power of pressure-group politics reflecting the ordered segments of society.'' A general version of the theory has been applied to economic growth, government regulation, and various types of public spending, but a more specific version needs to be applied to the aged and social welfare spending. Whatever the version, the theory offers two essential propositions and empirical predictions that differ from those of the other theories: (1) economic and demographic changes affect the structure of group resources and demands for welfare spending, and (2) the existence of democratic political institutions facilitates the realization of group interests.

The first proposition is that economic and demographic changes have expanded group resources for collective political action and diversified group interests in the welfare state. Nonclass ascriptive groups, in particular, have become crucial for government policy. In advanced industrial democracies, a general diversification of interests occurs as the economy becomes more specialized and universalistic (Lehner and Widmaier, 1983; Berry, 1984; Murrell, 1984). This reduces the organizational potential of classes but provides a resource for collective action among groups defined by ascriptive characteristics (Nagel and Olzak, 1982; Nielsen, 1985). The retired and aged are a prime example of such a group: they have changed from a relatively small group identifying with families and local communities (Davis and van den Oever, 1981) to a larger, high-voting, politically active group with common age-based interests (Fox, 1981). The expansion of political rights and the incorporation of formerly excluded groups into the political system of advanced democracies further contribute to the growth of groups competing for public resources (Janowitz, 1976; Gronbjerg, 1977). This creates growing demands on the state from a variety of interest groups for higher welfare spending. It also implies the existence of a stratification system segmented by nonclass elements such as age, race, language, occupation, and region that transcend and fragment class boundaries (Parkin, 1979).

The accumulation of interest groups in advanced industrial democracies is not only the result of economic diversification and political modernization, it is the necessary result of the dynamics of collective action. Olson (1982) argues that since collective action is difficult to organize, given the free-rider problem of group action, effective interest groups (or *distributional coalitions*, in Olson's terms) emerge slowly. The longer a nation offers a stable democratic environment, without upheaval or interruption, the more groups accumulate. Once groups exist, Olson argues, it is rational for them to act in their own interest rather than in ways that benefit the collective good: the rewards for special-interest activities are greater than those for actions on behalf of a collective good shared by all of society. Furthermore, the logic of collective action is such that once programs benefiting interest groups are implemented, there is little to be gained for other groups by eliminating the programs and more to be gained by advocating adoption of the group's own programs. Since one form of collective demand is for government programs, interest group action leads to escalating expenditures.

The second proposition of the theory is that government spending results from competition for votes in democracies. Liberal democracies can be defined as institutionalized arrangements for arriving at decisions by means of political struggles for people's votes (Schumpeter, 1975[1942]:269). The population seldom has a clear idea of political goals, voting instead on the basis of performance-related criteria and economic self-interest. Parties can be seen as loose coalitions designed for the purpose of winning elections rather than formulating policies (Downs, 1957; Schlesinger, 1984). Under such arrangements, latent interest groups may be organized by political leaders, or existing groups of varying size and power may demand the support of their representatives for particular programs in return for their votes. Government spending is thus an inherently political process (Tufte, 1978) in which the collective political action of groups in stable democracies furthers their own interests.

In these arguments, the central role given to voting in representative democracies stems from public choice models of politics. Public choice theorists, by assuming that persons are rational utility maximizers, depict voter choice as analogous to market choice (Mueller, 1979; see Hechter, 1983, for other sociological applications). A huge literature has grown from this perspective that investigates the behavior of self-interested groups (Buchanan and Tullock, 1980), voters (Downs, 1957), parties (Schlesinger, 1984), and public bureaucracies (Niskanen, 1971). Applied to the welfare state, public choice theory supplies a set of underlying microlevel postulates about human behavior that imply the need to consider the government response to voter demands for higher benefits.

Lacking a concise label, we use the term *interest group politics theory* to describe these arguments. Janowitz (1976) uses the name *mass society theory* to emphasize the extension of political rights, but *interest group politics theory* may be more general because it emphasizes the collective action of a broad set of groups in the political process. An interest group can be defined as "an organized body of individuals who share some goals and who try to influence public policy" (Berry, 1984:5). Similarly, Olson (19665:8) refers broadly to interest groups as individuals or firms that have common interests and, at least to some extent, share the benefits of concerted action to gain political power. Such groups may effectively advance their interests through the formation of formal organizations and the employment of lobbyists. Yet, they may also influence public policy through voting patterns or other informal means. We use the term *interest group* in its broadest sense, and refer to *interest group theory*, while recognizing that there are diverse arguments that make up the broader theory.[6]

Although the interest group politics theory is couched in general terms and may apply to a variety of groups, the aged deserve special attention. Besides being the prime beneficiary of the largest welfare programs, two key changes – growing numbers and homogenization of interests – expand their political influence and illustrate how the interest group processes work. The obvious increase in the percentage of the population over age 65 is found in all developed nations, but less obvious, and perhaps more important, is the greater increase in the percentage of voters who are aged. For example, the percentage of aged voters rose to 22.2 in Sweden in 1982 (Statistics Sweden, 1986) and to 32.5 in West Germany in 1984 (Statistiches Bundesant, 1986). Even if the aged do not vote as a single bloc, the threat of opposition by groups this large may sway the views and actions of legislators and candidates.[7] The size of the aged population may also be used advantageously by more formal lobbying organizations for the aged. Smaller groups may generally enjoy disproportionate power because large groups face greater problems in acting collectively (Olson, 1965, 1982). In the United States, however, organizations of the aged have been able to overcome the free-rider problem by offering selective incentives of insurance, travel, and pharmaceutical discounts with membership (Hudson, 1978). Their large membership can be mobilized against cuts in benefits or in favor of increased benefits or new programs. Through both voting turnout and effective lobbying, then, increasing numbers can translate into policies favorable to the aged.[8]

The second characteristic – homogenization of interests – results from changes in the labor force status of the aged. Retirement makes the aged dependent on the state, and low fertility makes families less reliable sources of support. Despite their diversity in status, location, and beliefs, nearly all aged persons benefit from increased public pension spending (Pampel, 1981). In fact, diverse group membership, including heavy representation of the middle class as well as the poor, offers a resource for collective action that can effectively be used when a group is united by common interests in government policy. A coherent, generalized ideology relevant to all issues or a dominant, encompassing age identification are unnecessary when older persons are united with respect to their financial stake in specific government welfare policies.

The implications of the theory for the three classificatory dimensions follow logically. The interest group theory, like the social democratic theory, takes politics seriously. The state may act autonomously in ways that are harmful to the economy and opposed by capital or by the working class; it need not act in ways that meet the technological imperatives of industry or the needs of monopoly capitalism. In fact, the state itself develops its own interests that may conflict with those of various economic groups (Skocpol, 1985b). The political demands of a variety of groups, perhaps including state managers as well as the aged, classes, and state constituents, and the political processes by which these demands are negotiated, occupy a prominent place in the interest group theory.

Unlike the social democratic theory, however, class conflict is not the only or dominant political force in the expansion of the social welfare state. Janowitz (1985) argues that stratification includes dimensions of age, sex, and ethnic-racial-religious groups that interact in complex patterns; he uses the term *ordered social segments* to capture this complexity. Labor and capital are important parts of these social segments, but they do not subsume all other bases of stratification (Parkin, 1979). Instead, the welfare state responds to the needs and demands of the increasingly large and specialized social segments, transcending class-based categories (Janowitz, 1985). Among the social segments, perhaps the most important for social welfare spending is the aged. Demographic changes in age structure must be considered to explain adequately the levels of welfare spending.

Like the monopoly capitalism theory, the interest group theory claims that the welfare state is not necessarily redistributive – in fact, it may be harmful to the interests of the disadvantaged (Janowitz, 1985). Instead of being a mechanism to the needy, the welfare state can be viewed as a mechanism for the relatively advantaged (drawn particularly from the middle classes) to maintain their position. For the aged, retirement income in the United States has not been redistributive (Boskin, 1986:38), and several authors have noted the discrepancy between funding for medical, disability, and pension benefits, much of which goes to the affluent aged (Crystal, 1982), and funding for poor children and single-parent, minority families (Preston, 1984). More generally, welfare spending advances political competition at the expense of economic competition as a source of social mobility. Yet, disadvantaged groups may have greater opportunity economically than politically (Olson, 1982): There is greater inequality in the opportunity to create and maintain powerful distributional coalitions than there is in productive abilities. The poor, in particular, have difficulty organizing, and as a result often benefit less from welfare state spending than do other organized interest groups (Alford and Friedland, 1975). Instead, government spending goes to more powerful groups, resulting in little tendency for inequality to decline. A spiral of expenditures may weaken social regulation and the ability to meet political goals (Janowitz, 1976), create an entitlement ethic (Bell, 1976), and slow economic growth and efficiency (Olson, 1982).[9]

Rather than reduce inequality, welfare spending may be a consequence of lower inequality previously brought about by economic change. As educational attainment and income are equalized during industrialization, and as the middle classes grow, the population that stands to benefit from redistribution, is articulate enough to sponsor policies, and can mobilize necessary political power grows in size (Wildavsky, 1985). Accordingly, Peltzman (1980) shows that historical increases and decreases in government spending in the United States, Great Britain, and Japan follow with a lag of several decades decreases and increases, respectively, in inequality. Income inequality has changed little since 1950 in advanced industrial democracies, but reductions before then created the conditions – a politicized middle class – to increase spending. Although the arguments of Peltzman and Wildavsky apply to all government spending, they are consistent with the arguments of the interest group theory concerning the aged – most of whom come from the middle class – for welfare spending. Rather than focusing on the extremes of income distribution, such as the poor or occupationally defined classes, and how benefits to these groups reduce inequality, the interest group theory considers the role of middle-income groups in welfare spending and maintenance of inequality (see also de Tocqueville, 1945:222; Meltzer and Richard, 1981).

Critique. Many claim that the interest group theory is based primarily on exaggerated, negative interpretations of current events (Thurow, 1981; Mishra, 1984; Skocpol, 1985). The financial problems of the welfare state, the failure of many programs to live up to expectations, and the ungovernability of modern democracies have all been overstated. Moreover, the attack on the welfare state may stem primarily from ideological beliefs and political goals. More dispassionate presentations of the theory and tests of its predictions are needed.

Such empirical support for the interest group theory is only just emerging. Many case studies examine the influence of interest groups on legislative action (see Pratt, 1976, Estes, 1979, or Williamson, Evans, and Powell, 1982, for examples involving the aged). Yet, quantitative studies are few. Gronbjerg's (1977) study of states in the United States shows that expenditures for Aid to Families with Dependent Children are explained by levels of political modernization and citizen political participation rather than financial need. Other single-nation studies show the influence of ethnic group mobilization on voting patterns (Ragin, 1979; Nielsen, 1980; Olzak, 1982). Economists have related spending trends in the United States to trends in voter incentives for transfers (Peltzman, 1980; Borcherding, 1985; Mueller and Murrell, 1985; North, 1985). Particularly problematic in all these efforts, however, is measurement of the concepts. Aggregate, cross-national measures of interest groups and lobbying efforts are of dubious validity and often can be interpreted as indicators of concepts from other theories. This suggests the need for some different approaches to testing the theory, such as examining the facilitative impact of democratic politics on the relationship between various groups and welfare spending.

Tests of other propositions of the theory – that economic development determines inequality, whereas welfare spending has no effect – are more straightforward. However, here the evidence in support of the theory is mixed. The literature review of Danziger, Haverman, and Plotnick (1981) shows benefits of welfare spending in the United States. Recent cross-national studies present evidence that economic development fails to predict inequality when controlling for economic dependency (Bornschier and Chase-Dunn, 1985) or union strength and social democratic government incumbency (Stephens, 1979). This evidence is by no means complete, and suffers from the same methodological problems mentioned earlier, but the burden of empirical proof for the interest group theory remains.

State-centered theories

In addition to the previous theories, which focus on the demand by societal groups and classes for spending, we can consider a set of less developed, supply-based theories of the welfare state. Such theories do not offer a clearly specified set of logically related propositions that answer all three questions we have raised. They do, however, suggest a number of state characteristics that may autonomously influence the level of welfare spending regardless of external group demands. The state-centered theories may overlap in some ways with the demand-based theories; the interest group theory, for instance, views the state bureaucracy as a set of organizations concerned with maximizing their budgets, just as any group desires to increase its benefits. Yet, the interest group theory, as well as the others, attends primarily to demands of external groups on the government. Here we focus on arguments strictly concerned with effects of state structure.

Much of the work of the state-centered approach, particularly that of Theda Skocpol and colleagues (Skocpol, 1980; Skocpol and Ikenberry, 1983; Orloff and Skocpol, 1984; Weir and Skocpol, 1985; Skocpol and Amenta, 1986), stems from a historical, qualitative research tradition. Because state characteristics must be studied in their historical and structural context, advocates of this approach avoid abstract generalizations that apply to a large number of nations and quantitative measures that can be used in statistical analyses. Further, much of the work in this tradition addresses the historical emergence of initial welfare legislation in the early decades of the twentieth century. We note here the similarity of Skocpol's work to the state-based explanations of welfare spending from 1950 to 1980, but we cannot claim to offer a test of her work.

Instead, we discuss five state characteristics that others have found important in quantitative studies of welfare spending. First, the centralization and corporatist organization of the state may expand the ability of state managers to implement desired policies for social welfare spending (Wilensky, 1981). Opposition to welfare spending from dispersed and isolated factions can be more easily overcome where the government, union and corporate elite are highly centralized. In fact, Mishra (1984) argues that problems of legitimacy and efficacy of the welfare state in nations such as the United States, Canada, and Great Britain result from the failure of these nations to integrate the welfare state into the economy. When considered as an integrated rather than a differentiated (or residual) part of the economy, social policy can be closely coordinated with economic management of both production and distribution, demand and supply (Wilensky and Lebeaux, 1958). This requires cooperation, economic bargaining, and a centralized pluralism among capital, labor, and the state. Given such a corporate structure, as exists in Sweden or Austria, a national consensus may emerge to implement welfare policies or increase spending without divisive conflict (Mishra, 1984). Several aspects of centralization may also be relevant to an explanation of welfare spending. Nations in which decision making is most concentrated in the central government rather than located in subnational and local governments should be better able to minimize the influence of fragmented opposition and expand national welfare spending (DeViney, 1983, 1984). Conversely, nations composed of federations of subnational units should show lower spending. Finally, centralization of labor and business elites, and their coordination with state managers (i.e., corporatist organization), should also increase welfare spending (Wilensky, 1976).[10]

Second, the bureaucratic strength of administrative agencies may increase spending. Assuming that the goal of government bureaucracies is to expand their budget, those with the most resources – employees, administrative budgets, powerful constituents – may best be able to reach their goals (DeViney, 1983). Thus, the power of state welfare agencies, like that of external groups, must be studied.

Third, the structure of state taxation may influence spending (Cameron, 1978). Nations in which the tax structure is based primarily on direct taxes and payroll deductions may find it difficult to raise funds for continued welfare spending. Reliance on indirect taxes, the cost of which is less obvious to taxpayers than that of direct taxes, creates a fiscal illusion and engenders less opposition to expanding taxes and spending.

Fourth, the electoral cycle specific to each nation may influence the timing of spending (Tufte, 1978; Griffin and Leicht, 1986). The political business cycle involves government spending as a stimulus to the economy shortly before an election in the hope that a burst of economic growth will predispose voters toward the incumbents. The reasoning here is consistent with a public choice, interest group theory of government, but the timing of elections is often mandated to occur at specified times or intervals. This constrains the timing of cyclical trends in spending and must be taken as an exogenous determinant of spending.

Finally, expenditures of states for competing programs, primarily military ones, may constrain the funds available for social welfare spending. If revenues set some sort of upper limit for spending, expenditures for social welfare must compete with military expenditures for available funds. During periods of war, priority may go to the military and welfare spending may remain low. Some nations spend more for defense than others, because of historical and strategic reasons, and may spend less for social welfare. It is difficult to claim that one type of spending causes the other, but the potential trade-offs are at least worth considering.

Although nearly all these arguments and studies predict a direct influence of state characteristics, a more sophisticated reading of the state literature may suggest an interactive argument. It may not be possible to determine a priori how state structures affect spending. Instead, state capacity may increase the ability of nations to respond to citizen demands rather than determining itself what these demands are (Pampel and Stryker, 1989). This suggests that state characteristics may facilitate the influence of demands of class and status groups. Hence, in addition to the additive effects, the interactive effects of state or supply factors must be considered.

In summary, this list of state characteristics hardly offers an integrated theoretical argument that describes the workings of the state apparatus. Despite the early developmental state of this perspective, the ad hoc nature of these arguments still offers something unique to the explanation of social welfare spending. Unlike the other theories, state-centered theories predict the effects of state characteristics regardless of class or demographic structure. They focus less on the potential demands of constituent groups and more on the ability of state managers to meet their own goals in dealing with external groups. As for the consequences of welfare spending on inequality, the effects of state structure are unclear. For example, in Wilensky's (1976) conception of corporatism, cooperation among elites allows them to implement programs that benefit the poor and reduce inequality. In Schmitter's (1982) conception, officially designated representatives of labor may come to accept the procapitalist interests of business and the state rather than those of their members. Corporatism may therefore not lead to lower inequality. The essence of the argument, then, concerns the determinants of welfare spending rather than the consequences.

Summary

The goal of this chapter has been to differentiate theories of the welfare state and draw out predictions that can be empirically tested. Our focus, therefore, has been on arguments and theories that are amenable to quantitative, cross-national analyses and that specify abstract propositions concerning the operation of economic, political, and social forces across nations. This limits the scope of our review somewhat, yet still allows coverage of the major arguments and traditions in the field of stratification. Accordingly, we offer a scheme that clarifies, compares, and contrasts the theories, and thereby provides some organization to the field that is currently lacking.[11] A summary of the predictions is presented in Table 2.1. Although each theory shares fundamental arguments with the others, they can be distinguished when studying welfare spending, equality, and democratic politics together.

Another way to contrast the theories is to consider the groups that each treats as dominant in driving up welfare spending. The industrialism theory views the needs of the poorest groups as most important, although all members of society benefit indirectly. The monopoly capitalism theory considers the other end of the stratification system – the needs of the capitalist class for state support of capital accumulation. The social democratic theory argues that the working class is the prime proponent and beneficiary of the welfare state, and the interest group theory argues that middle-income groups benefit the most.[12] Finally, state-centered theories see all of these groups as active, but dependent on the response of state structures and managers for determining levels of welfare spending.

Put in this perspective, the theories need not be seen as exclusive or encompassing views of the welfare state. By considering the individual programs that make up the welfare state and the groups they may benefit, the theories may prove complementary. For example, social insurance programs for public pensions and health care may favor the aged and middle-income groups and support the nonclass theories; means-tested public assistance and unemployment spending may favor the poor and working classes and support class theories. In evaluating theories, we must consider the domain of programs to which each may best apply. All this discussion, however, is no more than an introduction to testing the theories. It is necessary to delve into the predictions of each theory for specific dependent variables in more detail. With basic arguments, assumptions, and supportive research presented and discussed, we can proceed with such efforts.

Notes

1. It is not possible, of course, to pigeonhole exactly all the work on the welfare state. Theory and research may be seen as lying along a continuum on the three dimensions we have identified, differing as much in emphasis as on fundamental assumptions. It is nonetheless useful to identify the dimensions on which the theories differ and to offer rough groupings of theory and research along the dimensions. Such categorization organizes and simplifies a bewildering variety of ideas that otherwise are difficult to compare and contrast.

2. Attempts to test Wagner's law over time and within nations have not offered support for the

causal influence of economic product (Bird, 1971; Wagner and Weber, 1977; Cameron, 1978). However, no studies have examined the effects of percentage aged on spending over time within a number of developed nations.

3. O'Connor considers various types of expenditures that contribute to the fiscal crisis of the state, which makes his conceptualization of spending much broader than it is for those in the industrialism camp. However, there is overlap that allows comparison of the different theories.

4. Stinchcombe (1985) offers an appropriately named *functional theory of social insurance* that is similar to versions of the monopoly capitalism theory. Social insurance programs, according to Stinchcombe, are the result of compromise between heterogeneous class groupings in which capitalists maintain control over investment and workers obtain social protection. The programs reduce class tensions while preserving the essential capitalist structure. Like other functional theories, this one predicts convergence in the levels and types of social insurance spending.

5. For purposes of presentation, we include a number of scholars with different arguments, especially in their view of the relationship between capital and the state. O'Connor (1973) sees the state as a partner in capital accumulation, Offe (1984) as the outcome of the contradictions of capital accumulation, and Poulantzas (1978) as an autonomous body mediating class conflict. Despite these differences, the theories are linked by their assumption that the state is embedded in the capitalist system and ultimately acts in ways that benefit continued capital accumulation. It is this underlying similarity rather than the variations that exist in the basic argument that is most important for our research strategy.

6. In contrast to traditional pluralism, no assumptions are made that the state regulates and controls interest group activity, that all groups find representation in the political process, or that cooperation among groups contributes to equilibrium and the societal good. Instead, theorists focus on lack of social control, political divisiveness, and economic inefficiency.

7. The way the aged influence public policy may differ from the way classes or ethnic, religious, and linguistic groups do. Many assume implicitly that necessary conditions for the political influence of an interest group include (a) group characteristics as the primary source of identification; (b) a generalized, ideologically coherent collective orientation toward a variety of issues; (c) identification of interests with a single party; and (d) active participation of formal group organizations in the implementation of legislation. None of these conditions may in fact be necessary for the political efficacy of the aged. A preexisting, dominating age consciousness may be unnecessary when group consciousness can be activated by financial interests in public policies. A single generalized ideology among the aged may be unnecessary when mobilization occurs over specific issues. Identification with a single party may be unnecessary when the aged influence politicians within each of several parties and promote a nonpartisan consensus. Finally, the aged need not initiate, draft, or physically represent themselves in the implementation of legislation when external political pressure is present to shape the final outcome indirectly. Thus, the means the aged use to influence policy may be quite different – yet still effective – from the means used by class, racial, religious, or ethnic groups.

8. Size initially hinders collective action (Olson, 1965) but may, over time, prove to be a resource for groups such as the aged in modern political democracies. In Nielsen's (1985) model of ethnic group mobilization, economic modernization reduces the inhibiting effects of size on group organizational potential through improved communication and transportation technology, and political modernization increases the facilitating effects of group size on potential control over events through increased importance of electoral strength. Nielsen's arguments for ethnic groups also apply to other ascriptive groups like the aged.

9. Neoconservatives take these arguments a step further by arguing that expectations for governments have become so excessive that they exceed the capacity of governments to meet them (Brittan, 1975; Kristol, 1978). Similarly, Bell (1976) sees crises emerging from the revolution in entitlements brought about by capitalism (not coincidentally, Marxists such as O'Connor and

Offe predict much the same). Whether expectations are excessive or not requires some value-based definition of excess that belongs in the realm of political debate.

10. Cameron (1978) argues that for total government spending, federal and decentralized state structures disperse spending authority to multiple organizations, which attempt to use their influence by expanding their budget. When authority is fragmented, the central government is unable to control these internal bureaucratic pressures for spending. However, this argument does not apply to welfare spending, which generally is not driven by local or subnational units. Moreover, Cameron finds effects in the empirical analysis in the opposite direction: Spending is highest in unitary, centralized governments.

11. Hasenfeld et al. (1987) recently offerred a classification of the theories similar to our own.

12. The identification and measurement of membership in the middle class present a number of theoretical and methodological problems that have been addressed, if not solved, by a number of researchers (e.g., Wright, 1985; Vanneman and Cannon, 1988). More important here than precise measurement is recognition that the interests of the middle class or those in contradictory class locations differ from those of workers and capitalists.

3. Social welfare spending in advanced industrial democracies

Theories of the welfare state discussed in the last chapter make different predictions concerning the influence on welfare spending of class-based political parties and democratic political participation relative to economic and productive structures. They also make different predictions concerning the importance of class cleavages and power relative to economic and demographic groups such as the aged.[1] State-based theories add the organization and power of the state as explanatory factors in the growth of welfare spending. We begin testing these theories and the predictions they make by examining the determinants of social welfare spending in advanced industrial democracies. In so doing, we help to identify the major structural forces that drive social welfare spending and the nature of the welfare state. To what extent is it a response to economic needs of the population, an object of class struggle, or independently shaped by democratic politics, partisan parties, and state structures? Each theory provides a different set of answers to these questions, and evaluation of the theories offers a way to make sense of the complex processes and structures that make up the welfare state.

In this effort, we focus on high-income democracies to the exclusion of low, middle-income, and nondemocratic nations. The causal processes in nations where surplus income is high enough to support extensive transfer payments and democratic procedures allow the nonelite to organize politically no doubt differ from those in nations where income is low and democratic freedoms are few. Furthermore, the rich sources of data on politics and class structure in the advanced industrial democracies make their detailed study especially useful. Figures on welfare spending, unions, corporate assets, elections, and party incumbents are available back to at least 1950 for these nations. Because the figures show much variation across nations and over time, and are reasonably accurate, they are ideal for studying the economic, class, and political causes of welfare spending.

Despite the importance of studying advanced industrial nations, and the advantages that come from studying nations rich in data on politics and class power, there are limitations to this strategy. Because all the nations considered are highly democratic, it is difficult to examine how variation in democratic procedures

50

affects spending. This creates problems when trying to distinguish the industrialism and interest group theories, which differ not in the structural characteristics of nations they predict to influence spending, but in the mediating democratic mechanisms. Indeed, most literature on the welfare state fails to distinguish or test the two theories. We deal with the similarities in democratic procedures by measuring voting turnout and political party competition as components of democratic action and by examining their interaction with economic and demographic variables. Still, the results of this chapter must be interpreted in tandem with those of the next chapter, where we compare social welfare spending across democratic and nondemocratic, developing nations.

Given the overview of the theories in the last chapter, we need not repeat all the details of the arguments. We do, however, draw out more specific predictions of the theories as they apply to the welfare state in advanced industrial democracies, and discuss the concepts and measurement strategies implied by each of the theories.

Nonclass theories of social welfare spending

The industrialism theory argues for a pluralist model of welfare spending that suggests little if any independent influence of class-based politics. The state serves as a mechanism for meeting the needs of groups disrupted and dislocated by industrial and technological development. A variety of groups that transcend class boundaries, such as the aged, unemployed, sick, and divorced, benefit from the welfare state. The predictions of the theory are straightforward: The higher the level of technological development, and the larger the size of the aged population, the higher the level of welfare spending.[2] These predictions are implicitly additive: The industrialism theory posits a more or less automatic process in which needs for support translate directly into spending.

The interest group theory places more emphasis on the politics of welfare spending (but not on class-based politics). A variety of economic, demographic, and bureaucratic groups influence spending, not by demonstrating objective needs but through a variety of political activities and institutions. Higher spending is not an automatic response, but results from the combination of socioeconomic changes with democratic politics. The theory thus predicts the influence of economic development and the size of the aged population, along with the influence of political variables. The greater the political activity of the population and its representation in the political process – as shown, for instance, by the level of voting participation – the higher the level of welfare spending (Gronbjerg, 1977). Although all these nations are democratic in the sense that they offer competitive elections, political liberties, and voting rights for all adults, they differ in the percentage of the population that uses the right to vote. Electoral participation reflects the incentives that citizens have to vote and measures the use of existing formal channels to influence the political process (Powell, 1986; Jackman, 1987). Similarly, the degree of competition among political parties may also be important, as a large number of similarly strong parties increases the influence of interest groups relative to situations where two encompassing parties merge diverse interests (Olson, 1982:51).

Another way to differentiate the theories is to examine how demographic change combines with political structures to influence spending. A large aged population should have more influence on welfare spending where political participation and electoral competition are high and interest groups are most influential. Similarly, the effects of percentage aged may increase over time as the political resources of the aged grow and they are better able to translate growing numbers into higher spending. Janowitz (1976) and Gronbjerg (1977) suggest that welfare spending grows with interest group activity and the incorporation of excluded groups into the political processes, both of which have become more important over time. During the post–World War II period, the definition of "need" for welfare benefits expanded such that the welfare state diffused upward throughout the stratification system. The same characteristics (such as percent aged or economic product) may therefore lead to higher spending in later time periods. If such interactions exist, they may suggest an integration of the industrialism and interest group theories. Welfare spending, initially directed at the most needy, who face serious economic problems, may later expand to favor less deprived, more politically active groups.

Class theories of social welfare spending

Increases in spending, according to the monopoly capitalism theory, depend on the profitability and investment of capital. With respect to social insurance programs, spending serves monopoly capital by creating a more disciplined labor force. Workers develop a sense of security and commitment to work organizations when they can count on receiving benefits for unemployment, retirement, or sickness. Since workers need these benefits only because capitalist development makes them redundant and vulnerable in the first place, social insurance programs are ultimately programs for capitalists and corporations rather than for workers (O'Connor, 1973:138). Other social welfare spending in the form of poverty and government relief for the surplus population is also an inherent feature of capitalist development (O'Connor, 1973:158). Monopoly capitalism creates imbalances or disruptions that adversely affect or create a surplus population, and social welfare spending offers a way to limit protest from that population and maintain the legitimacy of the system.

These arguments imply that government social welfare spending is highest where the process of capital accumulation and centralization (i.e., monopolization) is most advanced. Both the secular trends and the cyclical rhythms of monopoly capital influence spending (Devine, 1985). Secular trends in the concentration of capital in advanced capitalist nations provide a steady impetus for continued spending. Cyclical increases in economic growth translate into unemployment (especially in the monopoly sector) and higher social welfare spending.

Labor also takes a part in determining spending. Institutionalized wage bargaining in the monopoly sector involves cooperation of capital and labor, and both groups may favor public spending as a form of deferred wages. Noninstitutionalized class struggle, such as disruption of labor through industrial disputes and strike activity, also may compel governments to quell the protest by developing new welfare programs and expanding existing ones.

If industrial and capital concentration leads to higher social welfare spending, external trade and market forces that affect industrial concentration may likewise affect spending. Smaller nations with fewer natural resources and smaller markets must depend on the import of raw materials and the export of goods for foreign markets. This subjects the economy to fluctuations in world markets and prices, and encourages the growth and concentration of monopoly capital to better withstand harmful external forces. Social welfare spending is similarly necessary to protect the population from the exigencies of the international market.

The arguments of the social democratic theory overlap those of monopoly capitalism, since both focus on class structure. Yet, the social democratic theory claims that capital opposes social welfare spending: The political efforts of labor to overcome this opposition are the force behind the growth of the welfare state. When centrally organized, unions can mobilize effectively in their collective interest and elect labor, socialist, or social democratic parties that implement social welfare programs favoring the working class. The social democratic theory uniquely emphasizes the importance of class-based politics: Labor has greater political power than market power to use in its struggle against capital (Esping-Anderson, 1985a). This translates into different predictions concerning the effects of political parties. If the capitalist economy constrains democratic outcomes, as argued by the monopoly capitalism theory, then differences in party philosophy will make little difference in welfare spending. In contrast, the social democratic theory predicts positive effects from leftist party incumbency and negative effects from rightist party incumbency.

Where the monopoly capitalism theory sees the effects of labor disputes and trade dependency operating through corporate concentration, the working-class strength theory sees them operating through democratic election of leftist parties. In the working-class strength theory, labor militancy and industrial disputes may be seen as a means to influence the government when direct political means fail and rightist or centrist parties control the government. The working-class strength theory also sees effects of foreign trade. In nations vulnerable to fluctuations of the world economy, political support for leftist parties, which are most willing to use government programs to protect the population from such fluctuations, is high. Even though the two class theories share the same predictions regarding these variables, the reasoning behind the predictions differs.

State-centered theory

The class and nonclass theories focus on the demands made by external groups on the government, perhaps neglecting the influence of state organization on spending (Orloff and Skocpol, 1984). Much of the work of the state-centered approach, particularly that of Skocpol and colleagues (e.g., Skocpol, 1985b; Skocpol and Amenta, 1986), advocates a qualitative historical approach that avoids the quantitative measures, statistical analyses, and abstract generalizations over a large number of nations used in this study. Nonetheless, other quantitative studies likewise suggest the need to control for a variety of state characteristics such as the degree of centralization (DeViney, 1983), federalism, coalition cabinets (Castles, 1982), corporate organization (Wilensky, 1976), bureaucratic power (DeViney, 1983), taxation policy (Cameron, 1978), electoral cycle, and budget constraints (Griffin et al., 1983).

Research design

Most previous studies of advanced industrial democracies are limited by the reliance on cross-sectional designs. A cross section of developed nations at one time point effectively eliminates much variation in the industrialism variables. This truncation is not a major problem in describing the association of spending with political control or union power, but it does limit the ability to test for these factors relative to the industrialism variables. Nearly all support for class theory has come from studying samples in which the industrialism variables are held nearly constant. Furthermore, even if variation in all the variables is high, a cross section of advanced industrial democracies fails to provide the necessary degrees of freedom for multivariate analyses. To control for all relevant industrialism, class, and political variables simultaneously, additional cases are needed. Combining nations at varied levels of development increases variance and cases but merges groups with substantially different causal processes. The variance of the variables and the degrees of freedom must be increased by other means if the net influence of measures stemming from each of the theories is to be estimated.

An alternative approach, pooling cross-sectional and longitudinal data for advanced industrial democracies over the last several decades, offers several advantages. First, examining cross sections over a relatively long time span – from 1950 to 1980 – increases the variation of all variables. In contrast to cross-sectional studies, which truncate the industrialism variables, the use of longitudinal data allows substantial change in GNP or percent aged, as well as in the class variables. Time-series data are an equally important source of variation in social welfare expenditures and their determinants and, indeed, are crucial for testing the interest group theory. Second, correlations from such analyses, because of the additional variation, are usually lower than for time-series data alone, limiting collinearity problems among variables. Third, the pooled cross-sectional and time-series design increases the sample size and allows multivariate analyses. The use of *n* (countries) times *t* (time periods) cases leaves sufficient degrees of freedom for reliable analysis of many variables.[3] The additional variation and degrees of freedom make comparisons of the effects of most relevant variables possible, even for the subset of advanced industrial democracies. The theories can be appropriately tested without inappropriate clustering of heterogeneous nations.

The use of pooled cross-sectional time-series data favors variables that track both changes over time and differences across nations and penalizes variables that differ across nations, but not over time, or vice versa. With the pooled data, we can describe general, abstract processes that minimize peculiarities specific to individual nations or time points and the influence of single-country and time-specific events on social welfare spending (Griffin et al., 1986). This does not mean that all contextual differences are ignored; the multiple nations and time points allows tests for the constancy of relations across subsets of nations and time points. Yet, the design minimizes problems of generalizability of single cross sections or time series and helps clarify the temporal and geographic domains of the models.

With these points in mind, we select the 18 advanced industrial democracies used in nearly all studies of the welfare state (and identified by the World Bank, 1983, as industrial market economies) for seven time points between 1950 and 1980. These nations include the major Western European democracies,[4] Canada, the United States, Japan, Australia, and New Zealand. There is some disagreement over whether Japan should be included, since it does not share Western culture (Stephens, 1979). However, it has reached the levels of industrial and democratic development required for class factors to operate. The time points to be studied are 1950, 1955, 1960, 1965, 1970, 1975, and 1980 (data for the years between these time points are not available for many of the variables for the full time span. The pooled cross-sectional time-series data provide a sample size of 126 – sufficiently large for multivariate analysis and containing much longitudinal and cross-national variation. However, since the time series within nations are not independent, special methods of analysis will be needed to deal with the statistical problems that result.

Measuring welfare spending

Our definition of social welfare spending, presented and discussed in Chapter 1, includes government cash and in-kind benefits for protection of households from loss of income, such as for pensions, unemployment, sickness, medical care, injury, public assistance, family allowances, and public health. Our measure of social welfare spending includes the same benefit expenditures by the government for each of these programs. It is the most commonly used measure in the literature, and the object of efforts by the ILO (1985) to make figures comparable and reliable (Appendix 3.A lists the sources for all variables used in this chapter). Consistent with our definition of welfare spending, the measure excludes spending for education, corporate infrastructure, and private pensions and medical insurance (see Chapter 1). Like virtually all previous researchers, we divide these expenditures by GNP to obtain a measure of welfare effort and control for available resources.

It is also useful to disaggregate social welfare spending into more internally homogeneous problems (although the data do not allow breakdowns before 1960). One distinction is between social insurance and means-tested (i.e., public assistance) programs, since the former are more likely to benefit the middle class, which contributes most to their funding, whereas the latter are aimed at the poor.[5] Further disaggregation of social insurance programs into pension, health care, family allowance, unemployment, and occupational injury categories would also be instructive. However, there are reasons why the study of general social welfare expenditures is still necessary. First, the general measure provides a useful summary in which each program is weighted by its proportion of the total. Separate analyses treat small programs the same as much larger programs. A measure that reflects the relative contribution of each program to the total avoids exaggerating the importance of small programs. Second, analysis of separate programs may be misleading to the extent that nations use different program strategies to meet the same goals of social protection. Some nations, for instance, may provide less for pensions because they offer free medical care. Nation-specific programmatic emphases may distort models for individual programs but balance out in the total model. Therefore, we begin with the analysis of the general measures of social welfare spending for the complete time span and move on to the analysis of the separate programs from 1960 to 1980.[6]

As a check on the results, we also examine another measure, based not on the type but the form of expenditures (Hicks and Swank, 1984). This measure includes cash transfer payments designed for income maintenance. National account statistics include as cash transfers spending for social security and related pension and income maintenance schemes, social assistance grants and aid to nonprofit organizations serving households, and unfunded employee benefits. The disadvantage is that it does not include in-kind benefits. While similar to the ILO measure, cash transfer expenditures are used to check the sensitivity of the results to measurement error.

Measuring independent variables

The discussion of the theories in the last chapter and this one indicates the complexities of the processes determining social welfare spending. The correspondence of a single variable to each of the theories would make for a simple test but no doubt would oversimplify things. Each theory considers a variety of influences on welfare spending, and there is often overlap in some of the arguments. We must discuss a large number of variables corresponding to the multiple hypotheses derived from each theory and explain technical details of measurement. For many of the variables, a summary of the standard operationalization used in nearly all previous research is sufficient. For others, however, more detailed discussion and justification of our choices are warranted.

The first industrialism variable, economic development, is measured by GNP per capita in thousands of 1975 U.S. dollars. The second, percent aged, is measured by the number of persons aged 65 and over divided by the total population (times 100).[7]

The interest group theory predicts, besides the effects of percent aged, the importance of political variables unconnected to class ideology. Political participation is measured as the percentage of the population aged 20 and over that voted in the last national election (the reported figures do not adjust for differences across nations or years in age of eligibility, but the small number of persons aged 18 to 19 excluded from the denominator should not greatly bias the measure). Political party electoral competition measures the equality of the share of votes received by participating parties against the perfectly competitive situation (where each party receives an equal share of the votes). The maximum value is one and the minimum value is zero (where one party receives all votes).[8]

The measures of monopoly capitalism should reflect structural pressures toward concentration of capital – a difficult task with cross-national data. One measure from Hicks and Swank (1984) divides the assets of the world's largest 250 industrial corporations with central headquarters in each of the nations by the nation's GNP. Hicks and Swank interpret the positive effect of this measure on growth in welfare spending as the result of the strong political capacities of capital. A more direct measure of monopolization from Stephens (1979) is based primarily on business establishment size, but is estimated by gross domestic product (GDP) for seven of the nations and is available only for 1970. Taking another approach, Griffin et al. (1983) argue that the effects of capital concentration occur indirectly through the creation of surplus capital and the resulting labor force dislocations. This suggests that the unemployment rate mediates the effect of monopolization and should be used as a direct determinant of spending. However, since the effect of the unemployment rate may also be seen as the response of leaders to societal needs or of leftist parties to political demands of their constituents, it cannot offer unambiguous support for the monopoly capitalism theory.

The degree of industrial conflict, as an indicator of economic protest that must be allayed to maintain social legitimacy, may also raise welfare spending, according to the monopoly capitalism theory. Yearly data were collected on the number of industrial disputes, the number of workers involved, and the workdays lost. To smooth the yearly fluctuations, the figures were then averaged over the five years up to and including the year of measurement. Finally, the figures were divided by the size of the labor force to control for the number of workers and workdays. In preliminary runs, the days-lost measure had the strongest effects, as might be expected, since it summarized the workers involved and the duration of the disputes. It is the only one of the three measures presented in our equations.

The social democratic theory emphasizes the strength of organized labor more than that of capital (although both class theories share a concern with the features of class structure and conflict). To measure labor's economic power, we combine union membership with union centralization, as suggested by Hicks and Swank (1984). Union membership as a percentage of the labor force was collected from statistical yearbooks of individual nations. It corresponds to the figures gathered and presented by Stephens (1979) for the years 1950, 1960, and 1970. Union centralization is measured as a recode of Stephens's (1979) measure of union bargaining power. Hicks and Swank (1984) find that a dichotomous recode of Stephens's original scale is correlated 0.99 with the more detailed measure and has a larger effect on social welfare expenditures. We also use this recode, in which Sweden, Norway, Finland, Denmark, Austria, Belgium, and the Netherlands are coded 1 and other nations are coded 0. A number of studies suggest that centralization and density interact; that is, density has more influence when union bargaining is centralized (Hicks and Swank, 1984; Myles, 1984). To capture this interaction, we follow Hicks and Swank by creating a variable, called *union scope,* equal to centralization plus 1 times density.[9]

The working-class strength theory uniquely predicts the importance of class-based political party control. Ruling parties are identified as left, right, and other by Castles (1982).[10] For each year since 1945, each party type received a 1 if it was ruling and a 0 if it was not (Stephens, 1979). For participation in coalitions, a party received a score between 0 and 1, depending on the proportion of legislative seats it had relative to the number of seats of all parties participating in the government. Nearly equivalent to party cabinet representation, this measure performs better than electoral strength or legislative seats because it captures the ability of a party to implement its program (Stephens, 1979). To adapt the measure to our longitudinal design, we calculate the cumulative years of party rule since 1946 for each party rather than party rule during the year of measurement.[11]

There are also a number of measures of state organization that may influence public spending. State centralization is measured by the percentage of revenues that go to the central government (DeViney, 1983). A dummy variable in which 1 indicates a federal system measures the converse of centralization, and another dummy variable in which 1 indicates the existence of coalition governments may also be important (see Castles, 1982:64, for a list of the countries with federal and coalition systems). Corporatism measures the appointment power of the central government, along with the centralization of labor union federations, and reflects the ability of elites in central governments to implement policies (Wilensky, 1976:50).[12] The percentage of social welfare expenditures that go to administrative costs measures the bureaucratic power of the social welfare agencies. The percentage of government revenues that come from direct rather than indirect taxes may limit the ability of governments to increase taxes and spending (Cameron, 1978). Defense expenditures as a percentage of GNP may compete with and lower social welfare spending (Griffin et al., 1983). Finally, the years to the next election, or whether or not a year is an election year, may measure the political business cycle; the closer the year is to an election, the higher the spending may be (Griffin et al., 1983).

Finally, our measure of trade vulnerability and potential economic dislocation is imports and exports as a percentage of GNP measures (Cameron, 1978). Another variable, which is difficult to tie to any single theory, is the consumer price index (1975 = 100); it reflects automatic escalation of benefits in response to inflation.

Estimation

The use of time-series data with the cross-sectional data means that the sample units are no longer independent and the model errors may be correlated over time. In other words, each new time point does not add a wave of completely new and independent information. Because of different population sizes and measurement techniques, the nations also may not have constant error variances; those with large errors may contribute disproportionately to the statistical results. With these problems – serial correlation and heteroscedasticity of the errors – ordinary least squares (OLS) estimates are unbiased but inefficient without a lagged dependent variable. Unless adjustments are made, serial correlation in the OLS residuals means that the degrees of freedom are overestimated because of the time redundancy. Heteroscedasiticy underestimates the error for nations with large error and overestimates it for nations with small error. Although these create problems in estimation of standard errors, they may have more serious effects – bias and inefficiency – in the presence of a lagged dependent variable.

To deal with these problems, we estimate generalized least squares (GLS) models, beginning with a relatively simple error specification of a single first-order autoregressive process and error variances unique to each nation. The model thus assumes a common autoregressive process wherein the errors are a function of values at the previous time point times an autoregression coefficient plus random error.[13] The two-stage estimation uses OLS residuals to estimate the error parameters and then uses GLS to transform the data matrices and obtain adjusted estimates (Stimson, 1985, presents the assumptions of the models mathematically and gives details of estimation). In effect, the procedure subtracts out over-time redundancy in the variables, so that each time point approaches independence from the others, and weights nations in inverse proportion to their error variance. Later we examine results for a more complex specification, but we find that the results are robust with respect to the estimation technique.

Pooling assumes, of course, that the models are constant over time and homogeneous across subsets of nations. We explicitly test for changes over time later when testing for predicted interactions, and are able to relax the assumption. As for differences in trends across nations, our relatively homogeneous subset of nations lessens this problem. Nonetheless, we did divide nations into large populations (the United States, Canada, Japan, Australia, West Germany, Great Britain, and Italy) and other, small populations that are more dependent on external trade (Stephens, 1979) to check for the constancy of the processes. At the .05 level, the models were not significantly different across groups. Otherwise, we examine models separately for strong- and weak-union nations, and for corporatist and noncorporatist nations, later in the chapter when we explore interactive class and state arguments.

Before examining the multivariate results, we present descriptive statistics and correlation coefficients with social welfare spending (Table 3.1).[14] Beyond providing some familiarity with these data, the table illustrates that the time-series

Table 3.1. *Means (all years, 1950, and 1980), standard deviations, and correlations with social welfare spending over GNP, advanced industrial democracies, 1950–80*

Variables	$\overline{X}$	s	$\overline{X}_{50}$	$\overline{X}_{80}$	r
Soc. welfare/GNP (%)	12.3	5.7	7.66	19.4	1.00
GNP ($1,000)	4.19	2.28	2.31	7.32	0.567
Aged pop. (%)	10.6	2.32	9.04	12.4	0.764
Vote/pop. (%)	75.9	14.2	74.1	79.8	0.384
Elect comp. (%)	83.5	6.66	84.4	83.4	0.146
Left rule	6.2	6.8	2.1	10.8	0.560
Right rule	7.6	8.1	1.2	13.3	−0.063
Union central (= 1)	0.389	0.489	0.389	0.389	0.340
Union member. (%)	36.3	14.9	31.1	43.6	0.472
Union scope	54.2	37.3	44.6	67.3	0.503
Strike days	0.219	0.238	0.282	0.284	−0.079
Unemployment (%)	2.83	2.47	2.72	5.01	0.286
Mon. assets/GNP[a]	0.979	0.223	na	0.938	−0.105
Monopolization[b]	1.38	0.29	na	na	−0.113
Consumer price	70.0	43.6	31.7	158	0.667
Imp + Exp/GNP (%)	52.8	24.7	49.7	67.3	0.410
Central gov. (%)[c]	61.7	14.5	65.0	57.3	−0.215
Federal (= 1)	0.333	0.473	0.333	0.333	−0.096
Coalition (= 1)	0.500	0.502	0.500	0.500	−0.219
Corporatism	4.38	4.24	4.38	4.38	0.416
Admin. cost (%)[d]	3.38	1.13	na	3.09	0.053
Direct tax. (%)[c]	53.5	9.44	48.9	60.0	0.396
Years to elect.	1.9	1.2	1.61	1.44	−0.015
Election year (= 1)	0.111	0.315	0.167	0.278	−0.065
Defense/GNP (%)	3.47	2.46	6.16	2.54	−0.252

[a] Data for 1960–80.
[b] Data for 1970; Japan missing.
[c] New Zealand missing.
[d] Data for 1955–80.

component of the data adds substantial variation to the variables. The means for 1950 and 1980 show that major changes have occurred in most of the variables. The nearly threefold growth in spending certainly needs explanation, along with the cross-sectional differences. Since cross-sectional relationships cannot be assumed to hold for overtime data or vice versa, studies that neglect either type of variation may be incomplete.

The bivariate correlations show that variables that increase steadily over time, such as GNP, percent aged, leftist rule, union scope, and consumer prices have a high association with social welfare spending. Yet, variables with little or no time trend, such as percent voting or corporatism, also show strong correlations.[15] Among the independent variables, the correlations are smaller than those typically found in time-series designs, since the pooled data add variation across nations. All but a few of the correlations are below 0.5, and only one is above 0.65 (the correlation between leftist rule and union scope is 0.758).

Results: Total social welfare spending

Based on these data, Table 3.2 presents the GLS model for social welfare spending (column 1).[16] The results can be summarized simply: The strongest determinant is percent aged; percent voting, GNP, and inflation follow in importance; and unemployment and electoral competition have small but significant effects. The class variables have weak effects, often in the direction opposite to that of predictions. The lack of strong class effects is also evident for the measure of monopoly assets (available only since 1960). When included in the equation, it reduces the degrees of freedom and the significance of all variables, but itself has effects near zero (beta $= -0.053$). Similarly, a simple model for 1970 with controls only for percent aged shows that the other measure of monopolization has a standardized coefficient of only -0.07. Overall, age structure appears stronger than class, and nonclass political variables appear stronger than class-based party variables; politics appear important, but all parties respond similarly with social welfare spending to demographic conditions.

These results raise the question of why the class and class party variables have such weak and, at times, negative effects. To help answer this question, we consider (and reject) several hypotheses relating to the statistical properties of the model that may account for our findings.

1. The assumptions made about the error term are inappropriate, and the GLS estimates downwardly bias the influence of the class variables. The OLS estimates show that the size of nearly all coefficients is larger without the GLS adjustments, but the basic pattern of coefficients remains the same. Leftist rule has negative effects, and union scope has small positive effects. Another form of the GLS model (Kmenta, 1971:512) allows autocorrelation coefficients to vary across nations, but these estimates (column 2) are nearly identical to those in column 1.

2. Simultaneously controlling for all class variables, which may be components of a single factor, eliminates their common variance and their influence on welfare spending. To check for this possibility, we present coefficients for variables with controls for only two industrialism variables – GNP and percent aged

Table 3.2. *Coefficients (unstandardized above standardized) for GLS estimates of models of social welfare spending, advanced industrial democracies, 1950–80*

Independent variables	Social welfare spending					Cash transfers
	(1)	(2)[a]	(3)[b]	(4)[c]	(5)[d]	(6)
GNP/pop.	0.586**	0.623**	0.667**	0.357	0.181	0.615**
	0.233	0.248	0.265	0.142	0.053	0.304
% aged	1.18**	1.25**	1.72**	1.22**	0.396*	1.28**
	0.478	0.506	0.696	0.492	0.151	0.644
% voting	0.112**	0.127**	0.121**	0.159**	0.059*	0.139**
	0.277	0.315	0.299	0.394	0.146	0.427
Elect. comp.	0.121**	0.173**	0.091**	0.166**	0.095**	0.216**
	0.141	0.201	0.106	0.135	0.111	0.312
Left rule	−0.075	−0.108	0.105	−0.221**	−0.001	−0.244*
	−0.088	−0.127	0.135	−0.261	−0.001	−0.358
Right rule	−0.065	−0.087	0.029	−0.239**	−0.074	−0.061
	−0.092	−0.123	0.041	−0.340	−0.093	−0.108
Union scope	0.010	0.002	0.035**	−0.003	−0.003	−0.030
	0.065	0.013	0.228	−0.020	−0.018	−0.242
Strike days	−1.98	−2.05	−0.339	−3.35**	−0.249	0.941
	−0.082	−0.085	−0.014	−0.138	−0.010	0.048
Unemployment	0.278*	0.216	0.588**	−0.056	−0.106	0.173
	0.120	0.093	0.254	−0.024	−0.041	0.093
Cons. price	0.034**	0.041**	0.036**	0.050**	0.045*	−0.001
	0.258	0.312	0.274	0.383	0.177	−0.009
Imp + Exp/GNP	0.005	−0.010	0.038*	−0.020	−0.007	0.009
	0.022	−0.043	0.164	−0.087	−0.028	0.048
Soc. welf.$_{t-5}$					0.779**	
					0.640	
Intercept	−23.9	−29.2		−24.3	−13.8	−32.2
R^2 (OLS)	0.851	0.851		0.867	0.919	0.619
df	114	114		114	95	114

**$p < .01$; *$p < .05$.

[a] Allows cross-sectional correlation of errors and nation-specific autocorrelation coefficients.

[b] Coefficients for each variable added one at a time to the equation with "GNP/pop." and "% aged." Coefficients for "GNP/pop." and "% aged" control for no other variables.

[c] OLS estimates with variables measured as deviations from year-specific means of each variable.

[d] Independent variables are lagged to the previous time point; 1950 deleted.

(column 3 presents the coefficients for each variable added singly to the two-variable equation). The effects of union scope increase, as do those for percent voting and unemployment, but, all in all, the class effects remain small.[17]

3. The measure of cumulative control of leftist and rightist parties over several decades attenuates the instantaneous effects of party control. Measures of control over just the last five years, however, show correlations and net coefficients that differ little from the cumulative measures.

4. The strong time trend in percent aged and social welfare spending dominates the model at the expense of the cross-sectional relationships between class and spending. We can estimate a model in which all variables are measured as deviations from the year-specific means, which effectively removes the time-series component of all variables. The within-year results using these deviation scores are shown in Table 3.2 (column 4). Strike days lost shows stronger negative effects, suggesting that welfare spending is high not where disruption occurs, but where unions are strong enough to make only the threat of strikes necessary. Rightist rule shows negative effects here; it has a modest cross-sectional relationship with spending, but it does not covary well with the trend over time. Although the model excludes important variation in welfare spending, it offers some evidence for the importance of class-based parties.[18]

5. Outliers and influential cases (e.g., American exceptionalism, Japanese culture) hide the effects of class. To check for the disproportionate and misleading influence of a single nation, we systematically estimated 18 models, each with one nation deleted (Mosteller and Tukey, 1977).[19] This exercise shows that the estimates are robust; none of the standardized coefficients change by more than 0.10. The effects of percent aged remain strong and positive, the effects of leftist rule negative, and the effects of union scope near zero in all equations.

6. Class variables have no effect on the level of social welfare spending, but they may better explain short-term change. Table 3.2 (column 5) presents an equation in which social welfare spending is predicted by a lagged dependent variable and lagged independent variables. By controlling for spending in the previous time period, the effects of the independent variables on changes in spending five years hence can be shown (this requires deletion of the 1950 data, since none of the variables have lagged values back to 1945).[20] The inclusion of the lagged dependent variable, however, biases downward the effects of the other variables when there is serial correlation of the errors, and it becomes difficult to estimate the error parameters accurately from OLS residuals. This problem may be partly responsible for the weak effects of many variables; only percent aged and the nonclass political variables remain at all important. Although these results must be viewed with caution, they provide no evidence of the importance of class or the unimportance of age structure. Indeed, since the lagged dependent

variable summarizes the influence of other exogenous variables in previous time periods (this is the essence of the Koyck distributed lag model; Pindyck and Rubinfield, 1976:214), the importance of percent aged and nonclass political variables shows through both the lagged dependent variable and their own net effect.

7. The results are specific to the ILO measure of welfare spending. Column 6 presents the basic model for the measure of cash transfers. The effects differ little from those for the ILO measure. Other analyses show somewhat weaker but still strong effects of percent aged on total civilian government spending (results not reported). Despite flaws in these other dependent variables, the results further indicate the robustness of the results.

State structure

Do any of the variables measuring aspects of state structure change our conclusions about the effects of the demand variables? Although recognizing that we do not have a full set of propositions to test, we do have a number of relevant variables. When added one at a time to the basic model, none of the state variables changes the previous conclusions. Table 3.3 shows the effects of each variable, along with the effects of selected demographic, political, and class variables. Most state variables have little effect on spending, and none changes the effects of the other variables. Government centralization has a negative rather than a positive effect. Federalism, coalition cabinets, corporatism, administrative costs, direct tax revenues, and electoral timing have virtually no effect on spending. (Several have a small effect in part because they do not vary over time and can explain only cross-sectional variation.) Defense spending has a small negative effect but does not change the effects of any of the other variables.

Interaction models

The effects of percent aged and other variables in these models are additive; the influence of each variable is the same at all levels of the others. This assumption may need to be relaxed, particularly for the influence of percent aged, which may be facilitated by political and social conditions. The existence or nonexistence of such interactions has obvious theoretical implications. The industrialism theory predicts additive effects of percent aged as spending increases proportionally with the size of the population in need. The interest group theory predicts that the effects of percent aged are greatest where and when the political ability of constituents to influence policy is greatest. Even the social democratic theory might predict that leftist governments and union power facilitate the effects of percent aged, whereas rightist governments inhibit them.

Table 3.3. *Coefficients for state variables and selected other variables for GLS estimates of models of social welfare spending, advanced industrial democracies, 1950–80*

| State variables | Social welfare spending | | | | | |
	State[a]	% aged	% vote	Left	Right	Union
Central gov.	−0.096** −0.237	1.02**	0.145**	0.001	−0.085	−0.000
Federal gov.	0.757 0.063	1.17**	0.120**	−0.057	−0.065	0.008
Coalition	−0.710 −0.063	1.15**	0.106**	−0.074	−0.071	0.015
Corporatism	0.060 0.045	1.15**	0.105**	−0.061	−0.059	0.007
Admin. cost	0.208 0.041	1.18**	0.129**	−0.111	−0.091	0.009
Direct tax.	0.066 0.106	1.22**	0.113**	−0.058	−0.088	0.004
Years to elect.	−0.008 −0.002	1.18**	0.111**	−0.072	−0.063	0.010
Election year	−0.880 −0.049	1.18**	0.116**	−0.092	−0.072	0.009
Defense/GNP	−0.136 −0.059	1.21**	0.111**	−0.085	−0.091	0.008
None		1.18**	0.112**	−0.075	−0.065	0.010

**p < .01; *p < .05.
[a]Unstandardized over standardized; otherwise, unstandardized alone.

Table 3.4 shows the results of testing for the interactive effects of political and class variables with percent aged and total social welfare spending. Multiplicative interaction terms of percent aged times political and class variables were added one at a time to our basic model. Without presenting the detailed results, the table shows the unstandardized coefficients for percent aged, the other interacting variable, and the multiplicative interaction term. The results show that the effect of percent aged is largest where and when a high percentage of the adult population participates in democratic processes and the electoral competition among parties is strong. Class-based parties do not change the positive effect of percent aged, as none appear able to claim the voting support of the aged. Finally, union scope facilitates the effects of percent aged (or percent

Table 3.4. *Coefficients (unstandardized) for GLS estimates of models of interaction of political and class variables with percent aged population, advanced industrial democracies, 1950–80*

Interacting variables (X_i)	X_i (1)	% aged (2)	$X_i \times$ % aged (3)	% aged −1 sd[a]	+1 sd[b]
% voting	−0.123	−0.589	0.023*	0.830	1.48
Elect. comp.	0.094	−0.506	0.020*	1.03	1.30
Left rule	−0.357	1.10**	0.021	—	—
Right rule	0.064	1.34	−0.013	—	—
Union scope	−0.108*	0.826	0.010**	0.995	1.74
Time	−0.019	0.674*	0.026*	0.700[c]	1.48[d]

**$p<.01$; *$p<.05$.

[a]Calculated from columns 2 and 3 when the interacting variable takes a value one standard deviation below its mean.
[b]Same, but the interacting variable is one standard deviation above its mean.
[c]1950.
[d]1980.

aged facilitates the effects of union scope); union power may require a large aged population to raise welfare spending.

Because the interaction coefficients are difficult to interpret, we make some simple calculations to illustrate how the effects of percent aged change under varying societal conditions. We use the interaction terms to calculate the net effect of percent aged when the other interacting variable is one standard deviation below its mean and one standard deviation above its mean. This shows, for instance, that the effect of percent aged is only 0.830 when 61.7 percent of the population votes and 1.48 when 90.1 percent of the population votes. The last two columns in Table 3.4 thus show how societal conditions influence the way percent aged translates into higher spending. The same sort of interaction exists between a linear time variable and percent aged. Calculations show that the effect of percent aged is 0.700 in 1950 and 1.48 in 1980 – an increase of 0.480, or 69 percent. Something more than mere growth in the number of aged persons is involved, since the influence of the same number of aged persons expands over time or across various societal conditions.

It is difficult to separate the unique effect of each interaction. A combined model is uninformative, as all interactions are highly correlated. The exact source of the interaction, however, is less important than the point that a consistent pattern of interaction exists. The effects of percent aged rise as conditions conducive to their influence grow. Political participation may make the aged a more potent voting bloc, electoral competition may drive up political stakes for support of the aged, and union power may combine with aged power to raise benefits.

The increase in the effects of percent aged over time is one instance in which the assumption of constant effects over the time does not hold. We also tested for other instances. It is not possible to estimate models for single years, since the number of variables approaches the number of cases. We did, however, estimate models for three time groupings: 1950–60, 1965–70, and 1975–80. The models for the first two time periods are statistically identical, but the last time period shows some changes from the previous ones. The coefficients for several variables are stronger during the late 1970s, but in the direction and range shown in previous models. Perhaps most interesting is that the negative effects of rightist rule increase; this suggests that during a period of spending retrenchment, nations with a history of rightist rule have slowed welfare growth the most. Otherwise, our conclusions apply across the time span.

Tests for more broadly based interactions of class and state characteristics, in which the effects of nearly all variables differ across class and state contexts, also add some complexity and insight to the additive models. In this case, the arguments of Hicks, Swank, and Ambuhl (1989) and Pampel and Stryker (1989) for the interactive effects of union and state characteristics can be tested. Following Hicks et al., we divide the nations into those with centralized unions or societal bargaining and those without; then, level and change models are estimated within the groups of nations. Similarly, following Pampel and Stryker (1989), we divide the nations into those with corporatist, centralized rule and those without, and estimate separate models for each. The interactive influence of union centralization and corporatism will be similar, since the classifications differ only in the placement of Italy and France, which have decentralized unions but centralized state appointment power (Wilensky, 1976). Although separating the unique influence of each interaction is difficult, the analysis of both provides the broad outlines of potential interactive influences on spending.

Table 3.5 presents trimmed models of welfare spending, using the most important variables from the basic additive model. The models for level of welfare spending show weak interactive effects; the reduction in the error sum of squares from the separate equations is significant at the .05 level, but not at the .01 level. The separate equations by union centralization show significantly different effects only for the consumer price index, whereas the separate equations for corporatism show significantly different effects only for GNP. Although the reduction in the error sum of squares is larger for corporatism than for union

Table 3.5. Unstandardized coefficients and standard errors for group-specific GLS estimates of models of welfare spending, 1950–80

Independent variables	Level models					Change models[a]				
	All nations	Union decent.	Union central.	Non-corp.	Corpor-atist	All nations	Union decent.	Union central.	Non-corp.	Corpor-atist
GNP pop.	0.556**	0.349*	0.587‡	0.210	1.29**	0.222	0.008	0.534‡	-0.072	1.25**
	0.137	0.160	0.309	0.151	0.276	0.169	0.213	0.298	-0.215	0.368
% aged	1.21**	1.25**	0.671	1.08**	1.02**	0.378**	0.554**	0.576**	0.488**	0.644*
	0.170	0.188	0.445	0.223	0.322	0.134	0.178	0.266	0.170	0.254
% voting	0.109**	0.102**	0.139‡	0.089**	0.074	0.056**	0.058‡	0.230**	0.047*	0.246**
	0.024	0.028	0.077	0.029	0.064	0.018	0.024	0.054	0.023	0.059
Elect. comp.	0.123**	0.101*	0.069	0.035	0.136	0.087**	0.062	0.173*	0.055	0.131
	0.041	0.050	0.091	0.050	0.089	0.030	0.039	0.079	0.043	0.087
Right rule	-0.071	-0.015	0.111	-0.033	0.059	-0.059‡	-0.034	-0.204*	-0.048	-0.045
	-0.044	-0.042	0.174	-0.055	0.088	-0.034	-0.049	-0.089	-0.052	-0.059
Union scope	0.002	-0.060	0.020	-0.024	0.008	-0.011	-0.047‡	-0.020	-0.038	-0.046‡
	0.025	-0.042	0.047	-0.053	0.034	-0.017	-0.028	-0.023	-0.032	-0.027
Unemployment	0.270*	0.280‡	0.220	0.330*	0.229	-0.098	-0.048	-0.352**	-0.085	-0.165
	0.116	0.144	0.186	0.150	0.172	-0.089	-0.112	-0.133	-0.127	-0.148
Cons. price	0.030**	0.022*	0.059**	0.028**	0.014	0.040*	0.052*	-0.024	0.058*	-0.044
	0.008	0.010	0.018	0.010	0.014	0.018	0.024	-0.027	0.025	-0.032
SSB						0.794**	0.651**	1.01**	0.696**	0.833**
						0.086	0.120	0.102	0.116	0.141
Int.	-24.0	-19.3	-19.0	-12.4	-22.6	-13.1	-10.7	-36.5	-9.30	-33.7
R^2	0.833	0.797	0.894	0.773	0.870	0.919	0.876	0.976	0.891	0.935
N	126	77	49	63	63	108	66	42	54	54
df	117	68	40	54	54	98	56	32	44	44
SSE	588	319	188	221	275	284	181	38	111	118

$**p < .01$; $*p < .05$; $‡p < .10$.
[a] All independent variables lagged five years.

centralization, neither interaction appears to be substantively important. For level of welfare spending, the additive models (along with the various age interactions) prove suitable.

The interactions for the change models are stronger. Those for union centralization show stronger effects on changes in spending (i.e., controlling for previous levels of GNP), percent voting, electoral competition, rightist rule, and unemployment in centralized nations. Similar but weaker interactions occur for corporatism. Recognizing that the interactions hold only for the change models, the results nonetheless offer some support for class effects. Strong-union nations facilitate the influence of a number of variables and show the expected negative impact of rightist rule. State structure in the form of government centralization (measured on the basis of appointment power of the central government) may also facilitate the influence of demand variables. Such models of change would be better studied with yearly data (e.g., Hicks et al., 1989), but they suggest an appropriate means to extend the theoretical arguments and empirical support for the class and state theories.

Program-specific spending

Our focus shifts in Table 3.5 to program-specific spending for a shorter time span. Because of the fewer degrees of freedom, we include in the program-specific models only the most important independent variables from the previous equations. We delete leftist rule also because it overlaps with union scope. The first equation replicates the model of social welfare spending for the shorter time span and the trimmed set of determinants. The coefficients change little from those of the models in Table 3.2. The next two equations show separate models for public assistance (means-tested) and social insurance (contribution-based) expenditures. Social insurance makes up, on the average, 76 percent of all welfare expenditures and dominates the previous models, whereas public assistance makes up 9 percent of all expenditures.[21] Thus, the model for social insurance continues to show strong effects of the industrialism and political variables and of consumer prices. For public assistance spending, however, the effects of percent aged become small and those of union scope and unemployment increase. If union scope is replaced by leftist rule, class effects still dominate. As the one program most directly targeted to the poor, public assistance spending responds primarily to class structure and cyclical economic conditions.

Further disaggregation of social insurance spending into pension, health care, family allowance, unemployment, and occupational injury spending follows in Table 3.6. The effects of percent aged are always positive but are strongest for pensions, health care, and family allowance. Although the aged benefit most

Table 3.6. *Coefficients (unstandardized above standardized) for GLS estimates of models of program-specific spending, advanced industrial democracies, 1960–80*

Independent variables	Social welfare	Public assist.	Social insur.	Old-age pension	Health care	Fam. allow.	Unemploy.	Occup. inj.	Old-age pension[a]	Health care[a]
GNP/pop.	0.554**	0.059	0.420**	0.243	0.174*	−0.003	0.045‡	0.002	1.62*	1.30*
	0.220	0.116	0.202	0.234	0.194	−0.009	0.158	0.021	0.218	0.207
% aged	1.14**	0.076	0.976**	0.531**	0.250*	0.153**	0.008	0.015	1.73‡	−0.849
	0.460	0.152	0.476	0.519	0.283	0.445	0.029	0.161	0.236	−0.136
% voting	0.132**	−0.013	0.113	0.039*	0.029*	0.030**	0.004‡	−0.004	0.340*	0.286*
	0.324	−0.158	0.336	0.232	0.199	0.531	0.087	−0.261	0.283	0.281
Elect. comp.	0.130*	0.006	0.122**	0.026	0.034	0.034**	0.014	0.002	0.284	0.357‡
	0.146	0.033	0.165	0.071	0.107	0.275	0.139	0.060	0.108	0.160
Right rule	−0.112‡	−0.016	−0.091‡	−0.004	−0.041	−0.027*	−0.008	0.004	−0.044	−0.384‡
	−0.167	−0.118	−0.164	−0.014	−0.172	−0.290	−0.106	0.159	−0.022	−0.229
Union scope	−0.002	0.010*	−0.008	−0.001	0.006	−0.008*	0.003	0.000	−0.017	0.008
	−0.014	0.347	−0.068	−0.017	0.118	−0.405	0.186	0.019	−0.040	0.022
Unemployment	0.272‡	0.106*	0.196	−0.013	0.018	0.029	0.214**	0.013	−0.008	−0.004
	0.119	0.229	0.103	−0.014	0.022	0.091	0.826	0.151	−0.001	−0.001
Cons. price	0.029**	0.004	0.027**	0.009*	0.014**	−0.002	−0.002	−0.000	0.089*	0.141**
	0.222	0.151	0.250	0.167	0.300	−0.110	−0.135	−0.000	0.231	0.431
Intercept	−24.5	−0.54	−22.6	−8.41	−5.77	−4.94	−1.84	0.23	−44.3	−21.7
R^2 (OLS)	0.822	0.418	0.838	0.729	0.689	0.609	0.658	0.168	0.527	0.567
df	81	81	81	81	81	81	81	81	81	81
$\overline{X}$	13.9	1.2	10.7	4.5	4.1	1.1	0.5	0.3	39.2	36.4
s	5.8	1.2	4.8	2.4	2.0	0.8	0.6	0.2	16.9	14.4

**$p < .01$; *$p < .05$; ‡$p < .10$.
[a]Dependent variable standardized by size of aged population.

directly from pensions and health care, an elderly population may encourage some nations to use family allowances as inducements to raise fertility. Class variables have little influence on the other social insurance programs, but unemployment, not surprisingly, dominates unemployment benefit spending. Inflation drives up spending for pensions and health care but is typically low when unemployment and unemployment spending are high.

Entitlements and program spending

Overall, the results show that the size of the aged population dominates the largest social insurance programs. The interest group theory argues that at least part of this influence of the aged comes from political activity rather than from a mere rise in the number of recipients. If so, the size of percent aged should increase spending per aged person – at least for the programs that most strongly benefit the aged. The social democratic and class theories may also be further evaluated. Leftist governments may implement policies that entitle certain groups to benefits or index benefits to economic conditions. Growth of the aged population and inflation may automatically drive up expenditures due to entitlements and indexing, although the governments responsible for the initial policy may ultimately have been the cause of the rising expenditures. By eliminating the demographic effects of percent aged from our dependent variable, the true benefit increases implemented by leftist governments may emerge and show support for the social democratic theory.

If the effects of pension, health, and disability legislation implemented by leftist parties do not show until decades later, when workers covered under the legislation reach old age, the effects of leftist rule should show after a lag of some length. We examined the effects of leftist rule on spending 5, 10, 15, 20, 25, and 30 years later (as the lag gets longer, additional waves of data must be deleted). With controls only for percentage aged and GNP (both unlagged), the lagged leftist rule variable does not have large or significant effects. In fact, the correlations of spending and leftist rule, without any controls, show the concurrent relationship to be as large as the lagged relationships.

Turning to the test for the influence of entitlements, we study spending purged of automatic increases due to the rising number of aged recipients. The focus would thus be on politically mandated rather than demographically driven increases. It is unnecessary to do all this for all programs; only those that primarily benefit the aged should be standardized by aged recipients. We focus on to such programs – pensions and medical care. For each, we measure spending per aged person as a ratio to GNP per capita. This produces a conservative test of their influence, since the inability to control for nonaged recipients biases downward the effects of percent aged.[22] Nonetheless, it provides some additional insights into the processes that are operating. The last two columns of Table 3.6 show the equations for the age-standardized measures of pension and health care spending. The effects of all variables except percent aged change little: Voting, GNP, and inflation drive up spending beyond that due to an increase in the number of aged persons. For pensions, the effect of percent aged is positive, thus replicating the results of Pampel and Williamson (1985); for health care, percent aged has little effect, or perhaps even a negative one. Not surprisingly, percent aged has no effect on age-standardized spending for programs not directed to the aged, such as public assistance, family allowance, or unemployment, and we do not report their results. However, because pensions make up a large part of welfare spending, percent aged has small and insignificant effects on social insurance and total welfare spending. All this suggests that the political effect of the aged population operates only for pensions, whereas the demographic effect operates more broadly for health care spending as well.

Conclusions

We are now in a position to readdress the theoretical debates over the influence on social welfare spending of democratic politics relative to economic structures and of class cleavages relative to demographic groups. To some extent, the forces driving spending in advanced industrial democracies are specific to the program and its targeted beneficiary population. Momentarily ignoring some of the variation across programs, an overview of the results shows the crucial role of democratic politics and demographic structure relative to class structure and parties. The size of the aged population is the strongest determinant of welfare spending, followed in importance by nonclass political variables, percent voting, and party competition. The unemployment rate, national economic product, and consumer prices also contribute to growing expenditures in these nations. Most class and state variables, in contrast, have weak or inconsistent effects. Finally, there is some evidence of the interaction of percent aged with political variables and of the influence of percent aged even when the dependent variables are standardized by percent aged.

The conclusions apply best to the social insurance expenditures, primarily pensions and health care, which dominate welfare spending. Evidence of the influence of the aged, political and otherwise, is strongest for these programs but spills over to affect total social welfare spending. An exception to these generalizations is means-tested public assistance expenditures, which are determined primarily by union strength. Unemployment expenditures also differ from the other programs in the dominant role of the unemployment rate. However, since public assistance comprises less than 10 percent, and unemployment benefits less than 4 percent, of all social welfare spending, they and their determinants have contributed minimally to the growth of the welfare state over the last several decades.

Given these results, we can evaluate the theories and the support that exists for their predictions one by one. First, the predictions of the industrialism theory concerning the importance of demographic structure receive partial support. National product provides the resources for transfers, and demographic aging combined with increased retirement creates a population in need of transfers. The results here to a large degree replicate Wilensky's (1975) findings rather than those of his critics. However, the industrialism theory may underestimate the importance of democratic politics in translating economic and demographic structures into public policy. The welfare state is more political and less functional than is recognized by the theory, and continued efforts are needed to identify the mechanisms of political influence of the aged or other groups.

The monopoly capitalism theory proves most difficult to test. Measures of monopoly assets, monopolization, and industrial disputes, although less than ideal indicators, fail altogether to affect welfare spending as predicted. Perhaps most consistent with the theory is the positive effect of unemployment on social welfare spending. Unemployment can expand spending in many ways, and the statistical relationship we find cannot be attached unambiguously to the monopoly capitalism theory. Yet, the effects of unemployment on public assistance, as well as on unemployment spending, suggest that some types of welfare spending may be a general response to structural conditions of the capitalist economy. The theory fits social consumption or social insurance spending less well, but further efforts to deduce and measure indicators of the monopoly capitalism theory (as Griffin et al., 1983, do for the United States) are needed to further evaluate and advance this theory beyond the limited support it receives here.

The social democratic theory also receives only partial support. Although union strength affects public assistance spending, it has little net effect on the larger social insurance programs. Political party government control fails to show consistent, stable influences on any program, but rightist rule may have modest cross-sectional effects, particularly in the late 1970s. Although we must limit our conclusions to a specific historical period of remarkable growth, support for the welfare state appears to come from a variety of sources and political directions, and reflects less a democratic class struggle than more general group activities in the democratic process. This does not mean that labor and capital fail to influence spending altogether, or that union strength might not facilitate the influence of nonclass variables, but rather that these groups do not directly dominate the processes. Even though we have used the same measures of class as the advocates of the social democratic theory, class may have influences that are not measured here. In particular, the influence of social democratic parties may be shown in the egalitarian distribution of benefits and the low level of poverty rather than in the spending levels (Hedstrom and Ringen, 1987). Continued research is necessary, but in the meantime, the claims made in favor of class theories must be more precisely delimited to certain programs, types of benefits, or interactive influences.

The interest group theory receives support from the effects of percent aged, nonclass political variables, and the interaction between the two. At least for several of the largest social insurance spending programs, the theory is correct in its emphasis on the importance of democratic politics and the role of demographic change in the structure of interest group size and resources. Although the evidence is indirect, the effects of percent aged appear to involve more than demographic accounting or entitlements, at least for pensions, and are consistent with a view of the aged as an active political force in the welfare state. The role of the aged, then, is at once more important and more complex than is recognized by almost all previous work on the welfare st te.

Finally, we find little evidence for the direct, additive influence of state characteristics in explaining variation in welfare spending. Since our tests consist only of preliminary investigation of diverse and isolated hypotheses, we are not able to evaluate fully state-based theories, many of which address the historical emergence of welfare programs in specific countries. Moreover, since state and legal structures contribute to the shapes that political participation and party competition take, the state proves of indirect importance in our results. Our initial efforts to examine how the state mediates (or facilitates) public demands show more promise than the additive models and suggest an approach for future research.

In summary, there is some evidence to favor nearly all the theories. Union strength favors programs for the poor, and the aged favor social insurance programs that benefit the middle class. Pension spending responds to political influence of the aged, health care spending to demographic influence. Democratic politics are important in translating interests into policy even if class-based parties do not differ in the expected directions. Class theories receive support once the domain of their propositions is delimited, but they do not deal well with the major source of growth of welfare spending – pensions and health care – or with the growing importance of the aged population in political democracies. Future theory and research may need to deal further with the growth of middle-class programs and their ascriptively defined constituents.

Notes

1. The other question we examine in this book – the consequences of the welfare state for equality – is considered in subsequent chapters. Here we focus on the causes of social welfare spending.
2. Another variable associated with advocates of industrialism theory is years of social insurance program experience (SIPE). For this group of developed nations, nearly all nations (with the exception of the United States) had instituted the five programs used in the measure long ago. As a result, there is little variation across nations, and the variable serves as little more than a time counter for our select sample. SIPE shows more variation among developing nations and receives more attention in the next chapter.
3. Strictly speaking, the number of cases is equal to $n \times t$ only when the points are independent and serial correlation of errors over time does not exist. Statistical adjustment for serial correlation, by purging the data of redundancy, is necessary to maintain the full potential of the sample size.
4. Sweden, Norway, Denmark, Finland, West Germany, the United Kingdom, Ireland, Belgium, the Netherlands, France, Switzerland, Italy, and Austria.
5. The distinction between social insurance and means-tested programs is not always clear. For instance, Australia offers means-tested pension benefits, and the United States offers means-tested medical care for the nonaged. More typically, however, pension benefits are based on earnings contributions or on some combination of earnings contributions and a universal, flat-rate benefit, and medical care is available to all persons or contributors. The classification of programs as either social insurance or public assistance, although not perfect, proves useful in the analyses to follow.
6. The analysis of program-specific spending for 1980 requires adjustment of the reported ILO figures. Beginning in 1977, the ILO reclassified spending for public health. Some expenditures were deleted altogether from the published comparative tables, and had to be obtained directly from the ILO and added to our 1980 figures. Other expenditures were shifted to the medical insurance category, making it necessary to combine public health and medical insurance into a single category for all years. In all, this makes the trend data comparable, despite changes in the procedures of the ILO, without distorting the conceptual classification of the programs.
7. Other related age structure measures, such as the percentage of the population under age 15, the fertility rate, labor force nonparticipation, or the dependency ratio, are also related to welfare spending. Because all have effects equal to or smaller than those of percent aged, and can introduce problems of causal direction, they are not included in the models. We experimented in most detail with a measure of the number of children (aged 0–14) over the number of women aged 20–44. Perhaps low fertility and a young rather than an old age structure are responsible for welfare state growth. Since the two are closely related, the effect of the child/woman ratio has little effect net of percent aged, and percent aged remains significant. This may be due in part to the small variation in family size – compared to percent aged – across these nations and years. But in addition, percent aged contains information on past and recent fertility and appears to reflect the most important characteristics of age structure in determining welfare spending.
8. The computation formula for electoral competition, presented in Myles (1984), is 1 minus the sum of $(P_i - 1/N)$ squared, where N is the number of parties competing and P_1 is the proportion of each party's vote. The maximum value is 1 when each party receives an equal share of the vote; the minimum value is 0 when one party receives all the votes. In the rare case where no election had been held in the last five years, figures for the most recent election were used to measure formal political participation and other electoral variables.
9. We find that the union scope measure, used alone, adequately summarizes the information contained in all three measures used together. The R-square adjusted for degrees of freedom using union centralization, membership, and scope is 0.824; using the scope measure alone, the ad-

justed R-square is 0.825. Further, collinearity between the three measures is eliminated, and interpretability of the coefficient is increased, when union scope is used alone.

10. Stephens (1979) classifies leftist parties slightly differently than Castles (1982). Stephens includes communist parties, whereas Castles does not, a difference that affects only the scores of Finland. When we measured leftist control according to Stephens's classification, we found no significant difference in the results.

11. Since the spending programs of leftist parties will persist after these parties are replaced in office, and since the slow spending of rightist parties cannot be overcome immediately by newly elected leftist parties, the cumulative measure of rule seemed most appropriate. The starting point of 1946 marks the beginning of postwar growth, but it means that 5 years of leftist rule is the maximum in 1950, whereas 35 years is the maximum in 1980. The cumulative nature of party rule corresponds to the trend in spending and the measures used by others (Hewitt, 1977; Stephens, 1979). Note also that the total years since 1946 minus cumulative leftist and rightist rule equals the years of rule of centrist, ethnic, religious, and other parties. The coefficients of leftist and rightist rule may be interpreted relative to the spending of the omitted parties.

12. Although the measures of corporatism and union centralization overlap, they reflect important conceptual differences, especially concerning the scoring of two nations – France and Italy. In Wilensky's corporatism scale, both nations receive a 0 for union centralization but score high on the appointment power of the central government. When combined, the two scores give the countries' medium values on corporatism. Stephens (1984) argues that the two components should be multiplicative, not additive. Italy and France should score 0 on corporatism because of their low union centralization.

13. Examination of the residuals for the equations to follow suggests that the autoregressive assumption is appropriate. The correlation between the residuals and residuals lagged over all 18 nations declines exponentially as the lag increases – just as it should in a first-order autoregressive process (Berk et al., 1979). In fact, for the basic model, the correlation between the observed autocorrelation function and the expected function based on the first-order assumption is 0.97. Other techniques of panel analysis that assume a constant autocorrelation function, such as fixed effects or random components estimation (Fuller and Battese, 1974; Hannan and Young, 1977), are inappropriate for these models.

14. The figures presented in this chapter differ slightly from those in Pampel and Williamson (1985) due to minor improvements and corrections of some of the measures.

15. These variables can only account for cross-national variation in welfare spending, and their explanatory ability is limited. By virtue of their cross-sectional relationship, however, they may prove to explain at least part of the variance in spending when included in the multivariate models. It seems appropriate to us that the effects of the variables reflect their inability to explain variation over time.

16. The use of significance tests in a study such as ours is of debatable value. We analyze a population of nations rather than a random sample and make no attempt to generalize to a larger universe. We nonetheless report, but do not rely on, significance tests, along with the size of the unstandardized and standardized coefficients. In some instances, such as testing for the interaction of a large number of terms, statistical significance proves to be a useful summary of the information we desire. Otherwise, we focus on the substantive meaning rather than the statistical significance of the results.

17. We performed further tests for collinearity by regressing each independent variable on all the other independent variables. Except for leftist rule and union scope, which are closely related, the tolerance or unexplained variation never falls below 30 percent. For union scope and leftist rule, the tolerance falls to 20 percent, but the coefficient signs are relatively stable throughout the variety of models we estimate. For union strength and leftist rule, the effects on spending

are small even when the other, highly correlated variable is not included. At worst, the effects of their high correlation are shown in certain equations, where some insignificant standardized coefficients are larger than other significant standardized coefficients. The standard errors and tests of significance are affected by the degree of independent variation of the predictors, as well as the size of the coefficients. In later analyses, we estimate models with union scope or leftist rule included without the other.

18. This equation is equivalent to estimating a model controlling for period dummy variables. A similar procedure is to control for SIPE, which in essence represents a yearly time variable for all these nations. Except for the modest negative effect of rightist rule, there is little change in the results.

19. Traditional outlier and influential case statistics are less meaningful and less easily calculated with the GLS transformations. Further, elimination of a single case (i.e., a nation-year) is not possible with GLS estimation, requiring that all time points for a nation be eliminated in testing for influential cases.

20. Change over a five-year time span may fluctuate less, exhibit more stability, and be more difficult to explain than yearly change. Upward and downward fluctuations in the growth rate may balance out over the five years we study. Some of the effects of political variables that explain yearly changes may be hidden in these models. Yet, our focus here is on the longer-term growth in social welfare spending in the postwar period, not on the yearly fluctuations. Hence, the use of the five-year change models is appropriate.

21. Not analyzed separately in Table 3.6 is spending for public employee social insurance programs, war victims, and miscellaneous programs (about 14 percent of all expenditures). Such spending amalgamates programs for a variety of purposes and fails to define conceptually meaningful categories.

22. The measure (Expenditures/#65)/(CNP/Pop.) is equivalent to (Expenditures/GNP)/(#65/Pop.); that is, the new dependent variable is equal to the old one divided by percent aged. Percent aged as an independent variable must affect a dependent variable multiplied by its reciprocal. Furthermore, since the programs may have many nonaged as well as aged nonrecipients, the measure overcorrects for benefits per aged person and provides a most severe test of the effects of percent aged.

Appendix 3.A. *Sources of data*

Variable	Source
Social welfare, other program expenditures, administrative costs	*The Cost of Social Security.* 1981 and various years. Geneva: International Labour Office. Tables 1, 5, and 8.
GNP, consumer prices, exchange rates	*World Bank World Tables,* Volume I. 1983. Baltimore: Johns Hopkins. Economic Data Sheet I.
Percent aged, population	*Labour Force: 1950–2000.* 1977. Geneva: International Labour Office. Volumes I and IV, Table 2. World Bank World Tables. Volume II. 1983. Social Data Sheet 1.
SIPE	*Social Security Throughout the World.* 1981. Washington D.C.: Social Security Administration.
Percent voting, election competition, election year	*The International Almanac of Electoral History.* Thomas T. Mackie and Richard Rose (eds.). 1982. New York: Facts on File.
Leftist rule, rightist rule	*Political Parties of Europe,* Volumes 1 and 2. Vincent E. McHale (ed.). 1983. Westport, Conn.: Greenwood Press. *Political Handbook of the World.* Arthur S. Banks and William Overstreet (eds.). 1984. New York: McGraw-Hill.
Strike days, unemployment	*Yearbook of Labour Statistics.* 1982 and various years. Geneva: International Labour Office.
Union centralization	Hicks and Swank (1984).
Union membership	Stephens (1979), Korpi (1983), and *National Yearbooks.*
Monetary assets	*Fortune Magazine.* The Fortune 500 and International Fortune 500. Various years.
Monopolization	Stephens (1979).
Corporatism	Wilensky (1976).
Central government revenues, total government revenues, direct taxes, defense spending, imports, exports	*OECD National Accounts.* 1984 and various years. Paris: Organization for Economic Cooperation and Development.

4. Social welfare spending and democratic political context

Although most theories and studies of the welfare state focus on advanced industrial, high-income democracies, as did our analyses in the previous chapter, the study of low- and middle-income developing nations may be equally valuable. Developing nations show greater diversity than high-income nations in democracy, trade dependency, and industrial structure. Welfare spending in developing nations rarely reaches the levels in developed nations but still shows a surprising range – from near zero to 5 percent of GNP. Combined with variation in spending, differences in democratic and economic context in developing nations offer the opportunity to test the influence of additional variables and further evaluate the hypotheses. Indeed, studying the developing nations allows us to concentrate on the emergence and early expansion of the welfare state rather than the maturation of systems in high-income nations. The processes determining welfare spending differ in advanced industrial democracies and other nations (Cutright, 1967; Williamson and Pampel, 1986), and the processes in these other nations need study.

In this chapter, we use low- and middle-income developing nations to further address two theoretical questions raised in Chapter 1: (1) what are the relative influences of class-based and non-class-based (demographic and industrial) determinants of social welfare spending? and (2) do democratic politics and political environments influence social welfare spending? An important component of class dominance – the dependency of low-income nations on capitalist, core nations – can be studied with these nations. Further, variations in democracy, its direct influence on social welfare spending, and its role in facilitating the effects of demographic and social change on social welfare spending can also be studied with low-income nations. In so doing, we can further differentiate and test theories of the welfare state and extend our models of the causes of its growth.

Research strategy

To answer the first question on the class and nonclass determinants of social welfare spending, we examine the external relations of developing nations. Whereas

80

nonclass theories attend to internal structures of nations, such as industrial development and population structure, class theories claim that the struggle between labor and capital spills across national boundaries. As capital expands geographically in search of trade partners, inexpensive labor, and new markets, capitalist core nations come to dominate dependent nations and their workers, which leads to an international struggle between labor and capital (Wallerstein, 1974; Rubinson, 1976; Poulantzas, 1978). Although typically applied to advanced capitalist democracies, the class theories thus can be extended to consider other nations and the external relations of nations in the class-based, capitalist world system.

To draw out the logic of the dependency and class arguments, we must consider how social welfare spending mediates the relationship between external domination and inequality. Assuming that dependency increases inequality (which class theories assert, but have not proved), welfare spending may intervene in the processes in two ways. On the one hand, if social welfare maintains inequality, we would expect that dependency *increases* welfare spending. Welfare can be seen as a mechanism by which foreign powers and corporations maintain their dominance over the local population and economy. On the other hand, if social welfare spending reduces inequality, we would expect that dependency *reduces* welfare spending. In what follows, we discuss how class theories offer divergent predictions concerning the efficacy of social welfare spending for reduced inequality.

To answer the second question on the importance of politics, we study the facilitative effects of a democratic political environment. The mixture of democratic and nondemocratic political systems among developing nations permits separation of the influence of democracy from that of development. Some impoverished nations, such as India or Sri Lanka, have strong democratic traditions, whereas some higher-income nations do not. We can therefore examine how democratic political procedures, independent of economic development, may raise spending by providing institutionalized means by which groups act collectively to influence policy. Specifically, if democracy is important, developing democracies should be more similar to advanced industrial democracies than to developing nondemocracies. If democracy is unimportant, the processes of welfare spending should be similar among all developing nations, regardless of the extent of their political freedom.

This strategy might logically be extended by examining the industrial nations of Eastern Europe, where economic development has occurred without the existence of democratic political processes. However, centrally planned, socialist economies seldom publish data on welfare benefits or national product in forms comparable to those of other nations, thus making comparisons with nonsocialist nations hazardous. Later, when we examine outcomes of welfare that can be measured comparably, such as infant mortality, we study both socialist and non-socialist nations. For the present, we limit ourselves to nonsocialist nations.

Because the quality and availability of data in developing nations are limited, we must focus on a relatively small set of easily measured economic, demographic, and trade characteristics. Other political and social characteristics, such as party domination, political participation, corporatism, or union strength, are seldom measured accurately and, indeed, may have little meaning in low-income nondemocracies. As a result, we study the equivalent of reduced-form models that focus on exogenous economic, trade, and population structures rather than the mediating or intervening factors that we examined for advanced industrial nations in the last chapter.

For the industrialism and interest group theories, this strategy means that we focus primarily on three characteristics: economic development, size of the aged population, and social insurance program experience (SIPE). Population structures are assumed to represent changing needs of the population and expansion of self-interested and potentially politically important age-based groups. Economic development represents the growth of resources needed for welfare distribution, changes in industrial demand, family support, and the need for insurance against loss of employment. For the monopoly capitalism and working-class strength theories, this strategy entails the study of external trade and political dependency that shapes internal class characteristics of nations. The external characteristics include the (1) degree and concentration of trade, (2) penetration by multinational corporations and foreign investment, and (3) position in the world networks of trade, political, military, and economic relations.

Hypotheses

In specifying the predictions of the theories, we need to focus on the variables considered important by each theory, as well as how the effects of the variables may differ across democratic contexts. Class and nonclass theories differ in the types of variables predicted to affect spending and in their emphasis on internal structures or external relations. But within the class and nonclass categories, each theory makes different predictions concerning the importance of the democratic political context. Table 4.1 summarizes the predictions of each theory and guides the following discussion.

The industrialism theory argues for the importance of economic development and population structure. Social welfare responds more or less automatically to internal processes of economic change and the problems they create. Social welfare expenditures rise with the development of industrial structures and emerging needs for insurance against loss of income due to injury, sickness, unemploy-

Table 4.1. *Predicted effects for development, population, and economic dependency on social welfare spending by level of democracy in middle- and low-income developing nations*

	Industrialism Democracy			Interest group Democracy			Monopoly capitalism Democracy			Working-class strength[a] Democracy		
	Low		High	Low		High	Low		High	Low		High
Development	+	=	+	+	<	+	0	=	0	0	=	0
Population structure	+	=	+	+	<	+	0	=	0	0	=	0
SIPE	+	=	+	+	<	+	0	=	0	0	=	0
Economic/trade	0	=	0	0	=	0	+	=	+	−	>	−

[a] Comparison of effects of dependency by democracy refer to the strength or absolute values of the negative realtionships.

ment, retirement, and lack of family support. According to Wilensky (1975), economic and industrial development may operate indirectly on social welfare spending through percent aged: In the relatively more developed nations, with lower fertility and mortality, a larger part of the population is subject to retirement, sickness, and loss of family support. Given the dominance of economic and population structures, the existence of political democracy makes little difference for social welfare spending. For instance, Kerr et al. (1964) argue that there are multiple paths to industrialization, some involving democracy and some not. If there is a qualification to these arguments, it is that the effects of development are curvilinear (Jackman, 1975). At higher levels of development, a greater proportional increase in development is needed to raise expenditures, which implies a log curvilinear function between development and spending.

The arguments of the interest group theory partly overlap those of the industrialism theory. Both focus on economic development and population structure rather than on trade dependency, on internal structures rather than on external structures. The difference between the two theories lies in the importance of political democracy. According to the interest group theory, economic and population structures help define the size and resources of interest groups, but democracy is also important since it provides existing groups with the institutionalized means to influence government policy. Democracy alone may not directly determine spending, but it may allow for the political pressure of a large aged population and may increase the effect of percent aged on social welfare spending in democratic nations. Similarly, economic development, to the extent that it diversifies interests and mobilizes ascriptive groups (Nielsen, 1985), should have stronger effects in democracies, where such interests can be more freely expressed and acted on.

The major propositions of the interest group theory are that the older the population structure and the higher the level of economic development, the higher social welfare spending – with the strength of the relationship increasing with political democracy. Table 4.1 summarizes the hypotheses for both nonclass theories. The industrialism theory predicts the same effects of development and percent aged for both democracies and nondemocracies, whereas the interest group theory predicts stronger effects in democracies.

Additionally, years of experience with social insurance programs may increase expenditures (Aaron, 1967; Cutright, 1967; Wilensky, 1975). This may reflect expansion of technical knowledge of the government bureaucracy needed to implement new programs easily, the bureaucratic momentum in budgeting that makes limiting spending for existing programs difficult, or the development of influential constituent groups represented by the program. Consistent with previous arguments, the industrialism theory predicts additive effects of SIPE, whereas the interest group theory predicts interactive effects.

The remaining theories – monopoly capitalism and social democratic (working-class strength) – differ fundamentally from the previous ones by their focus on the external relations of nations and position in the world system. Although both class theories emphasize the need to consider external relations, their implications for social welfare differ. The monopoly capitalism theory predicts that dependency on foreign investment and trade leads to higher social welfare spending, whereas the working-class theory predicts the opposite effect.

Before presenting the arguments, it is worthwhile to mention briefly some of the terms and concepts common in the dependency literature. Some scholars focus on the network of relationships in the world system, arguing that nations fall into one of three groups, each with a different role in the system. *Core nations* are economically diversified, rich, powerful, and independent of outside controls; *peripheral societies* are economically overspecialized, relatively poor and weak, and subject to direct control by core powers; and *semiperipheral societies* fall midway between the core and periphery, having made some progress toward industrialization and diversification (Chirot, 1986). Despite this simple classification, where dependency is lowest in the core nations and highest in the peripheral and semiperipheral nations, position in the world network summarizes a variety of characteristics involving trade, political treaties, military ties, and economic dominance/subordinance (Snyder and Kick, 1979; Bollen, 1983). Others treat dependency more directly as level of trade, concentration of products and trade partners, foreign multinational corporate investment, and external public debt (Bornschier et al., 1978; Delacroix and Ragin, 1981). We refer to all these aspects with the term *economic dependency* in the discussion to follow, but pay more attention to the different components of dependency in the empirical analysis.

The monopoly capitalism theory argues that welfare spending grows in advanced capitalist societies in response to crises of overproduction and discontent among workers and the poor. O'Connor (1973) extends this argument in considering the relations of capitalist nations to less powerful, lower-income nations. Continued capital accumulation and employment in the monopoly sector depend on foreign economic expansion. In dealing with foreign nations, monopoly capital in advanced capitalist nations must "buttress the rule of the local bourgeoisies whose economic interests are based on export production, processing, and trade; and on outright military and nonmilitary aid" (O'Connor, 1973:119). Such efforts create dependent relations between dominant and subordinate nations, benefiting monopoly capital in the core nations and small, indigenous elites, and encouraging narrow, specialized, trade-dependent economies in the other nations (Rubinson, 1976; Chirot, 1977). These processes also create crises of legitimacy and restlessness among populations in the dependent nations (as they do in core nations). To maintain conditions of order for further capital expansion, social welfare programs grow. As O'Connor (1973:169) states, "The need for welfare programs, wars on poverty, foreign aid, and other ameliorative programs knows no limit, or, more accurately, is limited only by the boundaries or the application of modern technology and the spread of capitalism itself." In short, the theory predicts that among low-income nations, the greater the dependency on advanced capitalist nations, the higher the level of social welfare and government spending.

Among low-income nations, population structure and economic growth are of little importance. Economic development, unless it stems from expansion of monopoly capitalism, does not require social welfare. It may create more resources for redistribution, but without the presence of foreign capital, the need for welfare expenditures is minimal. Similarly, a changing population structure leads to the emergence of demographic groups that do not require public expenditures, except when they benefit the expansion of capital. These arguments also imply little difference between democracies and nondemocracies; democratic political processes in these nations cannot withstand the power of foreign capital. Economic dependency dominates all these other factors and explains levels of social welfare spending.

The working-class strength argument, as we have emphasized, has been applied to advanced industrial democracies in which social democratic parties have emerged to represent the interests of the working class. Yet, the argument can be extended logically, with only minor changes, to low-income nations. Unlike the monopoly capitalism theory, the working-class strength theory sees the welfare state as a response to working-class desires rather than to the needs of capitalism. In low-income democracies, the size of the working class may not be large enough for social democratic parties to emerge and social welfare spending to grow dramatically. Still, the existence of democracy in these nations provides some chance for the working class to gain political power, whereas in nondemocracies there is no opportunity.

Although the working-class strength theory emphasizes the importance of political democracy, economic dependency is also important because it limits the ability of the working class to organize. Several dependency theories argue that the alliance between foreign and local elites works to maintain inequality and limit the power of the workers (Evans, 1979; Delacroix and Ragin, 1981). This is done by weakening, through external threat, pressure, and cooptation, the power of the state to make structural changes. Repatriation of profits also lowers the income that can be redistributed and reduces the ability of even a small working class to realize its aims. Thus, economic dependency and foreign capital reduce social welfare spending by limiting the power of groups that benefit from it, reducing the ability of the state to implement political change, and supporting the indigenous bourgeoisie.

Given the importance of both democracy and dependency, there is likely some interactive effect between them on social welfare spending. The effect of dependency may weaken when political democracy gives labor the ability to use political power to counteract the effects of dependency and the power of foreign capital. Consistent with the arguments of the working-class strength theories for advanced industrial democracies, we can predict that among developing nations, democracy can inhibit the harmful effects of dependency. To put the theory in propositional form, according to the working-class strength theory, the higher economic dependency, the lower social welfare, with this negative relationship declining with political democracy (Table 4.1). The monopoly capitalism theory, in contrast, predicts positive effects that do not vary with the level of democracy.

The nations and measures of spending to be studied

The sample and the measures of social welfare spending to be studied in this chapter are intimately tied. Unlike the study of advanced industrial democracies, where a variety of measures are available for all the nations, the study of developing nations is difficult because so much data are missing. Figures on social welfare spending are not routinely available, especially for multiple time points. Some countries have no programs, many others do not collect or report spending levels, and still others have such primitive programs that standard accounting categories for reporting them do not apply. Rather than attempting to maximize the sample by accepting dubious figures or invalid measures of social welfare, our strategy is to rely on a relatively small subset of nations with complete, more reliable, and valid measures.

In choosing the nations for analysis, we again rely on figures presented by the ILO (1985). Excluding the 18 advanced democracies studied in the last chapter and the socialist nations of the Eastern bloc (where welfare spending means little in isolation from broader government control of the economy and income distribution), this leaves 32 nations with acceptable measures of social welfare spending and most of the independent variables. For these nations, data on welfare spending are unavailable before 1960, and data on trade dependency are seldom available for 1980. Therefore, we limit the analyses in this chapter to the time span from 1960 to 1975. With four time points, there are 128 cases – enough for multivariate analysis.[1] The sample is not representative, but it does cover all regions, levels of development, and degrees of political democracy. By region, the distribution of nations is as follows: sub-Saharan Africa (12), Middle East (4), Asia (5), and Latin America (11). Although these nations are only a small part of the 100 plus developing, low- and middle-income nations in the world, they offer the variation and sample size needed for analysis and for testing of our theories.[2]

With these nations, we analyze a measure of social insurance spending that sums spending for five separate programs: pensions, sickness-maternity, employment injury, unemployment, and family allowance. This measure differs slightly from the broader measure of total social security spending analyzed in the last chapter (including its availability only from 1960 on). The broader measure includes social insurance spending plus expenditures for military and government personnel, public health, war victims, and public assistance. This broader measure is desirable for its inclusion of additional programs. However, measurement and classification of these additional programs are difficult enough that a quarter of the nations are missing data on them (when data on social insurance spending are complete). To avoid serious loss of cases, then, we rely on dependent variables based on the five social insurance programs previously listed. In practice, this causes no major problem in interpretation, since the two measures have a correlation of 0.94 and give similar results (except for the different degrees of freedom).[3]

An advantage of using these 32 nations is that measures of the industrialism and democracy variables are complete for the sample. Percent aged again represents the relative size of the total population over age 65, and social insurance program experience equals the sum of years since 1934 that each of five programs – work injury, old age, sickness, family allowance, and unemployment – has been in operation (Cutright, 1965; Jackman, 1975). Since many of these developing nations have adopted new programs during the time span of study, SIPE does not merely increase by a constant over time, as in the advanced industrial nations, but also shows variability across nations and over time. Economic development is measured by GNP in constant 1975 dollars per capita.[4]

Classifying democratic nations

The best available measure of democracy comes from Bollen (1980), who has created a six-component scale reflecting political competitiveness and political liberties. The scale, which varies between 0 and 100, has been shown to be unidimensional, valid, and reliable (Bollen and Grandjean, 1981). However, the measure is available for only the two earliest time points – 1960 and 1965. This is not a major problem for the analysis for two reasons. First, because social welfare programs develop inertia (Wilensky, 1975), the effects of democracy at the beginning of the time period are likely to influence expenditures in the future, even if democratic procedures change in later time points. Second, in studying the democratic context of welfare spending, nations can usefully be divided into larger groups. Even if changes in democracy occur that are not measured for 1970 and 1975, in most instances they would not be large enough to shift nations across major groupings. The exceptions, and possible biases due to the time span limitation of this measure, will be considered shortly.

Modeling the interactive effects of democracy proves less cumbersome when democracy is dichotomized. A dividing point of 67.7 on Bollen's scale was used to distinguish low-democracy nations from industrializing high-democracy nations. There is no single cutoff point on the democracy continuum that distinguishes democracies from nondemocracies. Yet, the value used here divides the nations into roughly equal groups that make theoretical sense. One group includes developing nations with democratic experience, such as India, Sri Lanka, Mexico, and Costa Rica. The other group includes developing nations without democratic traditions, such as El Salvador, Nicaragua, and most African nations.[5]

Although this classification is somewhat arbitrary, there are several points to keep in mind when considering its usefulness in the analysis. First, dividing the nations into two groups provides ease of presentation and interpretation. We can parsimoniously compare models across the two groups while controlling for differences in development when the continuous democracy measure is categorized.

Second, with few exceptions, the classification of nations is stable over time. Without 1970 and 1975 data on democracy, division of the sample into larger categories minimizes changes across the groups. A review of the recent political history of all the nations in the sample (Banks and Overstreet, 1980) shows major changes in democratic procedures in only three nations. Brazil and Panama experienced military takeovers of democratic governments in the late 1960s, and the Philippines saw the institution of martial law in the early 1970s. Since these nations began the period with democratic procedures, levels of spending reached during this time likely persist, making it appropriate to include these nations with the more democratic ones than with the less democratic ones. Nonetheless, the models to follow were replicated with these nations deleted, without any major changes in the coefficients. Our inability to measure major changes in democracy in 1970 and 1975 does not appear to bias the results.

Third, the results are not sensitive to other changes in the classification. One of the nations in the middle group – Israel – might be included with the advanced industrial nations. When it is deleted, however, the coefficients in the models change only slightly. Similarly, nations on the border between low democracy and high democracy do not change the results when shifted to the other category. Overall, the differences found in the models within the groups are not due to the inclusion of outliers or to the misclassification of nations.

Fourth, the classification is similar but not identical to a classification of nations on the basis of development. Nations such as India and Sri Lanka, for example, have high democracy scores but low economic product scores. This shows in the mean of the democracy scale for the high-democracy developing nations (82.3), which is closer to the mean for the advanced industrial nations (97.6) than to the mean for the low-democracy nations (48.4). In contrast, the mean real GNP of low- and high-income democracies is similar ($410 versus $792), compared to that of advanced industrial democracies ($4,516).

In summary, this is not the only classification that might be used, and it may differ from those used by others, but it has several advantages. It meets our goals of analyzing relatively homogeneous and theoretically meaningful subsets of nations, and it allows tests for the facilitative effects of democracy. Further, the classification is not biased by changes over time in democracy or sensitive to outliers or minor changes in the categories. Some loss of information occurs in the grouping, but this loss is outweighed by the desire for clear results and ease in comparing coefficients across separate groups.

Measuring economic and trade dependency

In addition to the industrialism and democracy variables, we obtained multiple measures of trade and economic dependency. Perhaps the most general measure, as well as the one most often used, is a dummy variable indicating position in the world system. Qualitative, positional measures may better tap discrete gaps and groupings inherent in the world division of labor than quantitative, continuous measures. Snyder and Kick (1979), based on cluster analyses of trade, political, military, and treaty ties of nations from bloc-model analyses, classify nations as core, semiperiphery, or periphery. Since core nations are excluded from analyses, we code the more highly dependent, peripheral nations as 1 and semiperipheral nations as 0. This variable is available for 29 of the 32 nations we analyze (Guyana, the Congo, and Zambia are missing) and is assumed to be constant over the 15-year time span studied here.

We also use several continuous measures of trade level and form. Overall dependency on trade and vulnerability to fluctuations of the world economy are measured by imports plus exports over GNP (times 100). Concentration of export commodities and concentration of trade partners measure the form of trade (Taylor and Jodice, 1983). They vary between 0 and 1, with a high score indicating concentration (a 1, for instance, indicates export of only one commodity or to only one partner).[6] A final trade-based measure is a scale of export and import processing (Galtung, 1971). We reverse the original directional coding of this measure, so that a positive score indicates export of raw materials and import of processed products, and a negative score indicates a preponderance of raw imports and exports of processed goods. A high score thus indicates trade dependency. This variable is available only for three time points – 1965, 1970, and 1975.

Finally, we use two measures of the magnitude of foreign investments, both of which are available for only 1967 and 1973 (Bornschier and Heintz, 1979). One is the stock of foreign capital investment divided by GNP. This is the major indicator of foreign and multinational domination of the economy. The other is external public debt over GNP (times 100), a measure of the fiscal problems resulting from dependency on foreign lending. Since these measures are not for the years we study, we assume that they affect welfare spending with some lag (1967 values predict 1970 and 1973 values predict 1975). Further, when considering these variables, data for the years 1960 and 1965 and three nations must be dropped.

Trends in social welfare spending and political democracy

First, we examine the trends and levels of expenditures and their determinants over the time span 1960–75. Since it is possible that democratic context specifies the models – that is, the relationships differ for democracies and nondemocracies – it is worthwhile to examine the trends separately for these two groups. Table 4.2 presents the means for expenditures and the determinants for 1960 and 1975 for each group (values for advanced industrial democracies are presented for comparison).

Expenditure levels for the social security and insurance programs comprise a not unexpectedly small part of GNP. In 1960, less than 1 percent of GNP was spent for all five programs. From 1960 to 1975, however, the democracies and nondemocracies diverge. For nondemocracies, only small increases occur; for democracies, expenditures as a percentage of GNP double for most programs. The gap between the two groups has widened substantially.

Perhaps this divergence stems from higher economic growth and greater demographic change among the democracies rather than from the democratic political environment itself. The trend in real GNP per capita, however, shows growth in both groups of nations. Percent aged better tracks expenditures, since the nondemocracies show little increase, whereas the democracies show a more im-

Table 4.2. *Means of social welfare spending measures and determinants by year and by political and economic context*

Variables	Low-income nondemocracies (N = 19)		Low-income democracies (N = 13)		High-income democracies (N = 18)	
	1960	1975	1960	1975	1960	1975
Type of expenditure (over GNP)						
Social insurance	0.51	0.70	0.94	2.04	5.99	11.3
Pension, old age	0.02	0.14	0.24	0.84	2.84	5.80
Sickness, Matern.	0.12	0.19	0.68	0.94	1.46	3.21
Employment injury	0.08	0.10	0.06	0.12	0.32	0.34
Unemployment	0.00	0.00	0.01	0.03	0.32	0.78
Family allowance	0.32	0.28	0.03	0.13	1.05	1.18
Determinants						
GNP/pop.	246	327	592	992	3,017	6,015
% aged	2.77	2.88	3.60	4.08	9.90	11.8
SIPE	28.8	79.6	52.8	104.7	114.2	186
Democracy	48.4	48.4	82.3	82.3	97.6	97.6
Imp + Exp/GNP[b]	45.7	58.2	40.0	44.0	48.6	54.7
Trade processing[b]	0.58[a]	0.54	0.47[a]	0.41	0.02[a]	0.01
Commodity concen.	0.43	0.34	0.33	0.24	0.12	0.11
Partner concen.	0.36	0.18	0.29	0.23	0.17	0.15
Foreign invest.[b,c]	—	2.93	—	7.59	—	4.61
Ext. public debt[b,c]	—	6.46	—	7.19	—	2.69
Periphery	0.875	0.875	0.385	0.385	0.00	0.00

[a] 1965.
[b] *Ns* = 15, 13, and 18 (the Congo, Guyana, and Zambia missing).
[c] Available only for 1967 and 1973.

portant change. If we look for indicators of dependency that change little for nondemocracies and much for democracies, and therefore are consistent with the trends for expenditures, none appear relevant.

Before going on to the multivariate analysis, some simple standardization exercises can help interpret the meaning of the divergent trends found when comparing across levels of political democracy. The differences between low- and high-democracy nations may be due to differences in development rather than to democracy per se. That part of the divergence due to differences in real GNP or percent aged can be calculated and removed from the trends presented in Table

Table 4.3. *Mean spending adjusted for GNP and percent aged by year and democracy*[a]

Spending	Means				Mean differences	
	Nondemocracies		Democracies		Democracy– nondemocracy	
	1960	1975	1960	1975	1960	1975
Social insurance						
Gross	0.514	0.702	0.945	2.04	0.431	1.34
Net: GNP/pop.	0.514	0.608	0.549	1.18	0.035	0.572
Net: % aged	0.514	0.663	0.652	1.58	0.138	0.917
Pensions						
Gross	0.018	0.143	0.241	0.843	0.223	0.700
Net: GNP/pop.	0.018	0.122	0.115	0.586	0.097	0.464
Net: % aged	0.018	0.118	0.059	0.556	0.041	0.438

[a] 1960 mean for nondemocracies used as the standard.

4.2. Use of simple regression techniques allows calculation of the means by year and by democracy when energy and percent aged are held constant, and shows what changes would have occurred in expenditures had these two variables been constant over time and across the two groups of nations. In this regression procedure, the mean for nondemocracies in 1960 serves as a standard.[7] Table 4.3 shows the gross (or unstandardized) means for two expenditures – all social insurance and pensions. Below these, means net of real GNP and percent aged are presented. With one exception (social insurance expenditures net of real GNP), major differences between nondemocracies and democracies remain controlling for differences in energy use or percent aged. This is shown by the differences between the means, which are always positive. Further, the gap between democracies and nondemocracies grows over time, even with the controls. The differences increase in 1975 in all instances. Even if development or age structure were constant, expenditures would be higher, and would have grown more, in democracies than in nondemocracies. This simple exercise illustrates the potential importance of democracy, and does not replace the multivariate analyses to follow, but it suggests the need to consider the facilitative role of democracy for social welfare spending.[8]

Returning to the descriptive statistics, Table 4.2 offers further insights into the structure of social insurance systems. In nondemocracies, family allowances are the largest expenditure, whereas in democracies, sickness and pension programs are largest. For comparison, pensions and sickness programs are largest in advanced industrial democracies. This indicates some convergence in the structure (although not in the levels) of expenditures in democratic developing nations and democratic developed nations, despite quite different levels of real GNP per capita. Despite their differences in size, however, the programs comprise a single dimension, which warrants reliance on the measure of the five programs summed. We also focus in more detail on pensions because of their relevance to our theoretical concerns with the influence of the aged. Even for social insurance and pension spending, the low level of expenditures in nondemocracies within years and the small change across years indicate that there is little variation in the dependent variables to be explained for these nations. This makes it more difficult to find meaningful predictors for one group, and again suggests the need for separate models for democracies and nondemocracies.

Industrial development, population structure, and democracy

With this background, we can consider more systematically the influence of the industrialism variables and the way they interact with democracy. Table 4.4 presents the main effects of the industrialism variables for all nations together and for developing nations separately. Initially, the variables include real GNP (logged), percent aged, and SIPE. Democracy alone has no additive effects in the equations and is not included until the interaction terms are included. As in the last chapter, we present GLS estimates that correct for serial correlation over time and heteroscedasticity across nations.

The results for all nations show the dominance of percent aged and SIPE. The effects of both are smaller for developing nations than for all nations combined but are still important. The effect of percent aged is, as we would expect, stronger for pensions than for general social insurance expenditures.[9] Real GNP shows nontrivial effects only for social insurance in developing nations. Important differences in the models for all nations and the developing nations indicate the need to separate advanced industrial nations from the analysis to follow. But the industrialism variables do show effects both within and across groups. This contradicts assertions that the industrialism effects are mere artifacts of grouping developed and developing nations (Castles and McKinlay, 1979).

According to at least one theory, these additive effects misspecify the process of spending for developing nations. The model may average quite different processes in democratic and nondemocratic nations. Columns 3 and 6 test for the interactive effects of democracy by including the appropriate interaction terms.

Table 4.4. Coefficients (unstandardized above standardized) for GLS estimates of models of social insurance and pension spending, developing nations, 1960–75

Independent variables	Social insurance/spending			Pensions/spending		
	All nations	Developing nations		All nations	Developing nations	
ln GNP/pop.	-0.328	0.448**	0.100	-0.307	0.095	0.023
	-0.073	0.359	0.080	-0.129	0.184	0.045
% aged	0.715**	0.202*	0.125	0.427*	0.198**	-0.059
	0.655	0.184	0.113	0.742	0.436	-0.130
SIPE	0.032**	0.012**	0.007*	0.016**	0.005**	0.002*
	0.388	0.344	0.201	0.368	0.347	0.139
Democracy = 1			-5.14*			-1.96**
			-2.33*			-2.15
Dem × ln GNP/pop.			0.708*			0.111
			2.06			0.782
Dem × % aged			0.028			0.274**
			0.052			1.24
Dem × SIPE			0.013**			0.008**
			0.512			0.762
Intercept	-1.26	-3.04	-0.64	-0.12	-1.28	-0.01
R^2 (OLS)	0.818	0.524	0.638	0.834	0.527	0.688
df	196	124	120	196	124	120
n, t	50, 4	32, 4	32, 4	50, 4	32, 4	32, 4

$**p < .01; *p < .05$

The variance explained rises substantially with the interaction terms, especially for pensions (the F-tests for increment in explained variance are 9.4 and 15.5, both significant at the .01 level).[10] Further, the results make theoretical sense: The variables show stronger effects in democracies. For SIPE, the effects increase nearly twofold in democracies (0.007 vs. 0.007 + 0.013 in column 3). This suggests that SIPE represents the growth of bureaucratic, governmental interest groups and their constituents, who can influence budgeting in democratic political processes. If mere inertia in budgeting were responsible for the effects of SIPE, they would be the same in democracies and nondemocracies. Similarly, the effects of real GNP are seven times as large in democracies as in nondemocracies. Although the difference in the effects of percent aged does not reach significance for social insurance spending, it is large and significant for pension spending. Democracy alone fails to raise pension spending, but in conjunction with other variables, it facilitates the growth of the welfare state.

To summarize the results thus far, the evidence favors the interest group theory and the facilitative effects of democracy. The industrialism theory receives some support insofar as the variables it specifies do indeed affect social welfare expenditures. However, the theory and other previous empirical research in support of it fail to account for the facilitative effects of democracy. Even with crude indicators of interest groups, we find meaningful differences in effects across levels of democracies that are consistent with predictions of the interest group theory.

Effects of dependency

The effects of the industrialism variables and democracy describe only part of the process determining social welfare spending in developing nations. We now need to consider the role of economic dependency and the international components of class. This task is made difficult by the variety of measures of dependency, each available for slightly different subsets of nations and time points. Our strategy is as follows. First, each indicator is added one at a time to the main effects of real GNP, percent aged, and SIPE (the interactive effects of democracy are considered shortly). This provides the best opportunity for each to affect social welfare spending before being included in a more complete equation with other related indicators of dependency and maintains, at least initially, the maximum number of cases for the separate equations. Then the most influential variables are simultaneously included in the equations.

Table 4.5 presents the results. Only the effects of the dependency variables are shown here; we will look at a more complete model shortly. The coefficients of the dependency variables on social insurance spending show that only peripheral status and foreign investment have large effects. More importantly, how-

Table 4.5. *Coefficients (unstandardized above standardized) for GLS estimates of dependency variables on social insurance and pension spending, developing nations, 1960–75*

Dependency variables	Cases $n \times t$	Soc. insur./spending (1)^a	Soc. insur./spending (2)	Pension/spending (1)^a	Pension/spending (2)
Commodity conc.	32×4	0.106 0.020		0.073 0.034	
Trade partner conc.	32×4	0.534 0.080		0.125 0.045	
Imp. + Exp./GDP	29×4	0.002 0.046		0.001 0.017	
Periphery = 1	29×4	0.739** 0.314	0.657** 0.280	0.075 0.076	−0.048 −0.048
Trade proc.	29×3	−0.428 −0.071		0.018 0.008	
Ext. public debt/GNP	29×2	0.025 0.101		0.012 0.132	
For. invest./GNP	29×2	0.053** 0.327	0.050** 0.308	0.024** 0.388	0.024** 0.400

**$p < .01$; *$p < .05$.
^{a} Dependency variables are included one at a time; the column represents results from seven separate equations. All coefficients net of GNP/pop, % aged, and SIPE.

ever, all the effects, net of the industrialism variables, are positive. Economic dependency increases expenditures rather than reduces them. When both peripheral position and foreign investment are included simultaneously, their net effects remain strong and positive (this equation requires deletion of data for 1960 and 1965). For pension spending, only foreign investment shows nontrivial effects, but again, nearly all dependency measures increase rather than reduce spending. As a further check on these results, we included a dummy variable for sub-Saharan African nations to control for regional or colonial influences on spending. Yet, the dummy variable is insignificant and the two dependency variables remain strong.

Democracy, dependency, or both?

Although many of the dependency variables fail to have meaningful effects, at least two are important. Moreover, nearly all dependency variables, even when the effects are small, increase spending. This favors the monopoly capitalism theory over the working-class strength theory. It remains to evaluate further the interest group and monopoly capitalism theories. Do controls for dependency eliminate the effects of democracy, or does democracy remain important, perhaps even interacting with dependency? Answering this question requires a combination of the models in Tables 4.4 and 4.5. However, as the number of variables and interactions increases and the correlations among the variables rise, it becomes more difficult to separate meaningfully the net effects of each variable. With missing data on the dependency variables, the problems are exacerbated. Our strategy is to include in the equations the additive and interactive variables from Table 4.4, along with one of the important dependency variables. Still, we must interpret these results cautiously, being aware of the robustness of the estimates.[11]

Table 4.6 presents combined models for social insurance and pension expenditures. The first four columns look at the effects of peripheral world-system position, the last columns at the effects of foreign investment (for a shorter time span). The effects of the industrialism variables change little with controls for dependency: Real GNP, percent aged, and SIPE are generally stronger in democracies than in nondemocracies. At the same time, peripheral position increases social insurance spending (but not pensions) and shows effects that are pretty much the same across democratic contexts. Foreign investment raises both social insurance and pension spending and shows stronger effects in democracies. Thus, dependency continues to influence spending. Rather than eliminating the influence of dependency, democracy perhaps increases the impact of dependent relations.

Another way to test the theories is to examine the effects that the variables have on change in expenditures. This involves standard panel analyses in which the most recent expenditures are predicted by earlier values of the determinants. Expenditures lagged to previous years are also treated as an independent variable, so that the dependent variable represents a change from previous levels. This strategy has the drawback of eliminating most of the cases from the pooled analysis, as each nation counts for only one case in the panel analysis. The multiple independent variables further reduce the degrees of freedom. With these caveats in mind, however, the panel analysis usefully supplements what we have already done and may more clearly confirm some of the hypotheses we have been testing. Specifically, the panel analysis in Table 4.7 focuses on the change from 1970 to 1975, the period for which all variables, including foreign investment, are available. The table presents OLS equations (GLS being unnecessary when separate years are not treated as independent units of analysis) both with and without dependency measures.

The change models of social insurance and pension spending show that de-

Table 4.6. *Coefficients (unstandardized above standardized) for GLS estimates of dependency and democracy variables on social insurance and pension spending, developing nations, 1960–75*

Independent variables	Soc. insurance (1)	(2)	Pensions (1)	(2)	Soc. insurance (1)	(2)	Pensions (1)	(2)
ln GNP/pop.	0.162 / 0.128	0.186 / 0.147	−0.006 / −0.011	−0.001 / −0.002	0.156 / 0.108	0.553* / 0.385	−0.026 / −0.047	0.033 / 0.060
% aged	0.293 / 0.267	0.280 / 0.255	−0.028 / −0.061	−0.031 / −0.068	0.055 / 0.038	−0.274 / −0.189	−0.055 / −0.010	−0.105 / −0.190
SIPE	0.004 / 0.110	0.004 / 0.110	0.002 / 0.133	0.002 / 0.133	0.011 / 0.236	0.008 / 0.171	0.003 / 0.168	0.002 / 0.112
Democracy	−3.77* / −1.68	−3.80* / −1.69	−1.98 / −2.13	−1.99* / −2.14	−5.62** / −2.09	−4.91** / −1.83	−2.00** / −1.96	−1.89* / −1.85
Dem. × ln GNP/pop.	0.554* / 1.58	0.513* / 1.47	0.137 / 0.947	0.130 / 0.898	0.416 / 1.02	−0.006 / −0.015	0.060 / 0.384	−0.003 / −0.019
Dem. × % aged	−0.025 / −0.046	0.009 / 0.017	0.251* / 1.12	0.257* / 1.15	0.415 / 0.613	0.754* / 1.11	0.293* / 1.13	0.344* / 1.33
Dem. × SIPE	0.013* / 0.507	0.012* / 0.468	0.008** / 0.752	0.008** / 0.752	0.020** / 0.765	0.022** / 0.842	0.010** / 1.00	0.011** / 1.10
Periphery	0.728** / 0.310	0.550 / 0.234	0.063 / 0.065	0.028 / 0.029				
Dem. × periphery		0.315 / 0.107		0.062 / 0.051				
Foreign invest.					0.047** / 0.289	−0.112 / −0.687	0.020** / 0.322	−0.003 / −0.048
Dem. × for. invest.						0.166** / 1.04		0.025 / 0.408
Intercept	−1.87	−1.81	−0.00	0.01	−1.18	−1.78	0.15	0.06
R^2 (OLS)	0.677	0.679	0.692	0.692	0.768	0.805	0.760	0.769
df	107	106	107	106	49	48	49	48
n, t	29, 4	29, 4	29, 4	29, 4	29, 2	29, 2	29, 2	29, 2

$**p < .01$; $*p < .05$.

Table 4.7. *Coefficients (unstandardized above standardized) for GLS estimates of change models of social insurance and pension spending, developing nations, 1975*

Independent variables	Social insurance spending			Pension spending		
	(1)	(2)	(3)	(1)	(2)	(3)
Lag DV.	0.578**	0.570**	0.545**	0.786**	0.795**	0.896**
	0.559	0.551	0.528	0.651	0.658	0.741
ln GDP/pop.	0.120	0.117	0.105	0.046	0.061	0.071
	0.079	0.077	0.070	0.076	0.010	0.115
% aged	−0.292	−0.292	−0.275	−0.052	−0.051	−0.064
	−0.179	−0.179	−0.169	−0.079	−0.078	−0.097
SIPE	0.005	0.005	0.006	0.001	0.002	0.001
	0.099	0.096	0.112	0.042	0.085	0.023
Democracy	−4.58*	−4.55	−4.75	−1.50*	−1.75	−1.34
	−1.68	−1.67	−1.74	−1.34	−1.58	−1.21
Dem. × ln GNP/pop.	0.222	0.220	0.232	0.032	0.048	0.030
	0.527	0.524	0.552	0.187	0.282	0.174
Dem. × % aged	0.613*	0.628*	0.628*	0.166*	0.131	0.136
	0.854	0.874	0.874	0.566	0.447	0.464
Dem. × SIPE	0.019*	0.018*	0.019*	0.010**	0.012**	0.009*
	0.635	0.619	0.653	0.828	0.987	0.754
Peripheral		0.063			−0.190	
		0.023			−0.168	
Foreign invest.			0.008			−0.008
			0.034			−0.090
Intercept	0.09	0.08	0.09	−0.08	−0.07	−0.14
R^2 (OLS)	0.912	0.912	0.912	0.925	0.941	0.928
df	23	19	19	23	19	19

$**p < .01$; $*p < .05$.

mocracy combined with percent aged and SIPE explains growth in spending as well as levels. These effects are reduced to some degree by controls for peripheral status and foreign investment, but still remain strong and positive (even if not always statistically significant with the few degrees of freedom). This table is consistent with the descriptive statistics in Tables 4.2 and 4.3, which show that expenditures rose much more quickly in democracies than in other nations. In contrast to these results for democracy, the effects of dependency are small and insignificant. Although peripheral status and foreign investment relate to levels of spending, they do not contribute to an explanation of the growth between 1970 and 1975. This negative finding applies to only a brief period and is insufficient to cause us to reject the dependency arguments, but it does indicate that they have less generality than the democracy effects.

Conclusions

Although theories of the welfare state focus primarily on advanced industrial economies, important insights into the process of social welfare spending come from the study of low- and middle-income developing nations. The variations among these nations in political democracy and trade dependency – factors that are nearly constant among developed nations – allow us to examine two of our major questions in new ways. The question of the role of political democracy and politics in welfare spending can be studied by comparing processes across more and less democratic developing nations. The question of the role of class in social welfare spending can be studied by examining the power of international capital – centered in core nations – to influence state policy in developing nations. Moreover, the direction of the effect of economic dependency on social welfare spending, whether it grows or declines with intervention of foreign capital, tells much about the use of welfare spending in reducing inequality in these nations.[12]

The hypotheses stemming from the theories can be briefly summarized. The industrialism theory predicts additive effects of economic development (logged), SIPE, and population structure that do not vary with level of democracy. The interest group theory suggests that the effects of economic, population, and program structures are strongest in political democracies, where the means exist for emerging groups to act collectively. The monopoly capitalism theory claims that political, trade, and investment domination of developing nations by core nations and international capital increases social welfare spending, as welfare responds to the needs for capital accumulation in low-income as well as high-income nations. The working-class strength theory argues that economic dependency, by prohibiting the organization of the indigenous population and workers, lowers social welfare spending.

Our test of these predictions is not so clear as to allow rejection or acceptance of each theory on the basis of a single set of coefficients. To some degree, many of the predictions are supported. Our strategy involves more a process of whittling away the predictions to see which ones are left after tests are made under a variety of conditions. We accept as most compelling those predictions that are most general and robust.

We find the industrialism theory correct in its predictions of the importance of economic and demographic structures and institutional programs. It is impossible to understand social welfare spending without some reference to the internal structures of nations. Further, these results clearly demonstrate that the effects of the industrialism variables are more than artifacts of clustering developing and developed nations: They hold within and across clusters of nations. The failure of the industrialism theory is that it does not account for differences in processes across democratic and nondemocratic nations.

The interest group theory receives more complete support, since it correctly predicts that real GNP, percent aged, and SIPE increase spending more strongly in democracies than in nondemocracies. Democracy does not increase spending directly, but it does facilitate the effects of other internal structures on spending. Democracy's effects hold for levels as well as changes in spending and account for the growing gap in welfare spending between democracies and nondemocracies.

When the effects of economic dependency are considered, some evidence supports the predictions of the monopoly capitalism theory. Nearly all effects of economic dependency on social welfare are positive, although most dependency variables have only small effects. There is no evidence of negative effects, as predicted by the working-class strength theory. Thus, social welfare grows with domination by foreign nations and capital, and may be seen as part of the diffusion of Western power. Where capital is strong, so is welfare spending, which is consistent with the argument that capital benefits from social welfare. It does not take a strong working class, free from international control, for the welfare state to grow.

The evidence, then, supports both the interest group theory and the monopoly capitalism theory. However, the dependency variables fail to explain changes in expenditures where the democracy interactions explain both change and levels. The broader scope of the interest group theory, then, is a basis for arguing that it gets most support from the analysis.

What do these results tell us about the process of welfare determination in developing nations? First, political enfranchisement is crucial for growth of the welfare state. However, political development is not sufficient, since certain structural, bureaucratic, and demographic changes are also needed. Political pressure and preferences of populations combine with changes in the structure of the population to increase social welfare spending. This conclusion certainly fits with the results found in the last chapter for advanced industrial nations. Many of the same variables affecting spending in advanced industrial nations are found here to be of increasing importance in developing democracies. The similarity between the two types of democracies, despite vastly different levels of development, indicates the importance of democracy for the social welfare state.

There may, however, be another road to the welfare state that is unique to developing nations and does not require political democracy. This is through ties to core nations and foreign investment. Since dependent peripheral nations are less democratic than semiperipheral nations (Bollen, 1983; also see Table 4.2), dependency may provide an alternative, less democratic means to welfare spending. Diffusion of social welfare programs from core to dependent nations may occur in response to the needs of monopoly capital, even when appropriate democratic and development structures do not exist.

Based on these arguments, we would expect to find the highest social welfare spending in the relatively few nations that are both democratic and dependent on trade. Dependency would offer external support and democracy internal pressure for welfare spending. We find some interaction between dependency and democracy that lends support to this possibility. The positive effects of foreign investment are stronger in democracies than in nondemocracies. Popular political participation leads not to rejection of foreign influence but to use of the resources to increase welfare spending further. Perhaps the interest group and monopoly capitalism theories are not inconsistent, but apply to different parts of a larger process. Foreign relations with core nations provide resources for social welfare spending, but the structure of internal groups and politics determines how those resources are distributed and the growth rate of spending.

There are some other ways that the views of the interest group and monopoly capitalism theories converge. Both theories agree that social welfare spending is not an egalitarian force or a source of long-term economic prosperity. If dependency maintains inequality, as argued by early theory and research on the topic, and dependency increases social welfare spending, according to our results, social welfare spending must be seen as a means used by foreign capital to maintain inequality. Given the facilitative effects of democracy, this does not appear to be a process opposed by the masses in developing nations. Yet, both theories see welfare spending as resulting in crisis, rather than equality, in the long run. The interest group theory suggests that popular demand for special government programs, often in more populous urban areas, may reduce incentives for production and investment, particularly in rural areas (Lipton, 1977). The monopoly capitalism theory suggests that social welfare spending may maintain dominance of foreign control at the expense of independent development. The effects of social welfare spending on inequality are studied more directly in later chapters, but these results are intriguing for their implications for the meaning and effects of the welfare state.

Notes

1. There are six other nations with complete data for three time points. Use of these nations, however, would require deletion of 32 others for one time point, resulting in a net loss of cases. We chose to maximize longitudinal variation even at the expense of eliminating some nations from the analysis. See *The Cost of Social Security* (ILO, 1981), Table 5, for the figures used in the study.

2. To examine the representativeness of this sample, we regressed a dummy variable indicating missing social welfare expenditure data on the industrialism, democracy, and dependency determinants. The results show that nations with new programs, less democratic governments, and less dependency on trade with one partner are more likely not to report social insurance expenditures. It makes sense that reporting procedures would be less developed for new programs; that tabulation and publication of figures would be less common under dictatorships, which have the power to prevent publication of unflattering statistics; and that relations with core nations would allow adoption and use by dependent countries of the bureaucratic and statistical reporting procedures of the core nation. All this is not to discredit our analyses but to emphasize what is already obvious – that we do not have a random sample and cannot generalize to all developing nations. It means that we have more to say about nations with relatively more developed programs than about those with primitive programs. Studies comparing the adoption date of social insurance laws for nations with more primitive systems and no expenditure data might provide a useful supplement to our study. Nonetheless, for the purposes of testing growth and levels of expenditures, it is necessary and useful to examine those nations that actually do report expenditure data, even if these nations do not represent all developing nations.

3. In the last chapter, we found that social insurance spending dominated overall welfare spending. Public assistance spending, although only a small part of all benefits, still responded quite differently to class and demographic determinants. Only 9 of the 32 developing nations we study in this chapter, however, have public assistance programs, according to the ILO figures, and even for these 9 nations, such spending is small. To a large extent, then, social insurance spending is equivalent to total spending.

4. Summers and Heston (1984) present newly estimated figures for real gross domestic product that better measure national prices and actual standard of living. We replicated the results in this chapter, using the GDP figures, but found little difference. In fact, the standard GNP measure we use correlates 0.96 with Summers and Heston's revised measure. Additionally, we replicated the models in this chapter with real GNP replaced by energy use per capita. This nonmonetary measure of development provides results nearly identical to those reported for the real GNP measure and indicates the robustness of the results to the measure of economic development.

5. Of the 32 nations, 19 are classified as nondemocratic: Benin, Bolivia, Burma, the Congo, El Salvador, Ethiopia, Guatemala, Guyana, the Ivory Coast, Kenya, Mali, Mauritania, Morocco, Nicaragua, Niger, Senegal, Togo, Upper Volta, and Zambia. There are 13 democratic nations: Brazil, Colombia, Costa Rica, Cyprus, India, Israel, Malaysia, Mexico, Panama, the Philippines, Sri Lanka, Turkey, and Venezuela. Clear regional differences exist in these two groups: All but seven of the nondemocracies and none of the democracies are African. That many nondemocracies come from the same region is not, by itself, a flaw in the classification: Democracy is a concept that is more meaningful theoretically than similar geographical location.

Nonetheless, we make some effort to ensure that differences across democracies and nondemocracies are not due to unmeasured, regionally based variables in the analyses to follow.

6. The formula is equal to the sum of $P(i)$ squared where $P(i)$ is the proportion of the total exports in the ith commodity division (of a total of 56 divisions from the Standard International Trade Classification).

7. The gross means can be obtained from a regression of expenditures on a dummy variable for 1975, a dummy variable for democracies, and a term representing the multiplicative interaction of the two dummy variables. The net means are obtained with the same variables plus controls for energy use or percent aged. The intercept is standardized to the group mean for nondemocracies in 1960; that is, all differences between groups are calculated from that standard.

8. These results appear not to be due to the concentration of African nations among the nondemocracies. The same standardization exercise was performed with a control for a dummy variable representing sub-Saharan African nations. This dummy variable, however, was insignificant and did little to change the results. Similarly small effects of an African dummy variable are shown in other models to follow, suggesting that the classification of democracy represents more than common regional location.

9. Another measure of age structure – the ratio of children aged 0 to 14 over women aged 20 to 44 – reflects high fertility and a young age structure. Low fertility may increase spending, as adult children demand government support to aid in caring for aged parents (Entwisle and Winegarten, 1984). However, since the ratio is highly correlated with percent aged, it has only weak effects in the models and is excluded from the reported results.

10. The multiplicative interaction terms in columns 3 and 6 lead to high standardized coefficients, sometimes over 1. This is not unusual for such models. The coefficients for variables that are components in interaction terms should not be interpreted singly, but rather in combination with the interaction terms. Similarly, the negative coefficient for the additive effect of democracy has little substantive meaning in these equations and those to follow. It shows the differences in intercepts between democracies and nondemocracies when values on all other variables are 0. Yet, the zero points on the variables in this equation are not substantively meaningful. Moreover, given that the slope for percent aged and SIPE is greater for democracies than for nondemocracies (rather than parallel), the slopes will diverge toward infinity as the distance from the point of intersection increases. Thus, in the presence of interaction, the additive negative effect of democracy does not necessarily indicate that democracy lowers welfare expenditures.

11. The correlations among the independent variables do not go above 0.60, and the tolerance of the independent variables does not fall below 0.40. The exceptions, of course, involve the relationships of variables with their own multiplicative interaction terms. Even so, the results in general, and those for the interaction terms in particular, are robust across equations and dependent variables. Other statistical characteristics of the models are also quite strong. Neither deletion of outliers and influential cases nor estimation with alternative error specifications changes the results.

12. We have intentionally neglected state structure variables in both the theoretical discussion and the statistical analyses of this chapter. The neglect comes from the difficulty of transplanting state-centered arguments and measures for the advanced industrial democracies to the study of developing, sometimes nondemocratic, nations. The effects we find for most state variables make little theoretical sense, are quite small, and suggest that their influence on spending in developing nations needs to be rethought. Other variables, such as electoral timing, corporatism, and coalition government structure, are not measurable for the nondemocratic, nonindustrial nations in our sample. Our lack of success in finding any meaningful state effects might at this stage it reasonably be seen as an indication of the need to await additional data.

Appendix 4.A. *Sources of data*

Social insurance, pensions, and other program spending	*The Cost of Social Security.* 1985. Geneva: International Labour Organization. Table 8.
GNP/population	Bornschier and Heintz (1979).
Percent aged	*Labour Force: 1950–2000.* 1977. Geneva: International Labour Organization. Volumes I, II, III, and IV, Table 2.
SIPE	*Social Security Throughout the World.* 1981. Washington, D.C.: Social Security Administration.
Democracy	Bollen (1980).
Commodity concentration, trade partner concentration, imports, exports	Taylor and Jodice (1983).
Periphery	Snyder and Kick (1979).
Trade processing, external debt, foreign investment	Bornschier and Heintz (1979).

5. Economic growth, social welfare spending, and income inequality

In this chapter, we consider the consequences of social welfare spending for aspects of social equality involving the distribution of income. Income inequality, conceived as the relative share of income going to different groups in the population, particularly the poorest groups relative to the richest groups, dominates discussions of social equality. Most scholars view low income inequality and low poverty as fair and just, a goal toward which societies should strive. Among large agricultural and industrial societies, none has come close to perfect equality, but some have come further than others.

If agreement exists on the goal, the means to lower inequality is subject to considerably more debate. More so than in previous decades, strategies of economic growth and direct government income transfer are viewed as mutually exclusive. To the extent that it directs resources away from production and discourages upward mobility, welfare spending may retard the progress toward greater equality coming from economic growth. Alternatively, to the extent that it benefits the upper and middle classes, economic growth may not change inequality unless egalitarian policies redistribute income. Assuming that no contradiction exists between government intervention and economic growth – that they reinforce each other in reducing inequality – blunts the debate somewhat and offers another set of predictions concerning the determination of income dispersion.[1]

Considering the redistributive effect of welfare spending in developing nations further incorporates issues involving the importance of national characteristics, such as economic and demographic structures, relative to external relations in the world system. Traditional views consider income inequality as a characteristic of nations, separable from the structure of equality across nations. World-system critics argue that nations are inappropriate units of analysis, since class power and inequalities transcend national boundaries. The position of a nation and its citizens in this world division of labor are crucial for the inequality within a nation. If economic growth or age structure is associated with level of income inequality, it is only because of the common effect of economic dependency and world-system position on both.

This chapter thus addresses questions concerning the independent influences on income inequality of social welfare spending (particularly in developed nations) and of world-system position (particularly in developing nations). Further, it examines such influences relative to the influence of economic development. Those arguing for the importance of social welfare spending or trade independence often reject the view that economic growth brings lower inequality. We therefore must test the efficacy of economic growth in light of such criticisms.

Because of severe measurement problems inherent in the study of household or individual income, all scholars face limitations in studying income inequality. Self-reported household income data are error prone, even in the most bureaucratized industrial societies; in agricultural societies, cash income is rare, and household economic resources may be harder to measure accurately. Even if income were reported without error, variations in household size, tax rates, in-kind benefits, nonmonetary income, and the cost of living would blunt the connection between reported income and economic well-being. Further differences across nations in sampling techniques, population coverage, and question structure compound the problems of comparison. All these problems might recommend the study of more easily measured physical indicators of well-being – such as infant mortality. Yet, in defense of the study of income inequality, previous research has shown that, however poorly measured, the measures have theoretically meaningful relationships with economic structures. The consistency of findings, over different samples and data sources, means that something more than random error must be included in the measures. What we offer in this chapter, then, is a careful analysis of an admittedly flawed but theoretically important component of equality. Given the limitations, the results of this chapter should not be viewed in isolation, but rather seen as part of the larger study. To the extent that the results here complement those of the previous and subsequent chapters, and form a meaningful set of consistent findings, the study of income inequality, despite measurement problems, remains valuable.

Hypotheses: does welfare spending matter?

The questions we ask in this chapter correspond to the larger questions we raised in Chapter 1 and provide a basis for distinguishing the theories of the welfare state. Concerning the determinants of income inequality, the theories differ on (1) the consequences of welfare spending and (2) the relative influence of external class-based international relations and nonclass economic and demographic structures. The industrialism and working-class strength theories predict strong positive effects of the welfare state on equality, whereas the interest group politics and monopoly capitalism theories predict little effect. The monopoly capitalism and working-class strength theories predict dominant effects of class structure and economic dependency, whereas the industrialism and interest group politics theories predict dominant effects of economic and demographic structures.

The industrialism theory predicts that welfare spending reduces inequality. As Wilensky (1975:87) states, "the net impact of the welfare state is egalitarian." This point follows logically from the argument that welfare spending aims to meet the needs of groups adversely affected by industrial growth. The urban poor, sick, unemployed, retired, and members of broken families all benefit from welfare expenditures. Even if taxation policies are mildly regressive, welfare programs so clearly direct expenditures to the most needy that the net effect is to transfer income to the poorest groups in the population and to reduce inequality and poverty. Since, according to the industrialism theory, economic growth determines welfare spending and welfare spending reduces inequality, welfare spending mediates much of the relationship between economic growth and inequality. That is, economic growth affects inequality indirectly through welfare spending. Although economic growth also affects inequality directly through the growth of a large middle class and occupational mobility (Kerr, 1964), at least part of the effect of development operates through welfare spending.

These arguments treat the welfare state as one mechanism through which the functional imperatives of industrialization are met. Industrialism spawns a variety of social and political institutions that contribute to the continued growth of the economy. The welfare state is one such institution. Like industrial structures, it helps to lower inequality, since lower inequality is functional for society. The welfare state is thus not independent of economic forces, since economic forces lead to the emergence of the welfare state. Yet, if industrialization reduces inequality because it is functional for society, so should the other institutions that the industrial processes bring into being. In terms of predicting levels of inequality, then, we look for *consistency* in the effects of industrial and welfare variables: Both should lower income inequality.

A simple but incorrect interpretation of the industrialism theory considers only the effects of development. The term *industrialism* implies a sole reliance on industrialization as a determinant of income inequality. As the originating force toward equality, industrialism is primary, but the logic of the argument also requires that welfare spending reduce inequality. A tenet of industrialism theory is that social welfare spending goes to those who are superfluous to industrial labor needs, thus maintaining the social integration necessary for long-term economic growth. This admits that industrialization alone fails to raise the income of all parts of the population and that welfare spending is needed to redistribute income. If welfare spending has no net impact on equality, the welfare state must be superfluous rather than functional to society. This is logically inconsistent with the industrialism theory: There would be no reason for the welfare state to emerge if it did not contribute, above and beyond the influence of economic development, to the conditions for further economic growth. Both factors – development and welfare spending – work together to reduce inequality rather than one completely subsuming the other. Thus, the theory does not predict that the effects of welfare spending are spurious, but rather that they contribute, along with economic development, to the reduction of income inequality.

The interest group politics theory argues for the importance of economic growth and population structure, but not of welfare spending. Economic growth produces the major means to lower inequality by creating opportunities for mobility and movement out of poverty. The welfare state at best has not resulted in lower income inequality and, at worst, may actually maintain poverty by creating dependency and demoralization among the poor (Janowitz, 1976, 1985; Gronbjerg, 1977). The differences between the industrialism and interest group theories concerning the generation of income inequality stem from their different arguments concerning the causes of welfare spending. The industrialism theory sees welfare spending as the response of government to the needs of groups harmed by industrial growth. The interest group theory sees welfare spending as a political process reflecting the distribution of political power in society rather than economic need. Although they may have the economic need, the poor lack the political power to influence public policies strongly in their benefit. (Alford and Friedland, 1975; Olson, 1982). Political processes offer the opportunity for stronger, more politically effective interest groups – particularly those coming from the upper and middle classes – to implement programs to benefit themselves. Democratic political processes may be crucial for the growth of the welfare state, but then do little to reduce inequality (Bollen and Jackman, 1985a).

The interest group arguments imply independence of political processes from industrial needs. In fact, welfare spending, as a political process, operates to maintain inequality, whereas economic growth reduces it. The autonomy of political programs shows in their effects on inequality, which do not act in concert with those of economic growth. In contrast to the industrialism theory, which predicts positive effects of both development and welfare, the interest group theory predicts contrasting effects.

Class perspectives on equality

In low- and middle-income (or peripheral and semiperipheral) nations, the major influence of class comes through economic dependency. Both class theories assume that investment dependency, trade dependency, and peripheral location in the world system all reduce a nation's control over its economic product. The greater the domination of developing nations by core nations and multinational

Table 5.1. *Theoretical predictions for determinants of income inequality*

Determinants of income inequality	Theories				
	Indust-rialism	Interest group	Monopoly capital	Working class	State-centered
Economic development population structure	−	−	0	0	0
Class structure, economic and trade dependency	0	0	+	+	0
Welfare spending	−	0	0	−	−

corporations, and the stronger the power of indigenous elites and capital, the lower the strength of labor. Foreign investors are thus in a position to demand expatriation of the lion's share of the economic surplus that might otherwise have been spent to benefit the indigenous poor. Similarly, local elites with ties to foreign business may control local wealth, preventing diffusion to the poor of wealth created by trade. Even if there is economic growth and fertility decline, these will not translate into lower inequality in the presence of economic dependency (Evans, 1979; Bradshaw, 1985).

The theories differ over the effect of welfare spending. The monopoly capitalism theory claims that welfare spending benefits capital. In the short run, spending alleviates protest, but ultimately it maintains inequality and furthers capital accumulation. Change in productive relations rather than in government programs can eliminate inequality. The working-class strength theory, in contrast, argues that welfare spending emerges at the behest of the working class and poor, who are the primary beneficiaries of such spending. As a result, inequality is lowest where trade dependency is low, states are strong, and democratic experience is long (Rubinson, 1976; Muller, 1988). Similar arguments apply to advanced industrial, core nations. Both theories emphasize that inequality is lower where labor is strong relative to capital. However, working-class strength theorists argue that welfare spending has grown most in leftist nations dominated by labor unions, and it has reduced income inequality and poverty. The monopoly capitalism theory sees welfare spending as a form of social control that is highest where capital is strong and does little to reduce equality. Thus, the theories agree on the relationship between class structure and inequality but differ on the mechanism through which the inequality occurs – through welfare spending and political power or, more directly, through control of economic power.

A brief summary of these predictions is presented in Table 5.1. Determinants are grouped into three broad categories based on (1) economic development and population structure, (2) class structure and economic dependency, and (3) welfare spending. Each theory specifies the effects of a unique combination of these three factors. Industrialism and interest group theories differ from class theories with their focus on internal versus external characteristics; within these two groups, each theory is distinguished by the predicted presence or absence of an effect of welfare spending.[2]

State autonomy

The scheme may also be extended to consider state-centered theories. Since advocates of the theory use state power as a sensitizing concept to interpret qualitative differences across nations, it is difficult to specify a set of predictions generalizing over a large number of nations. However, by making a key assumption that state policies independently influence and change societal substructures, such as the distribution of income, the theory makes implicit predictions concerning the determinants of income inequality. Briefly stated, state autonomy may be shown in government policies that counteract, or are inconsistent with, the influence of economic development on income inequality. Rather than referring to an unmeasurable "potential autonomy," we conceptualized autonomy more concretely as the extent to which the welfare state actually counteracts economic forces.

This view of state autonomy – based on the congruence between development and welfare spending – helps distinguish among the four demand theories. The economic determinism of the industrialism theory shows in the complementary contribution of the welfare state to the process of income equalization brought about by industrialization. The interest group theory, in contrast, posits beneficial effects of industrial-demographic structures but asserts that welfare spending maintains, or at least has little influence on, inequality. In one case, spending has the same effect as economic development; in the other, it does not. For the class theories, economic development has little influence in either direction. The monopoly capitalism theory asserts that neither economic growth nor social welfare spending lowers inequality. Both processes fail to overcome the harmful effects of dependency, and show consistency in effects and lack of autonomy of the welfare state. The social democratic theory predicts no effect of industrial-demographic structures and beneficial effects of welfare spending. A simple view of Table 5.1 thus shows the existence of autonomous influence when the predicted effects of economic development and welfare spending *do not* match.

A state-centered theory might go even further by suggesting that the state structures, either alone or in addition to welfare spending, directly influence inequality. Without the presence of a strong state to implement redistributive programs, neither the level of national product nor welfare spending may have any necessary relationship to inequality. Instead, inequality may depend on the ability of the state to implement welfare programs and coordinate economic processes in an egalitarian manner. For instance, central, nonfederal, and corporate states may allow leaders to overcome special and local interests so as to direct welfare spending most effectively to the needy. State revenues based on direct taxes may likewise provide an egalitarian form of funding that reduces inequality. Perhaps these characteristics independently affect inequality, or perhaps they combine with welfare spending in their effects. Either way, state characteristics should be considered. Otherwise, the theory gives little attention to economic development or dependency, not taking their influence for granted as much as denying it altogether. Nonetheless, it is reasonable to claim for the theory that state structure, as reflected in the independent effects of welfare spending, dominates the process of income inequality.

Previous research

Although by no means complete, the research literature on income inequality provides tests of some of the hypotheses we have just presented. Perhaps most thoroughly documented by empirical research is the relationship between economic development and income inequality – a relationship that emerges when treated as curvilinear. Dating back to Kuznets (1955), economists and sociologists have demonstrated the inverted U-shaped relationship (Berger, 1986). Studies that argue that development fails to affect inequality when controlling for economic dependency (Chase-Dunn, 1975; Rubinson, 1976; Rubinson and Quinlan, 1977; Bornschier et al., 1978) are flawed by the specification of linear effects of development. These studies correctly measure national product as its natural logarithm but fail to include a quadratic term. The logged variable allows leveling off of effects at high income levels but ignores the changing direction of the relationships. Weede (1980), Weede and Tiefenbach (1981), Bollen and Jackman (1985a), and Muller (1988) demonstrate strong effects of economic development when the functional form is correctly specified.

The curvilinear relationship implies that initially the new wealth brought about by economic development goes primarily to the elite and exacerbates inequality. Technological changes in agricultural and traditional craft occupations may also disrupt labor markets at first and contribute to higher inequality in the early stages of development. As income continues to grow with economic development, however, labor opportunities and wages expand, pay differentials between skilled and unskilled workers decline, and wealth diffuses to the masses. Consequently, income inequality lessens with continued development. Since production depends more on the skills of middle-level occupational incumbents than in the past, the elite can do little to block the transfer of income to these groups (income of the elite increases in absolute terms from higher production but decreases in relative terms; Lenski, 1966).

After income inequality initially increases and then decreases, it levels off among advanced industrial nations. The United States, for instance, has shown virtually no change in income inequality in 40 years. Although data are rare, other developed nations show generally stable inequality during the post–World War II period. The lack of change might be expected in part for statistical reasons. If a certain percentage increase in national product is needed to lower inequality, the same percentage increase implies a much larger absolute increase in developed nations than in developing nations. Change occurs only slowly at the upper tail of the distribution of national income. More importantly, there may be structural limits to how much equality can be tolerated in capitalist or industrial economies without loss of efficiency. Major redistribution in such economies may require at least short-term disruption and loss of income by all workers (Przeworski, 1985). For these reasons, once economic and industrial development reach certain thresholds, further reductions in inequality come slowly.

All this suggests that the proper specification of the relationship requires that national product (or whatever measure of development is used) be logged and squared. Logging reduces the skew of income but also allows the different meaning of income at different levels. The same change in dollar income per capita is more influential at lower levels than at higher ones (e.g., a $100 increase means more to a nation with a per capita income of $500 than to a nation with a per capita income of $5,000). The natural log changes the metric to percentage change in income rather than dollar change. Squaring the logged term also allows the relationship to change direction.

Besides income, other development variables linearly affect income inequality. Of particular importance is age structure. Bollen and Jackman (1985a) show that a young age structure, with a high percentage of the population below age 15, increases income inequality. Conversely, an old age structure reduces income inequality. Age structure in this context mediates the effects of population growth on inequality. High population growth expands the young population, particularly among low-income groups (Ahluwalia, 1976; Boulier, 1977). A young age structure, then, requires that family resources be directed to the young. This may lower the productivity of the society, inhibit the mobility of parents, and maintain poverty (Bollen and Jackman, 1985a).

Whereas the curvilinear effects of development on income inequality have been well established, the effects of other economic, trade, and state policy variables are less clear. With appropriate controls for development, neither trade dependency nor position in the world system affects inequality (Weede, 1980, 1982; Weede and Tiefenbach, 1981; Bollen and Jackman, 1985a). Advocates of the dependency viewpoint, in response, argue that the effects of dependency show only among developing nations (Bornschier, 1981; Bornschier and Chase-Dunn, 1985) but offer only preliminary evidence for that view. Democracy also appears to have little impact on inequality. Early studies erred by measuring democracy as stability or political participation (Cutright, 1967; Hewitt, 1977; Rubinson and Quinlan, 1977; Stack, 1978). However, even with a more valid and reliable measure (Bollen, 1980), democracy has no effect (Bollen and Grandjean, 1981; Bollen and Jackman, 1985a). A study by Weede (1982) suggests that controlling for political participation (i.e., percentage of the population voting) allows the effects of democracy to emerge, but this finding needs to be replicated. Another study by Muller (1988) shows effects of years of democratic experience (rather than a nation's current level of democracy) and also needs to be replicated. Finally, state expenditures or revenues fail to reduce income inequality. Despite some early evidence that strong states (i.e., with high tax revenues as a percentage of GNP) have lower inequality (Rubinson, 1976), more recent studies show no such effect with proper controls for development (Weede, 1980). Otherwise, studies of specific program expenditures, such as for social insurance or social welfare, are still needed.

Among high-income nations, some evidence exists that socialist or social democratic governments lower inequality (Hewitt, 1977; Tufte, 1978; Jackman, 1980; DeViney and Parker, 1984; DeViney, 1987). Either because measures of socialist party strength are flawed in less democratic, low-income nations or because socialist governments have little control over income distribution in poor nations, there is no effect on income inequality of government control in developing nations (Jackman, 1975). This makes theoretical sense, since working-class strength arguments suggest that it is only in high-income nations that surplus income is available to leftist governments to redistribute (Stephens, 1979). However, among high-income nations, levels of development are truncated, thereby eliminating in part the competing influence of other variables.

Our review of the literature offers no complete consensus, and therefore does not eliminate the need for further study, but it does offer some guidance on what we can expect. Given the evidence, our first task is to replicate the curvilinear effects of economic development and related developmental variables. In this effort, we rely heavily on the previous work of Bollen and Jackman (1985a), who show strong effects of such variables in their model. We then consider the effects of economic dependency, government expenditures and revenues, and leftist governments, and try to address some of the inconsistencies in the existing literature. We further extend previous research by considering developed and developing nations both separately and together.

The relationship between development and income inequality

In attempting to replicate and extend the findings of the literature on income inequality, we begin with the study of nations at all levels of development for which data are available. Like previous researchers (but unlike the other chapters in this book), we must rely on a cross section of nations at one time point (circa 1970) because figures on household income are seldom available for more than one time point. Data for income inequality thus come primarily from the years between 1967 and 1972 and the independent variables from 1965.[3]

There are multiple ways to calculate the dependent variable, income inequality. The share of income going to each quintile of households can be examined, but usually some sort of summary measure can simplify the analyses. The Gini coefficient, one such summary measure, is highly influenced by middle income levels of the distribution (Allison, 1978). Another measure, the ratio of the top quintile over the bottom two quintiles, concentrates more on the income at the extremes of the distribution (Bollen and Jackman, 1985a). The higher the share of the rich relative to that of the poor, the higher the ratio and the higher the inequality. Although we examine results for other measures, we depend primarily on this income share ratio. For almost all nations, this ratio is based on pretax income, but we examine later posttax income for a small number of nations. Whatever measure is used, however, it is necessary to control for whether it is based on household or individual income data (Bollen and Jackman, 1985a). Income data on individuals, although the basis of income share computations for a minority of the cases, show more inequality, since the measure includes many individuals who may share the household income of others but who are themselves without personal income.

We begin with an analysis of all nations combined before proceeding to the separate study of developed and developing nations. With the combined sample, we can fully explore the effects of development on inequality, a necessary prerequisite for the study of other determinants. Specifically, we follow Bollen and Jackman (1985a) with the study of GNP per capita in U.S. dollars, logged and squared, and percentage of the population aged 0–14.[4]

First, consider the relationship between development and inequality (controlling for a dummy variable indicating household data) shown in the first column of Table 5.2. The unstandardized coefficients show a significant positive effect for the first-order term and a significant negative effect for the second-order term of our measure of development – real GNP per capita. Inequality initially in-

Table 5.2. Coefficients (unstandardized above standardized) for OLS estimates of development and dependency variables on income share ratio, all nations

Independent variables	Dependent variable: income share ratio						
	(1)	(2)	(3)	(4)	(5)	(6)	(7)
ln GNP/pop.	9.31**	5.97**	7.47**	5.86**	6.40**	5.97**	5.81**
(ln GNP/pop.)²	−0.727**	−0.411**	−0.516**	−0.402**	−0.433**	−0.411**	−0.392**
Combined[a]	0.526**	0.449**	0.513**	0.450**	0.524**	0.450**	0.475**
% youth		0.163***	0.196***	0.158***	0.186***	0.164***	0.181***
		0.699	0.857	0.667	0.814	0.701	0.777
HH data = 1	−1.09*	−0.756	−1.21*	−0.723	−0.905	−0.759	−0.727
	−.238	−0.171	−0.260	−0.164	−0.211	−0.172	−0.166
Semiperiphery = 1			−0.217				
			−0.048				
Periphery = 1			−0.813				
			−0.200				
Commod. concen.				0.005			
				0.005			
Partner concen.					−0.010		
					−0.075		
Imp. + Exp./GNP						−0.001	
						−0.004	
Foreign invest.							−0.004
							−0.078
Intercept	−23.6	−22.2	−28.0	−21.9	−24.5	−22.2	−22.4
R²	0.318	0.465	0.552	0.467	0.537	0.465	0.469
df	61	57	51	56	53	56	55
n	65	62	58	62	59	62	61

**p < .01; *p < .05.

[a] Standardized coefficient for quadratic terms combined (see text for calculation); other coefficients for GNP are unstandardized.

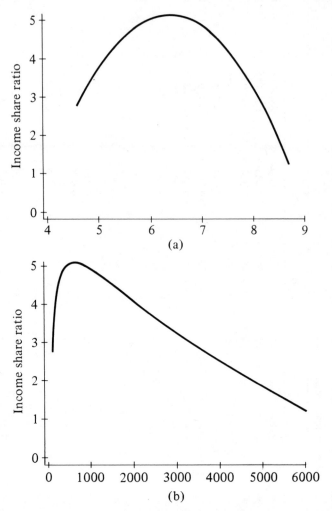

Figure 5.1. Plot of regression-based relationship between GNP and income inequality: (a) natural log of GNP in U.S. constant dollars per capita; (b) constant GNP in dollars per capita.

creases with development but then decreases with further change in development. Figures 5.1a and 5.1b graph the curve implied by these coefficients. Figure 5.1a plots the predicted values by the log of GNP and shows a curve equally balanced on both sides of the maximum point. Figure 5.1b shows the curve when plotted against GNP in its original metric. The curve is skewed, as many cases are packed on the low scale of GNP (when logged, these packed cases on the low end are spread out and distant cases on the high end are moved closer). In either case, the values of inequality are lowest at high levels of income. The curve in Figure 5.1b shows that income inequality peaks when GNP per capita is $605 dollars – the approximate level of Costa Rica or Turkey in 1965 – after which inequality declines. Improvement of only a few hundred dollars of GNP per capita thus brings nations up to the point where further growth lowers inequality.

The standardized coefficients for the GNP terms make little sense unless they are combined in some way. We obtain a summary standardized coefficient for GNP by calculating a variable equal to the unstandardized coefficients times GNP logged and GNP logged squared. The new variable then serves as a predictor replacing the two GNP terms and regressed with other independent variables on the income share ratio. The standardized coefficient of the new term indicates the effect in standard units of the curvilinear relationship.[5] In column 1 of Table 5.2, the standardized coefficient for the GNP term combined is 0.526 and indicates the importance of GNP to income inequality.

The next column adds percent youth to the equation. Since they are highly correlated, controlling for percent youth reduces the standardized coefficient for GNP combined to 0.449. Percent youth has a stronger effect. They are not so closely related that both cannot contribute unique explained variance. The obverse of this result is that high percent aged reduces inequality. Far from straining the capacities of society to care for them, the aged are most common in societies that are relatively egalitarian.

Additional influences on income inequality

The remaining columns in Table 5.2 add measures of dependency one at a time to the developmental variables. These measures include semiperipheral and peripheral positions in the world system, trade characteristics such as concentration of export commodities, concentration of trade partners, trade over GNP, and foreign investment (see Chapter 4 and Appendix 5.A for the definition and sources of these and other variables). None of the dependency measures has significant effects in the equations, and the largest effect, that of being in a peripheral position, reduces rather than increases inequality. In all cases, the effects of GNP and percent youth remain strong.[6]

Perhaps the failure of the dependency variables in Table 5.2 results from the inclusion of core nations in the sample. Because Bornschier and Chase-Dunn (1985) show that dependency has no effect in core nations, we replicate the models with core nations deleted.[7] The results in Table 5.3 for the subsample of

Table 5.3. Coefficients (unstandardized above standardized) for OLS estimates of development and dependency variables on income share ratio, developing nations[a]

Independent variables	Dependent variable: income share ratio					
	(1)	(2)	(3)	(4)	(5)	(6)
ln GNP/pop.	5.22	7.92	5.82	5.68	5.20	4.54
	−0.339	−0.546	−0.392	−0.363	−0.336	−0.283
(ln GNP/pop.)²						
Combined[b]	0.503**	0.589**	0.496**	0.573**	0.510**	0.487**
% youth	0.191**	0.215**	0.185**	0.207**	0.195**	0.200**
	0.466	0.546	0.451	0.524	0.476	0.493
HH data = 1	−0.932	−1.34*	−0.876	−1.09	−0.948	−0.873
	−0.204	−0.302	−0.192	−0.246	−0.208	−0.194
Periphery = 1		−0.600				
		−0.141				
Commod. concen.			0.005			
			0.045			
Partner concen.				−0.003		
				−0.021		
Imp. + Exp./GNP.					−0.002	
					−0.023	
For. invest.						−0.001
						−0.018
Intercept	−21.4	−30.5	−23.1	−23.8	−21.5	−19.7
R²	0.378	0.488	0.380	0.468	0.379	0.367
df	41	36	40	37	40	39
n	46	42	46	43	46	45

**p < .01; *p < .05.
[a] Except where noted, standardized coefficients are below unstandardized coefficients.
[b] Standardized coefficients for quadratic terms combined (see text for calculation); other coefficients for GNP are unstandardized.

developing nations indicate that none of the dependency variables has important or significant effects and that the standardized coefficients for GNP and percent youth remain strong.

Our next step is to consider the effects of various facets of social welfare spending, government activity, and political structure (Table 5.4) for all nations. Consider the social welfare variables – years of SIPE, social insurance expenditures over GNP, and social insurance expenditures in U.S. dollars per capita – added to the developmental variables in the first three equations. None of the variables has a strong effect. The largest negative effect comes from SIPE, an effect that is only half that of GNP or percent youth. Actual expenditures have virtually no effect on inequality. High government revenues are closely related to expenditures, and reflect the ability of governments to redistribute income, but have a positive effect. Percent direct taxes, which also reflects the extractive power of the state, likewise has a positive effect, as does socialist control of government (from Jackman, 1975). Likewise, neither political democracy nor political participation in elections has large effects on inequality, although they are negative in sign.

Finally, in Table 5.4 we include the natural log of a measure of years of democratic experience constructed by Muller (1988:55) for 40 nations. This variable shows an insignificant and weak negative effect on the inequality ratio, but it also reduces the effect of GNP. Although Muller (1988) concludes from similar results that the influence of democratic experience occurs indirectly through the election of governments that over time redistribute income to the masses, he presents no evidence on this crucial intervening process. Our results have revealed no such redistributive impact of the welfare programs, suggesting that the effect of years of democratic experience in Table 5.4 reflects something other than the election of redistributive governments. Bollen and Jackman (1988) argue that the measure of years of experience confounds stability with level of democracy, making it difficult to separate the influence on lower inequality of a stable economic environment from political democracy. Consistent with this interpretation, and indicative of a collinearity problem, is a multiple correlation coefficient of 0.737 between logged years of democratic experience and the logged GNP quadratic terms (using the data in Table 5.4). Additionally, Bollen and Jackman note that dichotomizing democracy as a characteristic either present in or absent from a nation introduces error into the measure. Democracy is a matter of degree, and selection of discrete dates before which nations are undemocratic and after which they are democratic creates validity problems. Given these problems and the weak effects in Table 5.4, we cannot conclude that the existence of democratic procedures alone reduces income inequality.

As a check on the robustness of the results obtained thus far, we estimated a

Table 5.4. *Coefficients (unstandardized above standardized) for OLS estimates of development and social welfare variables on income share ratio, all nations*[a]

Independent variables	Dependent variable: income share ratio							
	(1)	(2)	(3)	(4)	(5)	(6)	(7)	(8)
ln GNP/pop.	6.47**	6.53*	7.34*	6.09**	5.73**	7.10**	5.97	21.95
(ln GNP/pop.)²	−0.433***	−0.460*	−0.533*	−0.428**	−0.403*	−0.516**	−0.426	−0.199
Combined[b]	0.554***	0.355***	0.351**	0.408***	0.383***	0.333***	0.267*	0.231
% youth	0.142**	0.136*	0.160**	0.175***	0.171***	0.129**	0.130*	0.149**
	0.608	−0.242	0.719	0.748	0.731	0.602	0.611	0.648
HH data = 1	−0.676	−1.13*	−1.15*	−0.766	−0.734	−0.011	−0.456	−0.193
	−0.153	0.608	−0.249	−0.173	−0.166	−0.002	−0.088	−0.038
SIPE	−0.013							
	−0.261							
Soc. insur./GNP		−0.051						
		−0.087						
Soc. insur./pop.			0.004					
			0.168					
Gov. revs./GNP				0.034				
				0.150				
% direct taxes					0.017			
					0.139			
Left rule (Jackman)						0.020		
						0.232		
Democracy							−0.001	
							−0.083	
% voting							−0.015	
							−0.117	

	ln years dem. exp.
							−0.166
							−0.148
Intercept	−22.8	−22.2	−25.4	−23.4	−21.9	−24.8	−19.3	−11.4
R^2	0.493	0.553	0.558	0.475	0.472	0.570	0.525	0.455
df	54	39	38	56	56	26	26	38
n	60	45	44	62	62	33	33	43

$**p < .01; *p < .05.$

[a] Except where noted, standardized coefficients are below unstandardized coefficients.

[b] Standardized coefficients for quadratic terms combined (see text for calculation); other coefficients for GNP are unstandardized.

number of equations with different dependent variables, including the Gini coefficient and separate quintile shares. For the most part, the results change little: Developmental variables show strong effects, and position in the world system remains unimportant. SIPE increases the share of income for persons between the 20th and 80th percentiles by a standardized coefficient of 0.178. Although the coefficient is neither large nor significant, it suggests the benefits of social insurance spending for middle-income groups. Otherwise, we find little influence of any of the other spending variables for the income share of the high, middle, and low quintiles.

In summary, we find little effect of nondevelopmental variables on income inequality. Some variables, such as social welfare expenditures and voter participation, are available for only a subset of nations, generally higher-income, more democratic nations. Yet, analysis of these nations does not lead to artificially high effects of the variables. In fact, the smaller sample reduces the effects of GNP and percent youth, yet the expenditure and political variables still have tiny effects. Moreover, influence diagnostics (Belsey, Kuh, and Welsch, 1980; Bollen and Jackman, 1985b) show that when the most influential and outlying cases are eliminated, the results do not change. For instance, when the three most influential cases (Uruguay, Italy, and Pakistan) are deleted from equation 3 in Table 5.2, none of the standardized coefficients changes by more than 0.03. Similar stability is shown in other equations. With or without influential cases or outliers, then, the effects of development remain strong and the effects of other variables weak.[8]

Results: high-income nations

The weak effects of state and welfare variables found for the total sample (dominated numerically by developing nations) may be stronger when analysis is limited to the advanced industrial democracies. Because welfare programs are fully institutionalized and political or state structures are more easily measured, these variables can be more fairly tested. In fact, because a cross-sectional sample of high-income nations truncates the range and potential influence of the developmental variables, results for these nations favor the nondevelopmental variables. The choice of what to include among the high-income industrial nations, however, is problematic. Two strategies, both used by scholars in other studies, are possible. One selects a relatively broad sample of nations that includes some advanced developing nations, such as Argentina, Venezuela, and Trinidad-Tobago (Hewitt, 1977; Stack, 1978; Jackman, 1980). The other strategy defines the cutoff point higher and includes only advanced industrial nations, primarily Western European nations (Dryzek, 1978; Tufte, 1978; Stephens, 1979; De-

Viney and Parker, 1984). The latter approach selects a more homogeneous set of nations but greatly truncates development. Our strategy in previous chapters (where longitudinal data were available) has been to concentrate on this more homogeneous group, but here we also examine a wider set of nations. Regardless of the nations selected as having high income, the sample size will be small. The lack of time-series data combined with the select groups of nations limits the potential for multivariate analyses. More than in previous analyses, the results here must be considered exploratory, tentative, and subject to selection bias.

First, consider the results for the 16 advanced industrial democracies for which income data are available.[9] The first column of bivariate correlations in Table 5.5 shows that for these nations neither GNP nor percent youth has major effects on inequality (although both are in the predicted direction). Column 1 also presents the bivariate correlations of a number of government spending, power, and leftist control variables. None of the spending variables has large effects, but SIPE and measures of leftist government control strongly reduce inequality. Column 2 presents the standardized coefficients of these same variables controlling for GNP. This changes little the results found by the bivariate correlations, since GNP has such a weak relationship to income inequality.

A problem inherent in the study of a cross section of a small set of high-income nations is shown in these results: Variation in the developmental and inequality variables is seriously truncated. The problem is particularly acute for GNP, which is logged to compress values at the tail end of the international income distribution. To illustrate, the standard deviation of logged GNP is four times as large for the total sample as for the high-income nations, and the standard deviation among the high-income nations is only 1/25th the size of the mean. A similar reduction of variation occurs for the income inequality ratio. Partly for statistical reasons, then, GNP cannot have much of a relationship with inequality among the high-income nations. Given that the high-income sample selects nations for which the decline in inequality levels off, only a modest relationship might be predicted. With truncated variation in addition, GNP, not surprisingly, fails to affect inequality.[10]

Column 3 repeats these analyses, adding the three additional nations used by Hewitt, Jackman, and Stack (i.e., Argentina, Venezuela, and Trinidad-Tobago) and adding to the variation in GNP.[11] This changes the results drastically. GNP and percent youth now have strong relationships with income inequality. The correlation of the social welfare variables increases, and leftist government variables decline in importance (even reverse in one case). When GNP and percent youth are controlled (column 4), the net effects of nearly all other variables are small, with the exception of SIPE. Apparently, the results depend on the choice of the sample and the variability of the industrialism variables. Our analysis of

Table 5.5. *Coefficients (unstandardized and standardized) for OLS estimates of development, social welfare, and political variables on income share ratio, high-income nations*

Independent variables	Dependent variable: income share ratio					
	N = 16		N = 19		N = 10	
	r	Beta[a]	r	Beta[b]	r	r[c]
ln GNP/pop.	−0.162		−0.448		−0.142	0.013
% youth	0.106		0.725		0.230	0.156
SIPE	−0.485*	−0.522*	−0.731**	−0.366	−0.411	−0.087
Soc. welfare/GNP	−0.111	−0.128	−0.448	0.027	0.018	0.050
Soc. welfare/pop.	−0.117	−0.051	−0.509	0.076	0.035	0.096
Gov. revs./GNP	−0.031	−0.011	−0.308	0.208	−0.153	−0.118
% voting	−0.167	−0.326	−0.020	−0.052	−0.655	−0.715
Left rule (Stephens)	−0.297	−0.278	na	na	−0.557	−0.558
Left rule (Hewitt)	−0.573*	−0.585*	−0.303	−0.035	−0.763	−0.469
Left rule (Jackman)	−0.537*	−0.552*	0.357	0.259	−0.721	−0.584

$**p < .01$; $*p < .05$.
[a] Net of GNP logged.
[b] Net of GNP logged and % youth.
[c] Household standardized, posttax income share ratio.

these 19 nations is by no means the best sample; it was chosen to be consistent with previous studies. Yet, it does show the continued importance of development variables even among higher-income nations.

What can we say about the results for high-income nations? Here leftist governments, particularly those with long experience of social welfare programs, have lower inequality. However, the mechanism by which this occurs is unclear. None of the social welfare spending variables or government revenues significantly lower inequality. The typical argument is that leftist governments raise welfare spending, which redistributes income. We found in Chapter 3 that leftist governments do not increase welfare spending. This chapter shows that welfare spending does not redistribute income. Probably some other processes are operating that lead to the relationship between leftist government rule and low income inequality. Perhaps it is the power of strong, centralized unions in nations with socialist governments to extract higher wages and lower interindustry wage differentials rather than government spending that lowers income inequality (the correlation between percent union and income inequality is -0.55). In other words, wages rather than transfers contribute most to equality (Rainwater, Rein, and Schwartz, 1986). In any case, there appear to be some intervening or causally antecedent variables, other than social welfare spending, that are responsible for the relationship of leftist governments to income inequality.[12]

Even among these high-income nations, however, there may be measurement problems serious enough to cause us to question these analyses. The income figures used to calculate inequality are, in many cases, not comparable. Some data exclude self-employed persons, one-person households, nontaxable income, social security benefits, or rural residents (Sawyer, 1976). All the analyses we have done, and all those done by others, are subject to considerable error. In order to minimize such error, Sawyer (1976) selected 10 nations that have data based on complete samples and income figures (or that can be appropriately adjusted). To allow further for valid comparisons, he standardized for differences in household size across nations. Finally, he calculated posttax income shares among these 10 nations, thereby controlling for the progressivity of the tax system. As a check on previous results, we need to consider the pattern of income inequality for this more valid measure.

With only 10 cases, we avoid multivariate analysis. Column 5 shows the bivariate correlations of each variable with the posttax income share ratio standardized by household size. The results are generally similar to those we have already found: Leftist government rule is associated with low income inequality, whereas social welfare spending and developmental variables are not. To determine the influence of the sample, we also calculated correlations for the same 10 nations using the pretax, unstandardized measure of income inequality used in the other columns of Table 5.5. The difference in effects between these two columns is due to the different dependent variable rather than to the new sample of nations. The results show that the effects of SIPE, development, and leftist government rule are larger for the posttax measure than for the pretax measure.[13] These differences indicate that SIPE, development, and leftist government rule are associated with more progressive tax systems and lower inequality.

Although SIPE does not measure direct spending for welfare, it is closely related, net of development, to inequality in these equations. Perhaps these effects are evidence in favor of the benefits of the welfare state. Yet, we also find that SIPE generally has weak effects when controlling for leftist government rule (the correlations between SIPE and leftist government rule are 0.745, 0.538, and 0.574 for the 16-nation, 19-nation, and 10-nation samples, respectively). For the 16-nation sample, the net effects of SIPE decline by half and are no longer significant; for the 10-nation sample, the effects of SIPE become positive. It is only for the 19-nation sample that the effects of SIPE remain when leftist government rule is controlled for. Combined with the weak effects of welfare spending in all models, this does not provide reliable and consistent evidence for the benefits of the welfare state in reducing income inequality. Leftist governments and their association with wage equality are more important.

At the risk of overanalyzing, we checked finally for the influence of state variables (results not presented). Of the six variables examined – percent of revenues from direct taxes, percent central government revenues, defense spending over GNP, corporatism, federalism (equals 1), and coalition government (equals 1) – only one had a correlation over 0.15. Percent central government revenues has a small relationship of −0.23, but this disappears with controls for SIPE or leftist government rule. Tests of interaction of state variables with welfare spending, although entailing further statistical risks with the small degrees of freedom and lack of variation, offer evidence that corporatism facilitates the negative impact of welfare spending. Yet, given the statistical problems, we can only offer this as a suggestion for further research.

Conclusions

Theories of the welfare state differ in their views of the redistributive potential of welfare spending; in the importance of economic, demographic, and trade relationships to inequality; and in the congruence between the effects of welfare spending and structural forces. Autonomy of political forces, seen as crucial by several theories, shows not necessarily in the beneficial effects of welfare spending on inequality, but rather in the effects of welfare spending that counteract or fail to reinforce the influence of economic development or dependency.

Across a diverse group of nations reflecting all regions, levels of development, and positions in the world system, the results show the strong curvilinear effects of national product and the strong linear effects of age structure. At the lowest levels, increases in national product raise income inequality, but the effect soon reverses such that further increases in national product reduce inequality. Initial increases in wealth can be controlled by the elite, but further increases disproportionately benefit the increasingly powerful middle classes and the poor. Controlling for economic product, a young age structure also contributes to high inequality. Otherwise, economic dependency, social welfare spending, political structures, and state strength all have little or no effect on income inequality – at least for a sample of nations showing the full range of development.

Analysis of high-income nations shows different results. Among the most advanced industrial democracies, leftist government control emerges as a strong determinant of inequality while social welfare spending and development are of little importance. The weak effects of development are due to truncation of the sample such that variation in development is effectively removed. Broadening the sample to include just a few of the higher-income developing nations substantially raises the effects of development. Social welfare spending, however, has weak effects in all samples.

Measurement problems inherent in the study of income inequality require considerable care in analysis and interpretation. Reliance on reported household income, with all the variations in reporting and measurement, present the most daunting problems. We also faced these problems in considering high-income nations where sample sizes and variation in the variables are small and where the results change substantially with different subsets of nations. Otherwise, our results are robust with respect to measures of the dependent and independent variables, samples, and influential or outlying cases, and are consistent with a variety of other studies.

In matching the empirical findings and the theoretical predictions, the interest group politics theory receives strong but not totally consistent support. The weak effects of dependency contradict the predictions of the class theories. The weak effects of welfare spending are inconsistent with the industrialism and social democratic theories. If welfare spending is designed to meet the needs of groups most harmed by industrial change (as in industrialism theory), or to redistribute income in favor of the constituents of labor-based social democratic parties (as in the social democratic theory), it should have a stronger egalitarian impact. The interest group politics theory, in contrast, argues that welfare spending benefits the politically powerful as much as the economic needy, and that economic forces rather than political ones reduce inequality.

These results imply a disjuncture between the economic and political realms in many nations and, in some sense, lead to a rejection of economic reduction-ism. When development has strong effects in reducing inequality, welfare spend-ing has weak effects, and political institutions need not act in concert with eco-nomic forces. Whether autonomy shows in this manner or shows when welfare spending reduces inequality and economic forces do not, it still reflects the in-dependence of the two realms (Bell, 1976). Political institutions potentially have the autonomy to maintain, reduce, or increase inequality, but the structure of political power tends to maintain current structures of inequality.

The findings do, however, show effects of leftist governments and SIPE in high-income nations. This result is in part a methodological artifact, since it holds only for a set of nations in which development varies little. Moreover, the causal mechanism relating leftist governments to inequality is unclear. Social democratic theorists argue that leftist governments increase welfare spending, which in turn reduces inequality. Yet, the previous chapter showed that leftist governments do not increase welfare spending, and this chapter shows that wel-fare spending does not reduce inequality. Something other than social welfare spending must be responsible for the relationship. Perhaps the strong, centralized power of labor in some nations leads to both leftist governments and low inequal-ity through higher wage settlements (Stephens, 1979). In their study of family income of adults (aged 25–54) in Sweden, the United Kingdom, and the United States, Rainwater et al. (1986) likewise emphasize the importance of wage in-equality. They find that inequality in family income is due primarily to inequality in the husband's earnings. Taxes and transfers, in contrast, contribute little to intercountry differences in income inequality among the middle-aged.[14] The au-thors recommend that scholars focus more on the political and institutional forces that generate wage inequality and concentrate less on taxes and transfers (Rain-water et al., 1986:233).

Such conclusions concerning the contribution of social welfare spending to income inequality are controversial. Some claim, on the basis of trend studies in the United States, that the welfare state reduces inequality (Danziger and Wein-berg, 1986), whereas others claim that it increases inequality (Murray, 1984). We favor arguments that question any link between government policy and in-equality (O'Hare, 1985; Berger, 1986; Ellwood and Summers, 1986). William-son and Lindert's (1980) study of inequality demonstrates the importance over the last two decades in the United States of technological change, geographical productivity imbalances, and wage differentials by skill levels rather than gov-ernment programs (see also Williamson, 1985, and Lindert, 1986, on Britain). In another detailed study of income distribution in the United States from 1950 to 1970, Reynolds and Smolensky (1977:93) also fail to find strong evidence of the effects of government spending: "It appears to be a common view that, even in a predominantly market economy, the distribution of income, however defined, is subject to government manipulation. We are not convinced the conventional wisdom is correct.''

Given these results, we might ask: Why is it that social welfare and government spending do not affect inequality? How is it possible that the billions of dollars spent by nations to redistribute income can fail to do so? It may appear obvious that transfers go to the poor. The pretransfer and posttransfer income of the poor and the overall level of income inequality differ substantially in the United States and European countries, suggesting that welfare spending is indeed redistributive and that transfers benefit the poor (Hicks and Swank, 1985).

The first answer to the question of how the welfare state can fail to redistribute income is that the existence of transfer income to the poor is not sufficient to show the redistributive impact of such transfers. As Plotnick (1984) notes, pretransfer income is not independent of posttransfer income; one cannot assume that subtracting out transfers leaves the same income that the poor would have were there in real life no transfers. In the absence of the welfare state, the labor supply, living arrangements, and private transfers would be higher than they are with transfer income. If retirement pensions, for instance, did not exist, many older persons would not be retired and would not be dependent on transfer income. In other words, the transfer income, to some degree, replaces other sources of income and affects pretransfer as well as posttransfer income. The existence of transfer income does not, therefore, prove that it has a redistributive impact (Danziger et al., 1981; Plotnick, 1984).

Our strategy to deal with this problem is to compare the income inequality in nations where transfers are high and where transfers are low. This avoids unwarranted and artificial inferences about what the income would be in a nation were transfers eliminated. Instead, the approach can compare (at the risk of confounding the influence of other variables, of course) actual inequality. Our results, averaged over many nations and controlling for relevant variables, show that income inequality is no lower in high-spending nations than in low-spending nations. Our answer to the preceding question, then, is that welfare spending replaces other means of support of the poor, but without changing the actual income share of the poor. Transfer may be easier, less demeaning, and more reliable than other sources of income, but not, according to our results, more egalitarian.

A second answer to the question of how the welfare state can fail to reduce inequality is that the benefits go to those other than the poor. In developing nations, insurance programs clearly favor the urban elite and rely on regressive taxes (Midgley, 1984). In high-income democracies, middle-income strata may benefit most from the welfare programs (Jackman, 1980). Consider the beneficiaries of the biggest programs – pensions, sickness, occupational injury, and short-term unemployment. For pensions, few nations require a means-based qualification for pensions. In fact, as partial insurance programs, public pensions most often provide greater benefits to high-income workers, who contribute the most. Even if the rate of return to contributions is greater for the poor, absolute benefits are higher for middle-class recipients, who are also more likely to have other sources of retirement income (Boskin, 1986). Similarly, persons who face occupational injury, sickness, and unemployment are drawn from the large middle classes. Only the relatively small payments for public assistance go primarily to the poorest groups. Instead of redistributing income across classes, the welfare state smooths out life-cycle fluctuations in income (Page, 1983; Hedstrom and Ringen, 1987). Transfers may in fact reinforce existing inequalities because they are tied to market forces (DeViney, 1987). Welfare spending may level differences over the life cycle with generous means-tested or universal flat-rate benefits, but this form of program is rare and contributory or meager flat-rate schemes are common (Myles, 1984). Transfers may need to be better directed at the most needy in order to reduce inequality more effectively (Neugarten, 1982).

That benefits go to the middle classes, and do little to change the shape of income distribution in a nation, is not surprising given the political nature of the welfare state. Because welfare spending reflects, at least in part, the political power of groups in society, its programs should benefit the most powerful groups (Devine and Canak, 1986). This includes not just business but also organized labor, the aged, and other middle-income groups. Political processes, then, may be seen as a means by which groups maintain their advantage (Parkin, 1971). The poorest groups, in contrast, have little if any political power; as Alford and Friedland (1975) argue, the political system effectively disperses the interests of the poor and prevents their organization for political purposes. In fact, the most successful welfare programs attract and maintain widespread public support and do not strongly target benefits to the poor (Rainwater et al., 1986:238). Thus, the weak effects of political variables on welfare spending make sense. It is in the economic rather than the political realm that opportunities for redistribution are greatest (Olson, 1982).

We have consistently emphasized the difficulties in measuring income inequality and the consequent problems for multivariate analysis, especially for the high-income nations. To end this chapter, we can note several other limitations to our analysis, results, and conclusions. For one, the welfare state may have benefits for other components of equality that we have been unable to measure. We have not studied absolute poverty, for instance. Welfare spending may move persons and families above a designated poverty line even if it does not shift substantial income shares across quintiles. Welfare spending may ease the drop in income experienced by persons during old age even if the relative position of persons remains the same across life-cycle stages. Money is clearly being transferred, and many have come to depend greatly on such transfers over the last several decades. In reference to the goal of major redistribution, the welfare state may have had little impact, but in other ways it may have had benefits.

Another limitation is that we have been unable to adjust adequately for the influence of family change. In the United States, the growth of traditionally low-income groups such as female-headed families and unrelated individuals has raised income inequality (Treas and Walther, 1978). Within these groups, however, inequality has declined, in part because of transfer income (Treas, 1983). Our focus on overall inequality may disguise countervailing trends. Were it possible to decompose between-group and within-group inequality and examine the structural determinants of each, our results might be different.

Finally, for high-income nations, we have been unable to identify adequately just what it is that drives income inequality. The unresponsiveness of inequality in advanced industrial nations to both high public spending and economic growth suggests that other factors are involved. Productivity levels and skill-based wage differentials, family change, the political power of interest groups, and the form of capital ownership may all be involved in the stability of income distributions (Levy, 1987) and need to be investigated. Yet, to do so, new and different data are needed, and scholars will need to look for means other than those used here to move research forward.

Notes

1. Although less often advocated as a component of public policy, changes in the ownership of the means of production may be seen as a fourth strategy of redistribution. Programs for worker control of investment and the workplace provide an alternative to the more commonly debated strategies of economic growth and welfare spending.
2. Using path analysis terminology, the theories also vary in the specified direct and indirect effects. According to industrialism theory, welfare spending mediates the effects of development on inequality, whereas for the interest group theory, spending is unrelated to inequality, controlling for economic development. The working-class strength theory predicts that welfare spending mediates the effect of economic dependency, whereas the monopoly capitalism theory argues that welfare spending is unrelated to inequality.
3. For some nations, income data are available only for the late 1950s and early 1960s. Rather than discarding this information and these nations, we include them in the analysis, assuming that inequality has changed little over 10 years and that measures circa 1960 can serve as proxies for the missing 1970 figures. As it turns out, the results change little, if at all, when the analysis is performed only on nations with recent data (see Bollen and Jackman, 1985a, who make the same point). We therefore concentrate on the full set of available information in the analyses.
4. It would be just as effective to use percent aged here as to use percent youth. They are related closely enough to each other than both do not have independent effects. The choice of which

one to use is arbitrary. Percent youth has slightly higher effects than percent aged and is used by Bollen and Jackman (1985a). Moreover, percent youth better measures the population growth through which age structure contributes to income inequality. It would also be possible to replace real GNP with the real GDP figures of Summers and Heston (1984). For this cross section of nations at one time point, however, the two measures are nearly identical ($r = 0.96$). We rely on the GNP figures, where possible, and do so in this chapter.

5. In this case, let $X = 9.31 \times (\ln \text{CGNP}) - .727 \times (\ln \text{CGNP}^2)$. For other equations, the weights come from the appropriate unstandardized coefficients. Using the new X in the equations does not change the coefficients for the other variables or the variance explained. It merely translates a nonlinear relationship into a single variable that reflects the influence of two quadratic terms.

6. Equation 3 in Table 5.2 corresponds to the OLS equation in Table 4 of Bollen and Jackman (1985a). Given that we have the same measure of income inequality and the same independent variables, the size and significance of our coefficients are close to theirs. However, the coefficients are not identical. This is because we use a different source of data on income share and, as a result, a slightly different sample. Our figures on income share come from Bornschier and Heintz (1979), whereas Bollen and Jackman's data come from unpublished figures from the World Bank. Further, the World Bank includes data for some nations not listed in Bornschier and Heintz, thus leading to slightly different samples. Nonetheless, we do not view this as a problem and have not exerted a special effort to use exactly the same figures as Bollen and Jackman. We are encouraged that the same basic findings emerge even with slightly different data and samples. The models that they develop, and that we use here, are robust and insensitive to minor changes in the data.

7. Bornschier and Chase-Dunn model this effect by including an interaction term for core nations that adjusts for the different meaning of dependency in these nations. For ease of presentation and interpretation, we merely analyze the noncore nations separately. This avoids cumbersome multiplicative interaction terms and allows examination of the effects of development in lower-income nations. The list of core nations excluded corresponds to those analyzed in Chapter 3 and in the analysis to follow in this chapter. For a list of these deleted nations, see note 9 this chapter.

8. The results are also robust with respect to the year in which income inequality is measured. If only those nations with income inequality measures after 1965 are included, the results do not change. The effects of GNP logged and then squared are 6.95 and -0.501 (compared to 7.47 and -0.516 in equation 3 of Table 5.1). The effects of percent youth remain significant and large, whereas the effects of position in the world system remain insignificant and small. Bollen and Jackman (1985a) further strengthen the conclusions by estimating models for random subsets of nations and finding the estimates to be stable. They further find little change when estimating weighted least squares to correct for heteroscedasticity. All in all, the model shows remarkable stability with respect to the measures, sample, and estimation techniques used.

9. This includes the United States, Canada, Japan, New Zealand, Australia, Austria, Switzerland, West Germany, Italy, France, the United Kingdom, the Netherlands, Norway, Denmark, Sweden, and Finland. Of the advanced industrial democracies we studied in Chapter 3, only Belgium and Ireland are missing data.

10. Any analysis with only 16 cases must be suspect for other reasons as well. The results may be highly sensitive to single cases, for instance. However, reestimation of the equations in column 2 with influential and outlying cases deleted shows, in this instance, that the results do not greatly change. Deletion of Japan raises the effects of GNP and SIPE to -0.444 and -0.666; deletion of Finland raises the effects of both Stephens's and Hewitt's measures of leftist strength to -0.572 and -0.791. Although stronger, these effects do not change the direction or pattern of the relationships. They do suggest that these two nations reflect some unmeasured influence that is important for equality. With the small sample, adding multiple variables to explain such

unmeasured influence does little to make the model more acceptable. Perhaps all this indicates what we noted from the beginning: that data availability makes analysis of income inequality difficult.

11. Hewitt and Stack also included South Africa in their analyses. As noted by Jackman (1980), this is clearly inappropriate. South Africa does not meet the minimum conditions for democracy and is inappropriate for an examination of the influence of political parties on policy. Further, including South Africa in the analysis greatly distorts the results (Bollen and Jackman, 1985b). It is not included in the analyses here.

12. The egalitarian impact of the welfare state may depend as much on the form of the benefits and the criteria for their distribution as on the level. Egalitarian benefit formulas alone cannot make up for low benefits, but they may combine with high benefits to reduce inequality. Although the egalitarian distribution of benefits is difficult to measure, Myles (1984) has presented a scale that in part taps this dimension for pension programs. He measures the benefits for low-wage and high-wage workers. The higher the ratio of one to the other, the more redistributive the benefits. We rank ordered the nations on redistribution and multiplied their score by welfare spending. This combined measure of level and redistributive impact has a correlation of -0.160 with the income inequality ratio. The sign is in the correct direction, but the relationship is not strong. Myles's measure of means testing has an even weaker correlation with inequality. With these few nations and admittedly weak measures, we cannot make too much of this finding, other than to say that the relationship between the form of pension benefits and total inequality is not immediately apparent as a strong one.

13. The correlation of the income share ratio with percent voting is large in both columns and is likely due to sample bias; that is, even with the unadjusted measure of spending, percent voting has a stronger correlation by virtue of the truncated sample. Otherwise, social security expenditures and government revenues are weakly correlated with both measures of inequality.

14. Duncan et al. (1986) show that the income of the aged in the United States (in absolute dollars or as a ratio to needs) rose faster than that of children during the 1960s and 1970s. They also show, however, a drop in income among cohorts that entered old age over the same time period. That cross-sectional income increases while cohort income declines for the aged suggests that cohorts entering old age bring greater economic assets and resources with them. Duncan et al. therefore suggest that cohort replacement rather than transfer income may be responsible for the decline in poverty and the rise in income among the aged in the United States during this time period.

Appendix 5.A. *Means, standard deviations, definitions, and sources of variables*

Variables	$\bar{X}$	s	N	Definition (source)
GNP/pop.	1,265	1,605	72	Gross national product, U.S. dollars per capita (Bornschier and Heintz, 1979).
% youth	39.2	8.7	69	Percentage of the population aged 0–14 (World Bank, 1983).
Semiperiphery, periphery	.254 .493	.438 .504	67 67	Dummy variables indicating location in the world system, core nations omitted (Snyder and Kick, 1979).
Commod. concent.	42.1	21.9	72	Value of a nation's most important export commodity as a percentage of its total exports (Bornschier and Heintz, 1979).
Partner concent.	32.0	15.0	67	Value of a nation's goods exchanged with its most important trade partner as a percentage of its total foreign trade (Bornschier and Heintz, 1979).
Imp + Exp/GNP	46.0	28.8	71	Exports and imports of goods and nonfactor services as a percentage of GNP (Bornschier and Heintz, 1979).
Foreign invest.	57.6	41.3	71	Total stock of foreign direct investment as a ratio to the square root of energy consumption times population (Bornschier and Heintz, 1979).
SIPE	61.8	40.0	68	Years experience since 1934 with five social insurance programs (U.S. Social Security Administration, 1981).
Soc. insur./GNP	2.99	3.57	47	Expenditures in national currency for social insurance and family allowance programs as a percentage of GNP (International Labour Office, 1985).
Soc. insur./pop.	58.9	84.6	46	Expenditures in constant U.S. dollars for social insurance and family allowance programs per capita (International Labour Office, 1985).

				Description
Gov. revs./GNP	19.7	8.5	72	General government revenues as a percentage of GNP (Bornschier and Heintz, 1979).
Democracy	90.3	143.7	69	Political democracy index (Bollen, 1980).
% voting	68.0	16.7	35	Percentage of population 20 years and older that voted in a national election for the national assembly (Taylor and Jodice, 1983).
Left rule (Jackman)	23.8	24.0	43	Proportion of seats in the national (lower) legislature held by parties of the noncommunist left (Jackman, 1975).
Left rule (Hewitt)	27.9	16.8	20	Average post–World War II percentage of the Socialist Party in the legislature (Hewitt, 1977).
Left rule (Stephens)	7.3	7.4	16	Years rule of social democratic parties (Stephens, 1979).
Income share ratio (Sawyer)	4.3	2.2	68	Ratio of income share of the richest 20% to the poorest 40% (calculated from Bornschier and Heintz, 1979, Sawyer, 1976).
	2.3	0.6	10	

6. Infant mortality, equality, and social welfare spending

The concern of sociologists with income inequality perhaps has overshadowed an equally important component of equality: the provision of basic physical needs of the population and its poor. As much for its own sake, the value of an egalitarian income distribution may come from the ability it gives the poor to improve their physical well-being and quality of life. The way in which income distribution translates into the day-to-day life of a population reflects the dispersion of social rewards and deserves study in its own right.

Although there are many ways to study physical needs, well-being, or the quality of life (Morris, 1979; Estes, 1984), we concentrate on one commonly used indicator – the infant mortality rate.[1] The survival of infants depends strongly on the physical environment in which a child comes to term and is born. It closely reflects nutrition, sanitation, medical care, financial resources, education of the parents, and other aspects of physical well-being. Further, infant mortality is highly responsive to socioeconomic conditions and is more highly concentrated among the poor (Anderson, 1973; Gortmaker, 1979). Indeed, in an important sense, the decline of infant mortality reflects the diffusion of an acceptable standard of living from the elite to the masses and the poor. Because a biological limit appears to exist on how low infant mortality can go, the benefits of a declining rate must eventually extend to the poor. Unlike income, improvements in infant mortality cannot be monopolized by the rich; they must diffuse from advantaged groups to disadvantaged groups.

The infant mortality rate varies in meaningful and theoretically important ways, not only across levels of development but within groups of developed and developing nations.[2] Among high-income capitalist democracies, for instance, the United States ranks fifteenth in infant mortality despite having a per capita income among the highest in the world. Other historically less wealthy nations, such as Finland and Japan, have experienced steady improvements in their rank over the last several decades, but the rank of the United States has declined steadily. Perhaps equally surprising are the rankings of the Eastern European socialist nations. Infant mortality in these nations falls to the levels of some developing nations and lags well behind Western European capitalist nations. It

138

appears that the infant mortality rate of a nation – whatever its economic system or wealth – responds as much to the purpose to which income is put as to the level. In some nations, improvements in health may occur due to inexpensive public health programs, whereas in others, huge increases in income may fail to bring equivalent improvements. The determinants of infant mortality may be less obvious than expected and may include a number of factors unrelated to development and income.

Finally, there are methodological as well as theoretical advantages to the study of infant mortality. More than most indicators of equality, infant mortality can be compared directly and accurately across a variety of nations and economic systems. Socialist nations, excluded from the previous chapters because they lack comparable data on welfare spending and inequality, can be included in the study of infant mortality. Further, time series are often available, along with the cross-sectional data, at least for high-income nations, and therefore allow the kind of multivariate analysis that was lacking in the last chapter.

Despite the different nature of the dependent variable studied in this chapter, the issues addressed are much the same as those of the previous chapter. First, what effect does social welfare spending have on infant mortality? The last chapter showed that welfare spending does little to redistribute income, but perhaps at a minimum, it may serve to direct health care and nutrition resources to the poor and reduce infant mortality. Second, what is the role of class structure on equality involving the physical quality of life? This question can be examined in some new and different ways in this chapter. One way is to consider directly the influence on infant mortality of the income distribution. Along with dependency and other class variables, income inequality may reflect class power in a way that affects the quality of life of the less powerful classes. Another way to examine class structure is through the study of capitalist and socialist nations. Presumably, the power of labor is stronger, the power of capital weaker, and the role of the state in redistributing income greater in socialist nations than in capitalist nations.[3] In what follows, we first consider infant mortality in advanced industrial democracies; then we compare these results with those of Eastern European socialist nations. Finally, we examine infant mortality among developing nations.

Patterns of infant mortality: explanations and predictions

Background. Standard economic development and demographic transition theories offer one general explanation of the historic decline in mortality among Western nations that applies to infant mortality. Such theories suggest that the initial impetus to lower mortality comes from higher income and a better standard of living, which improve the nutrition, hygiene, and sanitary environment necessary for the health of adults, mothers, and infants (Dubos, 1959). Mortality may fluctuate with cycles of economic growth and unemployment but, more importantly, it shows a secular downward trend over the long term as income rises during industrialization. Improvements in medicine, increases in highly trained and skilled physicians, and easier access to medical care with urbanization also contribute to the survival of infants. In developed nations, the benefits of medical care followed improvements in the standard of living, but to a great extent preceded them in developing nations (Preston, 1977). As for fertility, declining parity and postponement of pregnancy to later ages may aid infant survival. Finally, high education of women encourages the development of life-styles supportive of good health and prenatal care in both developed (Fuchs, 1974) and developing nations (Caldwell, 1979; Hobcraft et al., 1984). All these changes – in economic product, unemployment, urbanization, medical care, fertility, and the status of women – although part of a broader process of modernization or development, may each contribute to declining infant mortality.

Although this explanation applies well to historical processes, scholars question its applicability to current patterns and changes. For instance, the high level of infant mortality in the United States, relative to other high-income nations, suggests failure of the developmental model among high-income nations. There may be thresholds in the relationships of economic and demographic variables with infant mortality such that above these thresholds, changes in determinants have little influence (Preston, 1975). As another example, the importation of public health programs or the redistribution of income may supersede the influence of development in currently developing nations. Sri Lanka, for instance, is often cited as an example of a poor nation with remarkably low infant mortality.

In response to these anomalies, and the weaknesses in standard developmental explanations they reflect, several alternative explanations have emerged. First, the extent of income inequality rather than income level may be crucial (Rodgers, 1979; Flegg, 1982; Weatherby et al., 1983). High national income need not mean that sufficient financial resources reach all groups in a society. Given the same mean income, those nations where income is more equally distributed will tend to have lower infant mortality.[4] Since a persistent and increasing socioeconomic status differential in infant mortality exists in developed nations (Stockwell et al., 1978; Pamuk, 1985), small reductions in the degree of inequality may produce thousands of persons better able to afford necessary prenatal and medical care. High U.S. infant mortality compared to that in Scandinavian countries – several of which have had lower income per capita but less income inequality – suggests that income inequality may be a relevant factor.

Second, researchers may need to consider the population heterogeneity of nations. Ethnic, linguistic, and social diversity creates multiple life-styles, health-related attitudes, and social backgrounds that may make it difficult to distribute high-quality health care to all parts of the population. Further, social distance and discrimination in heterogeneous nations may create social and geographic maldistribution of resources and raise infant mortality. Compared to the small, homogeneous Scandinavian nations, the diversity of larger nations such as the United States, Canada, and Great Britain may contribute to their high infant mortality.

These two factors – income inequality and ethnic diversity – likely reflect the influence of racial discrimination on infant mortality. Ethnic and linguistic diversity reflects the size of minority groups facing discrimination, and income inequality reflects the degree to which groups are economically disadvantaged. The situation of the United States, with high infant mortality, diversity, and income inequality, no doubt stems partly from the economic position of minorities. Perhaps income inequality and heterogeneity interact, such that nations with both high income inequality and large minority populations have high infant mortality.

Finally, government financial support for the standard of living in general and medical care in particular may come to replace economic development as the driving force behind lower infant mortality. Since the costs of medical care may exceed the resources of many persons even in high-income nations, generous public medical and social welfare programs may be necessary to increase access to health care and lower infant mortality. Again, the United States provides less public welfare support and fewer public medical benefits to the population than do European nations, many of which have socialized medicine or national health insurance (Sidel and Sidel, 1983). Similar processes of redistribution in developing nations may likewise speed the decline in infant mortality.

Theoretical predictions. The specific explanations of infant mortality relate to our general theories of the welfare state. None of the theories or their advocates focus explicitly on infant mortality. Yet, with a few inferences and extensions, the predictions made by the theories about income inequality can be applied to infant mortality. For instance, the industrialism theory focuses directly on development and the benefits it brings to society, including better health. The theory also claims that industrial growth brings a better quality of life to the poor partly through the growth of social welfare spending. Such programs are necessary to deal with pockets of the poor who are superfluous to the industrial process. Thus, welfare spending is egalitarian, directed to those most in need. Further, assuming that the underlying industrial processes are the same across nations, whatever the form of political rule, infant mortality may converge across socialist and capitalist nations. In both types of nations, industrial growth and the welfare programs that go with it contribute to lower infant mortality.

The interest group theory emphasizes economic and demographic change as the source of structural pressures toward social equality and shares the industrialism view of the importance of economic development for lower infant mortality. However, the interest group theory views skeptically the value of welfare spending and redistributive government activity as a means to lower inequality. The key difference between the theories centers on their view of the extent to which benefits go to the relatively powerless poorer groups that have the highest infant mortality rates. By claiming that benefits go primarily to more powerful middle-class groups, with relatively low infant mortality rates but greater political influence, the interest group theory predicts that welfare spending does little to reduce infant mortality. Instead, economic growth and related changes in medical care and fertility provide the major source of lower mortality to the poor.

The arguments of the interest group politics theory may also be extended to socialist nations, although in a modified form, since socialist nations lack the democratic procedures given prominent attention by the theory. Although Western-style interest group activity does not occur in socialist nations, political processes dominate the market in command economies (Parkin, 1971). Assuming that political intervention of the state administrative bureaucracy does not necessarily favor the most needy suggests that political processes contribute less than market-based, economic processes to greater equality. Rather than predicting the convergence across systems that industrialism theory does, the interest group theory claims that economic change unhampered by socialist bureaucracy and government intervention most effectively lowers infant mortality, and predicts higher infant mortality rates in socialist nations than in capitalist nations (Eberstadt, 1981; Berger, 1986).

Class theories all focus on the structure of power in society and only incidentally on the outcomes of this structure for infant mortality. But, again, we can make some inferences about the effects of power structure on the quality of life of the poor. The assumption we make is that class power is reflected in the structure of income inequality in a society. Even with high mean income, the skewed distribution of income limits the resources for health care and nutrition available to subordinate groups and classes and maintains high levels of infant mortality. The implication again is that development alone is not sufficient to lower infant mortality unless there is a major redistribution across classes of the wealth that development creates. Although inequality is partly – even primarily – a function of development (see Chapter 5), that component of distribution independent of the level of income should prove to be crucial in determining infant mortality. This argument can be further extended to consider the effects of ethnic heterogeneity combined with inequality. As we have suggested, their combined influence may reflect racial or ethnic discrimination as a factor limiting the decline in infant mortality in a nation such as the United States. Overall, then, the class arguments predict clear divergence of infant mortality from developmental patterns.

A logical extension of the class argument that infant mortality reflects class inequalities in capitalist nations suggests that infant mortality should be lower in socialist nations than in capitalist nations. Assuming that socialist nations restrict the power of capital, redistribute wealth, and provide equal access to medical resources, they should have lower infant mortality (controlling for developmental and demographic differences) than capitalist nations. Comparing richer Western democracies with later-developing, more agricultural Eastern socialist nations shows the latter to have substantially higher rates, no doubt due to their lower national product. Yet, statistically equalizing resources – such as national product, urbanization, fertility, education, and medical care – may show the Eastern European nations to be doing better than the Western nations in lowering infant mortality, or better than expected on the basis of their limited resources.

Both the social democratic and monopoly capitalism theories agree that the relative power of labor to monopoly capital – as reflected in lower income inequality and socialist government – reduce infant mortality. They differ, however, on the mechanism involved. The social democratic theory treats welfare spending as the crucial policy mechanism by which labor-dominated governments improve the quality of life of the poor. The size and strength of unions or of labor-based parties do not influence mortality directly, but do so through policies favoring government programs for the poor or through redistribution of income and lower income inequality. The monopoly capitalism theory, in contrast, sees welfare spending as less beneficial for the poor, even as ineffectual without structural changes in the system of wage labor. As before, the efficacy of the welfare state for infant mortality and the well-being of the poor distinguishes between the class theories.

To summarize, what we have done is to apply to infant mortality the predictions concerning income inequality presented in the last chapter (see Table 5.2). The standard demographic transition arguments are consistent with the industrialism and interest group politics theories. They predict that modernization and economic development variables explain variation in infant mortality among all nations – nations with high income, low income, and across capitalist and socialist nations. The main difference is their view of the efficacy of welfare spending. The class theory focuses on factors such as income inequality and socialism, as they vary independently of development. Monopoly capitalism and social democratic theories differ on the influence of social welfare spending.

Age, class, politics, and the welfare state

Table 6.1. *Infant mortality and social welfare spending, 1980*

Nation	IMR	Rank	IMR net GNP[a]	Rank	Soc. welf./ GNP	Rank
Sweden	6.9	1	7.5	3	31.4	2
Japan	7.5	2	7.4	1.5	9.3	18
Finland	7.6	3	7.4	1.5	18.3	10
Norway	8.1	4	8.7	4.5	20.5	9
Denmark	8.4	5	8.7	4.5	26.9	3
Netherlands	8.6	6	9.2	6.5	27.4	2
Switzerland	9.1	7	10.8	11	14.3	1
France	10.0	8	10.2	8	25.4	4
Canada	10.4	9	10.4	9	13.6	15
Australia	10.7	10	10.5	10	13.2	16
Belgium	11.0	11	11.6	13.5	25.1	5
Ireland	11.2	12	9.2	6.5	20.9	8
U.K.	12.0	13	11.2	12	14.3	13
W. Germany	12.6	14.5	13.6	17	23.0	6
U.S.	12.6	14.5	12.8	15.5	12.8	17
New Zealand	12.9	16	11.6	13.5	14.3	12
Austria	14.3	17.5	14.6	18	21.8	7
Italy	14.3	17.5	12.8	15.5	16.2	11

[a]Residual IMR from regression on the natural log of GNP/pop. added to the grand mean of 10.5.

Infant mortality in advanced industrial democracies

To begin the analysis, we consider infant mortality in those nations where differences in welfare spending may have the most effect – the advanced industrial Western democracies. It is among these nations that variation in infant mortality apparently diverges from levels of economic development and that alternative explanations may find support. The patterns of infant mortality across nations are shown for 1980 in Table 6.1. The figures show Sweden, Japan, Finland, and Norway as having the lowest rates. For Japan and Finland, this reflects a remarkable improvement from rankings among the lowest in the 1950s. The United States ties for fourteenth place. A slightly different pattern is shown in the next columns, where the infant mortality rate (IMR) is residualized on GNP (and added to the mean of 10.5 in 1980). If GNP were the same for all nations, Ireland and the United Kingdom would improve their position, whereas Switzerland's and West Germany's rankings would worsen.

The last two columns list and rank, for the same year, the percentage of GNP spent on social welfare. Although the ranks of some nations on infant mortality and social welfare spending match, there are some marked deviations. Japan, which has the lowest infant mortality rate, controlling for GNP, spends the least for social welfare. Nations with high spending, such as West Germany and Belgium, are among the highest on infant mortality. Although the low rank of the United States on infant mortality is consistent with the low level of spending, the nations with higher infant mortality rates – Italy and Austria – spend more on social welfare. It appears, then, that social welfare spending and infant mortality are only weakly associated.

Basic models. We can compare the effects of social welfare spending and GNP more directly, and consider the influence of other variables, with multivariate analyses. The independent variables to be used are listed and defined in Table 6.2, and their sources all described in Appendix 6.A. GNP and unemployment reflect the long-term and short-term economic situations of a nation. The total fertility rate and the percentage of births to teenagers measure the level and age of births. Urbanization, physicians, and hospital beds reflect access to medical care, and female school enrollment reflects the educational levels of mothers. Finally, the Gini coefficient, ethnic-linguistic fractionalization, and several types of welfare expenditures represent socioeconomic characteristics of the population that may affect infant mortality.[5]

In Table 6.2, we show the means and standard deviations of these variables and their correlations with several types of infant mortality.[6] The neonatal mortality rate (NNR) includes deaths from 0 to 28 days, the postneonatal rate (PNR) from 29 days to one year, and the infant mortality rate (IMR) from birth to one year. The three types of infant mortality are closely related, but they respond in some important ways to different determinants. In any case, the correlations in the table are based on all seven time points and reflect trends as well as differences between nations. The bivariate correlations for GNP are all large, as they are for urbanization, female education, and medical care variables. More modest in size are the correlations of unemployment, fertility variables, inequality, and ethnic diversity.

We also consider several different types of state expenditures. Medical, sickness, and public health spending is reported by the ILO only since 1960, but may be most directly relevant to medical care. General social welfare spending includes old-age pensions and disability, but is reported back to 1950 and includes nonmedical expenditures that may go for food, housing, and energy – perhaps more important than medical care for maintaining the health of infants. In any case, medical spending shows associations larger than those for general social welfare, but still not as large as those of GNP.

Since all these independent variables are closely related, they need to be ex-

Table 6.2. *Definition, descriptive statistics, and correlations of variables with mortality measures*

Variable	Definition	X̄	s	N	Correlations[a] IMR	NNR	PNR
GNP/pop.	Gross national product in thousands of 1970 constant U.S. dollars per head	4.20	2.28	126	-0.780	-0.783	-0.705
Unemp.	Unemployment rate	2.68	2.40	126	0.090	-0.472	-0.520
TFR	Total fertility rate	2.43	0.604	126	0.370	0.440	0.267
% teen births	Percentage of live births to females under age 20	7.1	3.8	126	-0.210	-0.137	-0.261
Fem ed.	Female enrollment in tertiary schools	12.0	10.8	126	-0.703	-0.714	-0.626
% urban	Percentage of the population residing in urban areas	65.3	12.7	126	-0.521	0.017	0.153
Phys.	Physicians per 1,000 population	1.34	0.431	126	-0.439	-0.419	-0.417
Beds	Hospital beds per 1,000 population	10.5	2.15	126	-0.400	-0.329	-0.432
Gini	Gini coefficient of income inequality	38.3	3.4	126	0.146	0.118	0.159
Ethl.	Ethnic-linguistic diversity index	0.237	0.218	126	-0.102	-0.058	-0.134
Soc. welf./GNP	Total government benefit expenditures for social welfare and social security as a percentage of gross national product	12.2	5.80	126	-0.443	-0.450	-0.395
Med. Exp./GNP	Government medical, sickness, and public health expenditures as a percentage of gross national product	4.13	2.04	96	-0.468	-0.543	-0.295
IMR	Infant mortality rate	23.2	12.4	126	1.00	0.952	0.952
NNR	Neonatal mortality rate	15.0	6.44	126		1.00	0.816
PNR	Postneonatal mortality rate	8.13	6.55	126			1.00

[a]Correlations are with the natural log of the independent variables.

amined in a multivariate context.[7] Table 6.3 shows several such equations. The first set uses general social welfare spending and covers the full time span. The last equations replace welfare spending with public medical spending. All three types of infant mortality are used to consider how the processes differ for early and late mortality.

We note, first of all, the strong effects of the developmental variables in these equations. First, both GNP and urbanization lower infant mortality. The effect of GNP is largest on the NNR, whereas the effect of percent urban is largest on the PNR. A higher standard of living may affect prenatal care, birth weight, and health behavior, whereas urban residence has more to do with access to medical care and infectious disease prevention for older infants (Khoury, Erikson, and Adams, 1984). In any case, these two developmental variables continue to reduce mortality in these nations, even if they work through different mechanisms. Additionally, controlling for these secular increases, unemployment raises both types of infant mortality. Short-term loss of income and the stress that goes with it affect both prenatal care and nutrition, as well as medical care for older infants.

Both the TFR and percent teenage births raise the NNR but have a small (or a negative) effect on the PNR. The social disadvantage and immaturity of teenagers affecting prenatal care and birth weight may lead to higher infant mortality. Even more important than age of childbearing and the number of children, however, is the education of the mother. Female tertiary enrollment has the strongest, most consistent effects on all three dependent variables. Higher education improves prenatal care and leads to the effective use of health care resources for postneonatal care. This result replicates microlevel studies of the importance of education in both developed and developing countries (Hobcraft et al., 1984; Trussell and Pebley, 1984). These results, combined with those for the economic variables, thus perform much as expected under standard explanations of infant mortality.

The effects of the medical care variables in Table 6.3 are mixed. The inverse effect of hospital beds on the PNR suggests that access to hospital care affects the survival of older infants, but no such effect appears for the NNR. The effects of physicians are more puzzling: Although not always significant, they are consistently positive. That the availability of more physicians apparently raises rather than lowers the infant mortality rate differs from theoretical expectations but replicates the positive effect found in other aggregate studies (Miller and Stokes, 1978; Grossman and Jacobowitz, 1981).

Finally, we have left three other variables for consideration: the Gini coefficient, social welfare spending, and ethnic diversity. The Gini coefficient has modest, significant effects on the NNR and little effect on the PNR (the same effects hold for share measures of inequality). Social welfare spending has sim-

Table 6.3. *Coefficients (unstandardized above standardized) for GLS estimates of models of infant mortality, advanced industrial democracies, 1950–80*

Independent variables	1950–80			1960–80		
	NNR	PNR	IMR	NNR	PNR	IMR
GNP/pop. (ln)	-5.35**	-3.80**	-9.22**	-3.14**	-2.18*	-5.36**
	-0.449	-0.313	-0.401	-0.290	-0.341	-0.332
Unemp. (ln)	0.726**	1.23**	1.96**	0.531**	0.582**	1.12**
	0.161	0.267	0.225	0.154	0.286	0.217
TFR (ln)	1.52	-4.66*	-2.92	3.22	-2.03	1.25
	0.058	-0.174	-0.058	0.166	-0.177	0.043
% teen births (ln)	2.66**	-0.061	2.62	2.35**	-0.166	2.18*
	0.269	-0.006	0.137	0.318	-0.038	0.197
Fem. ed. (ln)	-3.34**	-2.06**	-5.43**	-3.33**	-1.11*	-4.44**
	-0.516	-0.312	-0.435	-0.505	-0.285	-0.450
% Urban (ln)	-0.830**	-9.36**	-10.1*	-0.588	-3.91*	-4.42
	-0.026	-0.290	-0.166	-0.021	-0.238	-0.107
Phys. (ln)	2.43	1.20	3.93	2.63	1.06	3.79
	0.120	0.058	0.100	0.153	0.104	0.148
Beds (ln)	1.09	-6.82**	-5.76	0.873	-1.91	-1.04
	0.036	-0.222	-0.099	0.034	-0.126	-0.027
Gini (ln)	15.3**	0.662	16.3	9.31	-3.30	6.07
	0.210	0.009	0.116	0.168	-0.100	0.073
Ethl. (ln)	0.478	0.646	1.11	-0.157	0.172	0.017
	0.087	0.115	0.105	-0.038	0.069	0.003
Soc. welf./GNP (ln)	-2.46**	-2.75*	-5.23**			
	-0.188	-0.205	-0.207			
Med. exp./GNP (ln)				-3.22**	-2.28**	-5.50**
				-0.327	-0.394	-0.337
Intercept	-26.1	81.1	53.4	-12.5	49.1	36.1
R^2 (OLS)	0.792	0.686	0.770	0.796	0.596	0.780
df	114	114	114	78	78	78

**$p < .01$; *$p < .05$.

ilar effects on both the PNR and the NNR.[8] In Table 6.3, we also replicate these models, only substituting medical spending for social welfare spending and using a shorter time span (1960–80). Public medical benefits show stronger effects than the more general measure.[9] The effects of ethnic diversity are small in all equations.

Overall, variables relating to equality, at the very best, match the importance of GNP or female education. More commonly, however, the effects are small, less than half those of GNP or female education. Moreover, there is no evidence that income inequality and diversity combine to raise mortality: A multiplicative interaction term fails to have a significant effect on any of the dependent variables. These effects may partly be due to the overly broad measures of welfare spending and to the constant measures of inequality and ethnic diversity. Improvements in measures might raise the effects of the equality variables, but the results here do not show that equality comes to dominate economic growth in determining infant mortality.

Which variables contribute most to the high mortality in the United States? Among all these nations, the United States ranks first on teenage births, third on unemployment, third on ethnic diversity, and last on hospital beds. Each contributes in important ways to keeping infant mortality high, despite the benefits of high income and female education in the United States. The effect of teenage births, in particular, coincides with the finding that the high infant mortality rate in the United States is due to a high proportion of low birth-weight infants (Lee et al., 1980; see Geronimus, 1986, for a contrary view).

Time-invariant models. Having completed the basic analyses and offered some tentative conclusions, we can address a potential problem in what we have done so far. For infant mortality, the pooled cross-section and time-series models may overestimate the influence of variables that covary over time with infant mortality but not across nations. The problem stems from the development over time of superior medical knowledge, equipment, and techniques for the care of mothers and infants. Improved medical care may steadily lower infant mortality over the decades, but may also create a spurious relationship between infant mortality and any other measured variable that may coincidentally reflect the same trends. Since these developed nations are likely to share medical advances, the problem resides in the time-series component of the data. An attempt to adjust for unmeasured medical care that occurs over time across all nations in the sample would be a crucially important way to evaluate the robustness of the effects found thus far.

One such adjustment is to measure all variables as deviations from their year-specific means (this is equivalent to including dummy variables for all but one time period; Judge et al., 1980). This in essence removes the time-series variation from the variables and removes the potential spurious influence of changes over time in the medical care of infants and mothers. It leaves cross-national variation around identical means of zero for each time period. Table 6.4 presents OLS estimates of models of infant mortality with the time-invariant data (GLS estimates to remove autocorrelation are inappropriate with such data).

The main conclusion from an overview of these results is that the effects of national product remains strong, whereas those for social welfare spending decline. A nearly linear net decrease in infant mortality from the effects of time eliminates the influence of total welfare spending altogether and reduces the influence of medical care spending. The effects of welfare spending appear less robust in these results, and may more likely than GNP be due to unmeasured changes in medical care. The other variable to decline in importance in these models is female education; nearly all of its relationship with infant mortality stems from time-series covariation. We also note that the effects for the Gini coefficient and ethnic diversity remain small. Because all variables are measured as deviations from yearly means, the lack of time-series variation for the Gini coefficient and ethnic diversity in these equations places them at no special disadvantage. Still, they have little influence.[10]

To summarize, even for this sample of high-income nations, standard developmental and demographic variables are the dominant determinants of infant mortality. Economic growth in particular shows strong and robust effects, but urbanization, teenage fertility, unemployment, hospital beds, and perhaps female education also contribute to explaining variation in infant mortality. The alternative explanations receive less support. Inequality and ethnic diversity have weak and inconsistent effects, but medical spending (not total welfare spending) shows more consistently beneficial effects.

Infant mortality in Eastern European socialist nations

At first glance, the gap between capitalist and socialist nations is wide, with lower rates occurring among the Western capitalist nations. For the seven socialist nations in the sample – Bulgaria, Czechoslovakia, East Germany, Hungary, Poland, Romania, and Yugoslavia – the mean infant mortality rate is 22.3 compared to a mean in 1980 of 10.5 for the Western nations.[11] If all nations are ranked together, East Germany ranks thirteenth and the remaining socialist nations from twentieth to last.

The comparison is unfair, however, because of the lower economic product and level of urbanization of the East European nations compared to the Western nations. Controlling for relevant developmental characteristics would allow more

Table 6.4. Coefficients (unstandardized above standardized) for OLS estimates of time-invariant models of infant mortality, advanced industrial democracies, 1950–80[a]

Independent variables	1950–80			1960–80		
	NNR	PNR	IMR	NNR	PNR	IMR
GNP/pop. (ln)	−5.55**	−4.57**	−10.1**	−4.01**	−3.17**	−7.18**
	−0.467	−0.378	−0.443	−0.372	−0.499	−0.447
Unemp. (ln)	0.744**	0.938**	1.68**	0.884**	0.552**	1.43**
	0.165	0.204	0.194	0.257	0.273	0.280
TFR (ln)	−0.190	−3.61	−3.80	0.448	−2.87	−2.42
	−0.007	−0.135	−0.075	0.023	−0.251	−0.084
% teen births (ln)	0.958	−0.653	0.305	0.713	−0.395	0.318
	0.097	−0.065	0.016	0.097	−0.091	0.029
Fem. ed. (ln)	−0.424	−0.354	−0.778	−1.29	−0.314	−1.61
	−0.066	−0.054	−0.063	−0.196	−0.081	−0.164
% urban (ln)	−0.726	−6.70**	−7.42*	−0.951	−3.48*	−4.43
	−0.023	−0.208	−0.122	−0.034	−0.213	−0.107
Phys. (ln)	7.17**	1.86	9.03**	8.12**	2.01**	10.1**
	0.353	0.089	0.231	0.474	0.200	0.398
Beds (ln)	−0.042	−6.24**	−6.28*	1.23	−1.65	−0.412
	−0.001	−0.204	−0.108	0.048	−0.109	−0.011
Gini (ln)	10.9**	0.314	11.3	5.36	−4.35	1.01
	0.150	0.004	0.080	0.097	−0.133	0.012
Ethl. (ln)	0.330	0.534	0.863	0.158	0.317	0.475
	0.060	0.096	0.082	0.038	0.129	0.076
Soc. welf./GNP (ln)	−0.182	−0.238	−0.420			
	−0.014	−0.018	−0.016			
Med. exp./GNP (ln)				−2.29**	−1.76**	−4.05**
				−0.234	−0.305	−0.278
Intercept	−9.72	66.8	57.1	5.16	51.5	56.6
R^2 (OLS)	0.864	0.737	0.823	0.874	0.606	0.828
df	108	108	108	72	72	72

**$p < .01$; *$p < .05$.
[a] Models based on variable deviations from yearly means.

meaningful comparisons and might eliminate differences in infant mortality. We would then have a better picture of the "net" gap between East and West – the gap that would exist were the two groups to have the same developmental and demographic characteristics. To do this, the models of infant mortality must be comparable across both sets of nations, a difficult task given the differences in statistical accounting and data gathering. Female education, urbanization, the total fertility rate, percent teenage births, physicians, hospital beds, and ethnic diversity can be measured in socialist nations, as they were for capitalist nations in Table 6.3. However, we must use special estimates of GDP from Summers and Heston (1984), which are available for both socialist and capitalist nations. Summers and Heston note several potential sources of error in estimating national product and prices in centrally planned economies, but improve considerably over the figures on net material product reported by socialist governments themselves.[12] Further, we must eliminate two variables used in the previous models. Unemployment cannot be measured comparably for both groups of nations. Social welfare spending also has little meaning in socialist nations, where living expenses are heavily subsidized. Since levels of unemployment and social welfare spending are so closely tied to economic systems, we can allow their effects to show in the net difference between the two sets of nations. Otherwise, we must also eliminate the 1950 data point, since many of the socialist nations are missing data for this year.[13]

Table 6.5 presents the abbreviated models for both the Eastern and Western nations. The small number of Eastern European nations allows only 33 degrees of freedom and lowers the statistical significance of the coefficients. Only one variable is significant for the socialist nations – real GDP – but physicians and percent urban have modest if insignificant effects. The model for the Western nations replicates the results from the previous section but indicates some differences compared to the Eastern nations. Whereas physicians has a positive effect for Western nations, it has a clearly negative effect for Eastern nations. In general, developmental variables do more to lower infant mortality at the low levels of economic, medical, and demographic development that exist in the socialist nations than at the higher levels of development among Western nations. However, female education, teenage fertility, and ethnic diversity are more important among the Western nations.

We may view this gap in infant mortality more directly by combining the capitalist and socialist nations. Despite apparent differences in the coefficients in Table 6.5, only two of the differences are statistically significant. All but the coefficients for female education and physicians can be assumed to be equal and the differences to be due to the role of random error. Statistical significance is never a final basis for decisions such as these, but since we have already exam-

Table 6.5. *Coefficients (unstandardized above standardized) for GLS estimates of models of infant mortality, Western capitalist and Eastern European socialist nations, 1955–80*

Independent variables	East (1)	West (2)	Combined (3)	(4)	(5)
GDP/pop. (ln)	−30.2**	−20.7**	−22.5**	−23.3**	−19.6**
	−0.586	−0.840	−0.592	−0.614	−0.516
TFR (ln)	6.35	−1.99	2.90	3.30	1.09
	0.091	−0.054	0.046	0.053	0.017
% teen births (ln)	−2.17	2.70**	1.77	2.34	0.872
	−0.031	0.195	0.067	0.089	0.033
Fem. ed. (ln)	−1.66	−3.28**	−1.82	−2.12*	0.915
	−0.062	−0.315	−0.092	−0.107	0.046
% urban (ln)	−9.63	2.88	−2.30	0.063	−4.81
	−0.131	0.059	−0.036	0.001	−0.076
Phys. (ln)	−12.7	4.33	7.62**	8.29**	10.5**
	−0.213	0.141	0.144	0.157	0.198
Beds (ln)	−3.75	−4.91	−8.20*	−6.93*	−8.31**
	−0.042	−0.039	−0.114	−0.097	−0.116
Ethl. (ln)	−0.239	1.21	1.06	1.04	0.705
	−0.013	0.155	0.074	0.072	0.048
East. (=1)			19.2**	23.7**	6.55
			0.501	0.619	0.171
East. × fem. ed.			−1.50	−1.83	−3.53
			−0.097	−0.118	−0.228
East. × phys.			−28.6**	−27.6**	−31.9**
			−0.417	−0.403	−0.466
Gini (ln)				9.18	
				0.116	
Time					−0.442**
					−0.219
East. × time					0.287
					0.512
Intercept	331.3	197.6	235.3	194.4	247.7
R^2 (OLS)	0.912	0.734	0.893	0.897	0.902
df	33	99	138	137	136

**p < .01; *p < .05.

ined separate models, a more parsimonious combined model can offer useful insights. Our strategy is as follows. All nations and time points are pooled, with a dummy variable for the Eastern bloc nations included with the other independent variables. In addition, we multiply female education and physicians by the Eastern bloc dummy variable to allow their effects to differ for the two groups.

This equation is presented in Table 6.5 (column 3). The effects of the variables are similar to those in the previous equations. What is notable, however, is the coefficient for the Eastern bloc nations. It shows that, controlling for all other variables, infant mortality is still 19 deaths per 1,000 higher in the Eastern European nations. We have clearly not measured whatever it is that accounts for the difference between the two sets of nations, since the net gap is even higher than the gross gap of 12. But it is clearly not the measured development or demographic characteristics that are responsible for the poor performance of the socialist nations. We also know that the unmeasured variables that should lead to lower infant mortality in socialist nations – low levels of unemployment, widespread availability of government, and more equitable distribution of income – do little to benefit infant mortality. More precisely, if these characteristics offer benefits, they are outweighed by other unmeasured characteristics of socialist nations that are harmful to infant mortality. Averaged over all unmeasured characteristics, the net effect of socialist nations is clearly, then, to raise infant mortality. These results are quite consistent with the recent reversals in the level of infant mortality in these nations well before they reached comparable levels to the West (World Health Organization, 1982).

How might income inequality contribute to the differences across groups of nations? Given different sources, meanings, and measurement of income across the groups of nations, it is hard to determine reliably the role of measured income inequality. If we include the Gini coefficient in separate equations for both the Eastern and Western nations, we find that it has no effect on either group. When it is included in the pooled data (column 4, Table 6.5), it has only a small effect and increases the net gap. Even if it were measured correctly, income inequality could do little to explain the disadvantage in infant mortality unless inequality were substantially higher in the socialist nations. Controlling for the presumed more equitable distribution of income in socialist nations should only improve the relative position of the West. With or without controls for income inequality, then, the socialist disadvantage in infant mortality remains.

Our comparison between these two groups of nations is less than perfect. The lack of data on socialist nations makes modeling their levels of infant mortality difficult. Nonetheless, we have attempted to control for a variety of components of development that may account for the advantage of the capitalist nations. Yet, even adjusting for higher development, the Western advantage remains strong.

To the extent that low infant mortality reflects high equality, the socialist nations rank well behind the capitalist nations. Elimination of the power of monopoly capital, increased worker power, and the distribution of income that may have occurred in these nations do not improve the quality of life of the poor or lower infant mortality.

The results also fail to support predictions of convergence between capitalist and socialist nations. Convergence in infant mortality may be especially likely because of the availability to socialist nations of new medical technology and techniques. Prenatal and obstetric techniques from advanced capitalist economies may diffuse more easily than political and economic ideas. To check for this, we added a linear time trend variable to the combined models.[14] We then allowed this time trend to vary by multiplying it by the dummy variable for the Eastern bloc nations (column 5). Although the linear trend is negative for both groups, the difference between the two groups is not significant. At best, the decline among the Eastern bloc nations has been no faster than among the Western nations. Viewed differently, however, the positive effect of the time variable for the Eastern nations, although not significant, indicates that the net decline is slower for these nations. We might expect a faster decline among socialist nations on mathematical grounds alone: Having reached lower levels, Western nations might find it difficult to achieve further reductions. Yet, there is no evidence of convergence.[15]

Although these results are by no means final, unmeasured forces in socialist nations limit the decline in infant mortality. Unfortunately, we are not able to identify exactly what it is that is responsible for the socialist disadvantage. Some speculate that it is inefficient medical care or worker malaise (Davis and Feshbach, 1980; Eberstadt, 1981). Our purpose is more simple: to demonstrate that the gap is not due to developmental or demographic differences. Instead, political control of the economic system may do little to improve the quality of life of the poor, and the results favor a view that economic sources are most important for improvements in equality.

Infant mortality in developing nations

To move from the study of industrialized capitalist and socialist nations to the study of lower income, developing nations raises a number of new methodological problems. To be sure, the theoretical issues remain much the same: We desire further tests of the influence of development, inequality, and social welfare spending as means to evaluate the industrialism, interest group, and class theories. Yet, data and measurement problems in developing nations make this task more difficult than we have found so far in this chapter. For example, infant mortality often is underestimated in developing nations because of incomplete registration procedures, especially in the rural and poor regions. As a result, researchers looking at the same determinants of infant mortality find different results, depending on the source of infant mortality data. Rodgers (1979), who examines United Nations mortality data for 1970, finds little effect of inequality on the infant mortality rate. Flegg (1982), in contrast, incorporates corrected and adjusted figures and uses the best available data for any available year; he finds that inequality has a substantial effect on the infant mortality rate.

We are left with a choice, then, of how to proceed in modeling infant mortality. We may use error-prone data from a consistent source and common time period, or we may use adjusted data from different sources and covering different time points. We may replicate analysis of data that show either no effect or a substantial effect of inequality on infant mortality. While noting the varying consequences of the different data, we favor the corrected data from a variety of time points reported by Flegg (1982). These data offer the best chance for the effects of inequality to emerge. Since inequality has had little effect in our analysis thus far, and since we desire to provide every opportunity for it to do so, we use the data on infant mortality gathered and reported by Flegg.[16]

Our strategy of analysis is to examine the relative influences of development, inequality, social welfare spending, and, for these developing nations, economic dependency. With only one time point per nation and a relatively small number of nations with both infant mortality and inequality data (a maximum of 47), we do not have the freedom to construct complex models. Instead, we attempt to keep the number of independent variables small. Following Flegg, we begin with a simple model including national economic product and a measure of inequality. We then add to that equation several measures of welfare spending and economic dependency. Finally, we consider a more complete developmental model, which includes measures of education and medical care that mediate the effect that economic product has on infant mortality.

Several of the variables we analyze in this section come directly from Flegg's analyses and are new to our study. Since Flegg reports all the figures he uses, and matches the data of independent variables with those for infant mortality, we use his data where possible. His measure of economic product is GDP per capita. He also measures the percentage of the female population that is illiterate – a proxy for education – and the number of physicians and nurses per 10,000 population. To measure inequality, he uses the log of variance coefficient rather than the Gini coefficient.[17]

We add several of our own measures, again matched to the data with which infant mortality is measured. Government revenues over GDP, social security expenditures over GDP, and SIPE are the measures of social welfare spending.

Peripheral status in the world system and the foreign investment ratio are the measures of economic dependency (see Chapter 4 or 5 for definitions and sources of data).

Keeping in mind that our goal is to evaluate the independent influence on infant mortality of development, inequality, dependency, and social welfare spending, we present models for the developing nations in Table 6.6. Following Flegg (1982), all variables are logged. In the first equation, both economic product and income inequality have strong effects on infant mortality in the predicted direction. Together these two variables explain nearly 60 percent of the variance. When various measures of social welfare spending are added to the equation, none reduces infant mortality; all have positive effects instead. The largest positive effect, for social security expenditures, is based on only a small number of cases with the necessary data and is suspect. Yet, neither government revenues nor SIPE shows any evidence of improving infant mortality in developing nations.

Economic dependency also contributes little to the level of infant mortality. Peripheral status increases the IMR slightly, but the coefficient is not significant. Foreign investment has effects in the wrong direction. Neither variable appreciably reduces the effects of national product or inequality.

The final equation helps to identify the mechanisms through which economic product influences infant mortality by adding female illiteracy and the medical care variables.[18] Female illiteracy emerges as the strongest predictor, just as female education was strongest for the high-income nations. High numbers of physicians and nurses lower infant mortality. Although inequality remains significant, the effect of GDP is eliminated by the controls. Because of the high correlation of GDP with illiteracy, physicians, and nurses ($r = -0.641$, 0.831, and 0.546, respectively), GDP contains little net variation that can explain infant mortality. If we take GDP as causally prior to illiteracy, physicians, and nurses, we may interpret these results in the form of a causal model in which the intervening variables mediate much of the effect that GDP has on infant mortality. The difference between the standardized coefficient of GDP in the first and last equations of Table 6.6 shows the total indirect effect that GDP has on infant mortality through illiteracy, physicians, and nurses. This indirect effect of -0.525 is large indeed and shows the importance of GDP, if not directly, then through the influence it has on intervening variables.

In replicating Flegg's model, we do not include fertility variables. Flegg estimates a simultaneous model of fertility and infant mortality but finds that fertility shows little or no effect on infant mortality. Flegg deletes fertility from his final model, which we use as a basis for our analysis. The problem may be that fertility is so closely linked to illiteracy and GDP in these nations that it fails to have

Table 6.6. *Coefficients (unstandardized above standardized) for OLS estimates of models of infant mortality, developing nations, circa 1965*

Independent variables[a]	Dependent variable: infant mortality rate (ln)						
	(1)	(2)	(3)	(4)	(5)	(6)	(7)
GDP/pop. (ln)	−0.549**	−0.592**	−0.932**	−0.658**	−0.487**	−0.507**	−0.091
	−0.625	−0.679	−0.103	−0.820	−0.582	−0.624	−0.103
Var. coeff. (ln)	0.797**	0.701**	0.878**	0.675**	0.638*	0.580**	0.491*
	0.430	0.379	0.481	0.366	0.378	0.324	0.265
Fem. illit. (ln)							0.234*
							0.342
Physicians (ln)							−0.135
							−0.274
Nurses (ln)							−0.010
							−0.132
Gov. revs./GDP (ln)		0.034					
		0.021					
Soc. sec. exp./GDP (ln)			0.449*				
			0.459				
SIPE (ln)				0.178			
				0.248			
Peripheral = 1					0.147		
					0.136		
For. invest. (ln)						−0.031	
						−0.059	
Intercept	7.95	8.13	9.97	7.98	7.53	7.80	4.36
R^2	0.567	0.570	0.728	0.562	0.540	0.460	0.657
df	44	38	13	34	34	28	41

**$p < .01$; *$p < .05$.
[a]The first five variables are from Flegg (1982); the others are from sources listed in Appendix 6.A.

independent effects. Thus, we do not dismiss its importance altogether in reducing infant mortality, but we suggest that it does not bias the model we estimate here.

Overall, these results are similar to previous ones in this chapter: The effects of the developmental variables, in one form or another, strongly contribute to a reduction in infant mortality and an improvement in the physical quality of life of the poor. Unlike previous results, we find stronger effects of inequality and weaker effects of welfare spending among developing nations. Inequality, taken as a reflection of the concentration of power in the hands of the dominant class, does raise infant mortality. However, inequality does not explain away the effects of development and, in fact, has smaller effects than the developmental variables. Also, were other data analyzed, the effects of inequality would no doubt be much weaker (Rodgers, 1979). Moreover, as income levels rise, inequality declines in importance; or conversely, the distribution of income becomes more important when income levels are low. In addition to reducing inequality, then, rising income reduces the effect that income inequality has on the physical quality of life. Social welfare spending, in contrast, seems to have little beneficial influence, except in nations where income levels are already high. Finally, economic dependency has no effect on infant mortality.

Conclusions

The goal of this chapter has been to examine the determinants of one crucial component of equality: the ability of a society to provide for the physical well-being of its members. Infant mortality is thus treated in its larger context as a reflection of the socioeconomic conditions of a population. The lower the rate of infant mortality, the greater the diffusion of appropriate nutrition, health care, and financial resources to the poor. Although the study of infant mortality requires attention to some more technical demographic issues, we have otherwise tried to keep our focus on the ultimate goal of understanding equality.

The results in this chapter in some ways are similar to those in the last chapter on income inequality. However, the study of infant mortality offers much that is new. Income inequality data are seldom available for more than one time point, lack comparability across capitalist and socialist nations, and suffer from unreliable measurement inherent in the study of income. In contrast, infant mortality is available for multiple time points, allowing the study of changes along with cross-sectional differences. It can be compared across quite different political and economic systems, and offers our only chance to study socialist nations. Finally, the problems of measuring mortality are less serious than those of measuring income. For methodological as well as theoretical reasons, then, the study of infant mortality moves well beyond the study of income inequality.

The major finding in this chapter is that developmental variables show strong effects on infant mortality for a variety of nations. Among the advanced capitalist democracies, where income is high enough that differences might be expected to be of little importance, GNP has strong effects. The effect of development is just as strong or even stronger among socialist nations. Finally, national product has strong effects in developing nations until closely related controls for medical care and education are added. Developmental effects still occur indirectly through increasing female education, improving medical care, and reducing fertility. Just as for income inequality, then, we find development to be the dominant influence on quality of life.

What of the effects of social welfare spending? We find negative, but at times spurious, effects on infant mortality among high-income Western democracies. Among developing nations, in contrast, no evidence that government spending reduces infant mortality emerges. A comparison of infant mortality in advanced capitalist and socialist nations sheds further light on the influence of government intervention. Socialist nations lag behind capitalist nations in mortality reduction. Even controlling for development, the gap between the two types of nations remains quite large: A disadvantage of nearly 20 deaths per 1,000 births is shown in the socialist nations. We are not able to identify the exact cause of the poor performance of socialist nations here, but the results give no evidence that government intervention in socialist nations improves infant mortality or that the absence of monopoly capital translates into higher equality.

Finally, our results show the importance of income inequality as a determinant of infant mortality among low-income nations, but less so among higher-income capitalist and socialist nations. Where national income levels are low, the dispersion of income is important for the quality of life of the population. When national income levels are high, distributional variation declines in importance. The different findings for high- and low-income nations may also be methodological. Since income inequality changes slowly over time, it cannot explain the rapid reductions in infant mortality that have occurred in most nations in the last few decades. Income inequality better explains cross-national differences and has stronger effects in our analysis of developing nations at one time point.

No single means to lower infant mortality exists, and no single theory accounts completely for the variations across nations and over time. Economic development most consistently explains the trends and patterns of infant mortality, but other factors may likewise contribute in particular contexts. On the basis of these results, the interest group politics theory receives support by virtue of the strong effects of development and the weak effects of social welfare spending and government intervention among low-income and socialist nations. Welfare spending and government intervention as politically based sources of equality generally appear less influential than economic processes in increasing equality, but welfare spending shows some beneficial effects in high-income democracies. The industrialism theory also receives partial support in that it correctly predicts the effects of both development and social welfare spending in advanced industrial democracies. Yet, social welfare spending fails to show consistently strong effects across all samples and models. Further, despite predictions of the industrialism theory to the contrary, convergence between capitalist and socialist nations as they industrialize does not occur even with controls for developmental variables and data over a 25-year time span. The class theories receive modest support in this chapter from the effect that income inequality has on infant mortality among developing nations. If we take income inequality – net of development – as a reflection of the concentration of capitalist power, its effect on infant mortality is evidence in favor of the class theories. At the same time, however, income inequality has little or no effect among high-income nations, and the class theories do not account for the high levels of infant mortality in socialist nations.

Notes

1. Some researchers (Moon and Dixon, 1985; Williamson, 1987) study an index of the physical quality of life developed by Morris (1979). The index combines the infant mortality rate with life expectancy at age one year and the literacy rate. Others have suggested an even more extensive list of 10 dimensions of the social progress of nations, with each dimension including numerous indicators (Estes, 1984). In any case, combining empirically related but conceptually different variables in an index may make model building difficult. The theoretically specified determinants of each component in the index may differ. For this reason, we prefer to concentrate on one indicator at a time and, for the reasons we discuss, find the infant mortality rate especially useful for our purposes.
2. The other two components of the physical quality of life index – literacy and life expectancy at age one year – are much less useful than infant mortality for the study of high-income nations. Literacy has reached maximum levels among nearly all high-income democracies and does not offer an indicator of equality that varies among these nations. Similarly, the variation in life expectancy is smaller than that in infant mortality. Life expectancy also faces a problem of dealing with the delayed effects of World War II, especially for those nations occupied by foreign powers and suffering the greatest physical harm to their populations. Elderly mortality may increase from war experiences that occurred 30 years earlier. Infant mortality is less influenced by such historical forces. For all these reasons, then, infant mortality is the most appropriate indicator of the physical quality of life.
3. We avoid in these efforts any attempt to identify the fundamental processes in socialist societies that generate inequality. Scholars cannot agree on the appropriate means of referencing Eastern European societies, much less on the nature of the stratification within them. Appropriately, we do not endeavor to measure the political and economic processes within these nations, but merely contrast the rates of infant mortality with those in advanced industrial democracies, controlling for relevant demographic characteristics. Although only hinting at the underlying political causes of the differences, this strategy nonetheless can help to identify the net patterns of infant mortality that will need to be explained in other types of studies.

4. This assumes a relationship between income and mortality at the household level that is inverse and convex downward (Rodgers, 1979; Flegg, 1982). The assumption certainly holds in developing nations, where the range of income is high and the effect of inequality on infant mortality strong. In developed nations, however, the lower bound of household income typically is much higher than in developing nations, perhaps at a level where the inverse relationship levels off. As the relationship approaches linearity, the distributional aspects of income decline in importance. Since evidence shows that a status differential in mortality still exists, such a level has likely not been reached in developed nations. But the influence of inequality vis-à-vis developing nations may be smaller.

5. The Gini coefficient is available only for years around 1968, and ethnic diversity is available only for 1960. It is necessary to assume that these variables are constant over the time span of study. For most developed nations, this seems a reasonable assumption. In the United States, for instance, the percentage of income going to the richest or poorest fifth of the population changes by less than one point from 1950 to 1970 (U.S. Bureau of the Census, 1975). Other studies similarly point out the lack of change in overall inequality during this time period (e.g., Treas, 1983). There is no guarantee that the values are equally stable for other developed countries, but the U.S. evidence and the possible importance of inequality in explaining intercountry variation in infant mortality justify its use here, despite its limitations. For ethnic diversity, large fertility, mortality, and migration differentials among the ethnic and linguistic groups would change the diversity index. The assumption of constancy no doubt introduces error, but for most nations, changes in ethnic composition occur slowly and the relative positions of the nations change little during the time span.

6. We find that the effects of the independent variables logged are stronger than those of the untransformed variables. In the models to follow, we continue to log the independent variables. This means that the effects of the variables level off at their higher values, and the same proportional increase, yet a higher absolute increase, is needed to affect the IMR at higher values. To interpret the unstandardized coefficients in the original units, the coefficients of log (x) have to be divided by the value x at which the function is to be evaluated.

7. In general, because of the pooled data, the intercorrelations are lower than for the time-series or cross-sectional studies. All but a few are below 0.6, and none is above 0.71. Further, in the models to follow, the coefficients do not fluctuate greatly, and the tolerance (i.e., the unexplained variance in each independent variable when regressed on the other independent variables) never falls below 0.3 (see Pampel and Pillai, 1986, for related correlations).

8. Perhaps expenditures should be measured in absolute terms rather than relative to GNP. Yet, the coefficients for social welfare expenditures in constant dollars per capita are no larger than they are for expenditures over GNP. Regardless of how the expenditures are measured, GNP is controlled through residualization in the estimation process. However, because of their high correlation, the effects of GNP are substantially reduced with the inclusion of the collinear constant dollar measure. The tolerance for both variables falls to 0.12 and makes the results unstable. Given that the results for expenditures do not differ for either measure, we present the more robust models with expenditures over GNP.

9. These results for social welfare spending differ in some ways from those reported in a previous analysis of data for the period from 1950 to 1975 in Pampel and Pillai (1986). The results here show stronger effects of medical care benefits and weaker effects of total welfare spending. The divergence is due in part to the additional 1980 data and the more robust estimation techniques used here. More importantly, we have been able to create a combined spending category of medical, sickness, and public health spending for our analyses here that proves to be a better predictor of infant mortality than any of the separate programs alone.

10. The positive effects of physicians increase in these models. The upward trend in physicians and the downward trend in infant mortality partly hide the positive cross-sectional relationship. Here

this relationship is shown strongly. A number of possible explanations of this relationship are evaluated by Pampel and Pillai (1986), but the causal mechanisms involved remain unclear. In particular, a panel model shows that the causal effect is not reversed and that physicians predict changes in infant mortality in the following years. We note again that the positive relationship has been shown in other aggregate studies.

11. We are, unfortunately, not able to obtain sufficient data on the USSR to include in these analyses. The rising infant mortality in the USSR has received much attention (Davis and Feshbach, 1980). Its exclusion may thus tend to understate the level of infant mortality in socialist nations. This would be particularly true in the multivariate equations, where controls for development would further exaggerate the high infant mortality rates in the USSR.

12. We also estimated the equations with energy use per capita instead of national product. Although subject to variation from different climates, energy use can be measured comparably across nations. Its effects are slightly larger than for GDP, but they clearly reaffirm the results presented in the tables.

13. This is also advantageous, since it eliminates the year in which infant mortality is most likely influenced by the effects of World War II. The aftereffects of the war on infant mortality should decline during the later time periods.

14. The linear time trend may also serve as a crude means of removing time-series variation from the data and is similar to the models in Table 6.4. Variables that remain strong with controls for the linear time trend are again less likely to be spuriously related to infant mortality.

15. The fact that there is lack of convergence in infant mortality also allows us to dismiss the role of foreign occupation during the war as responsible for the high rate of infant mortality in socialist nations. If this were the cause, the gap should decline as the time from the war increases.

16. For instance, data from Guyana are for 1955, whereas data for the Philippines are for 1972. Use of the data requires the assumption that the time points make no difference, that is, that the processes are constant. When we add a variable to the basic equation that measures the year of the data, it has modest negative effects but does not change the effect of any of the other variables.

17. The formula for the coefficient of variation can be found in Atkinson (1973). Whereas the Gini coefficient attaches more weight to the middle of the income distribution, the coefficient of variation attaches more weight to the lower end. Although the results for infant mortality show similar effects of the two measures of inequality, those for the Gini coefficient are the smaller of the two. We thus use the measure most likely to show effects of inequality.

18. We are not able to match exactly the equation presented by Flegg, even though we use the original data as presented in his article. The differences, however, are minor and do not affect the interpretation of the results.

Appendix 6.A. *Variable data sources and adjustments*

Variables	Sources
GNP/pop.	World Bank. 1983. *World Tables*. Baltimore: Johns Hopkins University Press.
Unemp.	International Labour Office. 1980 and various years. *Handbook of Labour Statistics*. Geneva: International Labour Office.
Fem. ed.	UNESCO. 1979 and various years. *Statistical Yearbook*. New York: United Nations.
TFR	United Nations. 1978 and various years. *Demographic Yearbook*. New York: United Nations.
% teen births	United Nations. 1978. *Demographic Yearbook*. New York: United Nations.
% urban[a]	Davis (1969) and World Bank. 1983. *World Development Report*. London: Oxford University Press.
Beds, phys.[b]	World Health Organization. 1980 and various years. *WHO Statistics Annual*. Geneva: World Health Organization.
Ethl.	Taylor and Jodice (1983).
Gini[c]	Bornschier and Heintz (1979). *Compendium of Data for World-Systems Analysis*. Zurich: University of Zurich Press.
Soc. welf., med.	International Labour Office. 1985 and various years. *The Cost of Social Security*. Geneva: International Labour Office.
IMR	United Nations. 1980 and various years. *Demographic Yearbook*. New York: United Nations.
NNR, PNR	World Health Organization. 1980 and various years. *WHO Statistics Annual*. Geneva: World Health Organization.

[a] Data for 1955 and 1965 are estimated by midpoint interpolation. Data for 1975 and 1980 are from the World Bank, except where clearly inconsistent with Davis, in which case data are projected.

[b] For some nations, it was necessary to subtract out dental surgeons from the figures in order to make them comparable to those of other nations.

[c] Data for Belgium and Ireland obtained from regression-based estimates of Weatherby et al. (1983).

7. Conclusions: The causes and consequences of the welfare state

As is true of any detailed, thorough empirical study, our results are complex and general conclusions must be qualified. Yet, the diverse empirical results in our study lend considerable support to our claim that age structure, politics, and development should be taken more seriously in the study of welfare spending and social equality. With the perspective of the empirical analyses behind us, and a roughly defined interest group theory to make sense of the results, we can review these arguments and the evidence in favor of them.

The aged and the welfare state

The major influence on the rise of social welfare spending from 1950 to 1980, at least in political democracies, is age structure – primarily the rise of the aged population but secondarily the decline in the population of young children. This influence stems in part from automatic entitlements for the increasingly larger number of eligible aged persons. As the major program designed specifically for the aged, pensions respond in part to the sheer growth in the number of persons entitled to benefits. Direct demographic forces likewise prove important for medical care spending. The high rates of illness and medical care usage among older persons, and the expensive and difficult care needed for the very old, mean that the aged receive medical care benefits in excess of their representation in the population. Not surprisingly, then, those societies with the most developed welfare states have the world's oldest populations as well.

   At the same time, something more than demographic accounting – perhaps the political influence of a large, literate, and high-voting-age population – is involved in welfare spending. A number of findings emerge that cannot be explained by demographic accounting alone. We find that pension spending per aged person grows with percent aged in advanced industrial democracies, even though the spending measure controls for the number of potential aged recipients. We find that political participation and party competition interact with the size of the aged population to jointly raise welfare spending. We find that the effect of percent aged on welfare spending increases over time, thus showing

165

that the aged more effectively translate their numbers into greater spending in more recent time periods. Finally, we find that among lower- and middle-income nations, where the degree of democracy varies greatly, democratic political procedures amplify the influence of age structure and other development variables on welfare spending. All this suggests that democratic procedures furnish the opportunity for socioeconomic and demographic groups to influence public policy. Since the structure of such groups is determined by changes in the economy and in demographic composition, developmental change combines with democratic politics to raise welfare spending.

The aged, as both a demographic and a political force, are not the only influence on welfare spending. Economic growth, unemployment, and inflation contribute to the upward trend in spending in advanced industrial democracies, as do the aforementioned nonpartisan political participation and competition variables. Variables measuring the strength of organized labor and leftist parties emerge important in explaining public assistance spending directed to the poor. Whereas social insurance programs for pensions and medical care favor the aged and middle-income groups, means-tested programs target the poor. A variety of groups and forces thus influence welfare spending to one degree or another or for one type of program or another.

What appears special about the aged, however, is that the social insurance programs they most influence comprise such a large part of social welfare spending.[1] Pensions and medical care spending, including that for government employees, make up 76 percent of the total. With other programs related to an old age structure such as disability included, the proportion rises even higher. Programs with little connection to the aged, such as public assistance and unemployment, make up less than 15 percent of all welfare spending. Furthermore, when nations slow the growth or cut the level of welfare benefits, programs for the aged fare best.

Taken together, these facts and findings add considerable credibility to the thesis that changes in age structure have contributed enormously to the growth of the welfare state over the past several decades. Among sociologists, this insight has sometimes been ignored but more often denied. The orthodoxy is that labor, capital, and class-based political parties drive welfare spending, regardless of the size or political influence of the aged population. In this study, the orthodoxy fares poorly. We reject theories that dismiss the role of the aged and population, and recommend that researchers and theorists make room for age structure in their conceptualizations and empirical studies.

Several more general implications follow from the specific findings. First, conceptions of the stratification system must address more carefully the role of middle-class and ascriptive groups whose interests do not unambiguously coincide with those of labor or capital. Dominant conceptions in the field emphasize class relations to the means of production, occupational status, or work characteristics such as authority. When considering political components of stratification, however, nonclass ascriptive elements may also prove important. Since age, sex, racial, or ethnic boundaries increasingly come to intersect class boundaries (Nielsen, 1985), they contribute independently to a complex and diffuse pattern of social segmentation (Janowitz, 1985). In terms of the debate over Marxian and Weberian conceptions of the stratification system, our study favors a status-based theory that recognizes the importance of ascriptive and status groups (Parkin, 1979). Although some authors suggest the reemergence of class stratification in the 1980s (Piven and Cloward, 1982; Walton, 1986), we find the continuing importance of status and ascriptive groups in relation to the welfare state.

Second, although we lack direct evidence, our results support a view of the aged as an active political force in advanced democracies. Their political power may come normatively and structurally. The aged have normative legitimacy to their claims on the welfare state that is denied to most other groups. As a result, they have become symbolic representatives of the welfare state with full citizen rights to public income maintenance. Beyond public support, the aged gain political power structurally through large numbers, effective organization, and common interests in higher benefits. The aged do not need candidates who specialize in aged issues alone, but may use their symbolic and organizational power to pressure candidates from all political parties for support of their demands.

Third, the size and political power of the aged suggest increased spending in years to come (or at least growth in the programs designated for the aged). The simple projection of spending from numbers of potential recipients alone no doubt fails to capture all the contingencies involved (Furniss, 1986) or all the differences across nations (Myles, 1984). Still, the aged exert pressure to which governments must respond in some form or another. Since benefits are difficult to eliminate in the face of the political power of the aged, governments must raise taxes or rely on deficit spending.[2] Even if the rate of growth cannot continue as it did during the 1960s and early 1970s, the welfare state will remain strong by virtue of the political demands of the aged.

Given these speculations, much remains to be done to investigate the influence of the aged in the welfare state. Further research should examine how groups combine, compete, and intersect in the political process of implementing welfare spending. The aged must be given their due in such efforts, as should other groups. At the macrolevel, however, existing data make it difficult to provide more than indirect evidence on participation in the political process. Studies of single nations, the organizations for the aged that exist in them, and their relationships with unions and political parties would supply valuable detail to go along with multination, quantitative studies. Studies of low-income democracies might also provide an invaluable opportunity to study the treatment of the aged where their numbers are small and the welfare state is just emerging.

Another direction for research is to consider other types of expenditures and government activity. We limit ourselves to a set of programs based on social protection that make up a substantial part of nonmilitary government spending. Since mixing widely different programs in a single measure of spending hides the different causal processes that may be operating, delimiting the kind of spending to be explained has important advantages. However, others might study different components of government activity – regulation, educational spending, research and development, or a variety of other programs – and reach conclusions different from ours. Efforts to specify the domain of the various theories must continue.

Redistributive efficacy of welfare spending

Economic and productive structures have strong effects, whereas social welfare spending and broader government spending variables have weaker effects, on two components of social equality – income inequality and infant mortality. High national product and an older age structure reduce levels of income inequality; high national product, female education, urbanization, and medical care resources reduce infant mortality. In contrast, political democracy, economic dependency, social welfare and other government spending, and leftist government control have little effect on either dependent variable. We do not show that developmental variables completely explain the cross-national variation in equality, or that other variables are never important, but that the developmental variables have generally beneficial effects, whereas the other variables do not.

As a means to equality, political intervention appears to offer limited benefits. If welfare spending responds to democratic political processes, it may in large part reflect the demands of the politically powerful middle-income groups more than those of the poor. Having little influence in the political arena, the poor may not be as effective as higher income groups in pressuring for programs that most benefit them. If, as Olson (1982) argues, greater inequality exists in the opportunity to create distributional coalitions to protect interests than in the productive abilities of people, the ability of political programs to redistribute income is inherently limited. Efforts to understand how differentials in wages and hours worked may be more important to explaining national differences in income inequality than taxes and transfers (Rainwater et al., 1986).

The limitations of public spending as a means to redistribution are further illustrated by considering the implications of our findings on the political importance of the aged as a determinant of welfare spending. The major part of pension spending is based on age rather than on need. Despite wide diversity in resources among the aged, benefits under dominant social insurance programs go to aged persons based on previous contributions rather than current need. Even if lower-income pensioners may receive higher returns on the contributions, higher-income workers receive higher benefits by virtue of their higher contributions. Further, cost-of-living increases, applied to all recipients, favor those with the highest benefits. Those nations that opt for some form of flat-rate benefits seldom offer them at high enough levels to redistribute income. Social insurance programs have grown precisely because they can obtain the support of persons at all income levels; more redistributive programs gain weaker political support. As a result, there may be a contradiction between high benefits and progressive distribution. The end result appears to be that those who are advantaged during middle age remain most advantaged during old age, even when their dependency on government transfers increases. Perhaps political pressure of the middle class leads to benefits that are shared by the aged poor, and without the force of the more affluent aged, benefits would be meager for those most in need. Yet, this precludes redistribution, as wealth transfers occur across generations rather than across classes (Page, 1983; Hedstrom and Ringen, 1987).

Despite its failure to reshape permanently the distribution of income, welfare spending may have other benefits. We in fact show that it can contribute to lowering infant mortality; it may also contribute in important ways to the well-being of the poor in many ways that we have not studied. There are many justifications for welfare spending, and we do not desire to enter the political debate over the validity of these claims (see Eisenstadt and Ahimeir, 1985, for a presentation of alternative sides of the debate). We focus instead on the more exaggerated conceptions of the welfare state as a means to achieve substantial reductions in inequality or as the road to socialism.

Whatever the benefits of welfare spending, it does not replace economic and productive structures as the major source of equality. Our results confirm the existence of a relationship between economic development and equality, and show that it stands up to commonly asserted criticisms. Some claim that with appropriate controls, the effect of development on equality disappears. The antecedent cause of economic dependency, or the roles of government intervention and union power, eliminate any association that development may have with equality, and need only be controlled in statistical analyses to show the weak effects of development. Yet, our analyses show that these claims have little validity. In nearly all instances, economic dependency, social welfare spending, or leftist power have little influence on either income inequality or infant mortality.

Economic development, when properly specified as having a curvilinear relationship, has consistently strong effects regardless of the controls, as do some related developmental variables, such as age structure, fertility, or medical care.

Others claim that low-income nations can never repeat the historical economic experience of the Western nations or obtain the same benefits for equality from economic growth. The two groups of nations are fundamentally different, having begun industrial development during different historical periods and having occupied different positions in the world system. These differences make comparisons across the groups inappropriate and spuriously attribute to developmental differences what is really due to fundamentally diverse historical experiences. Even if high-income nations have greater equality, it is not possible to attribute it to economic development. In response to this criticism, we show that development has effects within these two groups of nations as well as across them. When analyzed separately, development strongly influences income inequality and infant mortality in developing nations. Similarly, development has strong effects on infant mortality among high-income nations. Only for income inequality among high-income nations, where variation is truncated due to lack of time-series data, are developmental effects weak. Otherwise, our results show clear effects of development within the historical classification of nations; the effects of development do not depend on artificial comparisons across strata in the world system.

Although our results indicate that the effects of economic development are not spurious, they show that the changes development brings about in equality come slowly and with difficulty. Among developing nations, there is little evidence of the ability of governments to unleash and maintain economic growth and then enjoy immediate and substantial reductions in inequality; among high-income nations, the responsiveness of inequality to economic growth decreases. Returns to economic growth in infant mortality are greater than in income inequality, but for neither has the gap between low- and high-income nations been eliminated. Expectations that equality should come quickly or easily make the slow pace of change seem unsatisfactory. Yet, we are unable to document empirically other means to permanent, sustained improvements in equality.

The weakest link in these arguments, however, stems from problems of data availability and measurement. We, like all previous researchers, lack time-series data on income inequality and are only partly able to overcome this gap with additional data on infant mortality. Even if multiple data points were available, problems in the measurement of household income used to compute income inequality are serious. Alternative explanations based on measurement error might explain the empirical relationships we find (Gagliani, 1987). Since existing data on income inequality have already been fully analyzed, new data points and more accurate measures are needed to move the debate forward. New and better survey data would be especially helpful in this regard (e.g., Hedstrom and Ringen, 1987; Rainwater et al., 1986). Besides income inequality, scholars might fruitfully focus on the more valid and easily available measures of the consequences of income distribution such as infant mortality.

Interest groups and political parties

Control of governments by particular political parties, of either the right or the left, most influences the level of spending for relatively small public assistance programs. For social insurance spending, the ideological perspective or union support of the victorious party is less central than nonpartisan components of democratic politics such as the participation of the population in elections and the number of parties competing in the democratic process. The class characteristics traditionally considered responsible for the power of partisan parties, such as union strength, monopolization, and strike activity, likewise have limited influence on spending. Our results show some cross-sectional relationships of class and party variables with spending, but little over-time relationship. The effects of the variables decline with controls for variables that track both over-time changes and cross-sectional differences in welfare spending.

In developing nations, class structure operates through the forces of trade dependency and world system position. The effects of dependency we find in the analysis are not as strong or robust as those for percent aged combined with political democracy, and we do not want to overemphasize their importance. Even so, the study of peripheral and semiperipheral nations provides some interesting insights into the causes of welfare spending. We find that ties to core nations increase rather than decrease social welfare spending, thereby contradicting assumptions that welfare spending protects labor from the power of capital. Class-based parties cannot be measured for most of these nations and cannot be expected to explain spending among them. But the idea that welfare spending reflects the interests of labor and of labor parties is contradicted by the way dependency raises spending. At a minimum, worker influence on public policy should be weaker and welfare spending lower in dependent nations, where the power of foreign capital is strong.

We also were generally unable to substantiate the causal impact of political parties on social equality. The redistributive impact of political parties should come through welfare spending advocated by leftist parties. Even assuming that parties actually do increase welfare spending (at best, only partly true), the level of social welfare spending has no effect on income inequality and only limited effects on infant mortality. Moreover, the only direct association we find between leftist governments and income inequality is shown among high-income democracies. This effect, however, is highly sensitive to the nations included in this group and disappears with the addition of new cases. Since welfare spending itself has no direct influence, it is more likely that the effect of leftist governments on income inequality is spuriously due to the power of labor and interindustry wage differentials. Structural forces rather than political intervention emerge as most important for equality.

All of this does not deny the importance of politics. Nonpartisan democratic politics remain central to welfare spending. Groups such as the aged, which transcend the distinction between laborers and capitalists, may pressure representatives of all parties for higher spending, particularly for programs such as pensions and medical care. Thus, the issue is not whether politics are important; clearly, they are (Burstein, 1985). The issue concerns the organizational units of political action relevant to welfare policy. Our findings suggest that the political participation of a variety of socioeconomic and demographic groups, the number and variety of competing parties, and the structural changes in group resources contribute more to variation in public welfare policy than party ideology. Neither structural forces alone nor class-based parties are sufficient to account for growth of the welfare state.

Taken together, the empirical results reveal an apparent contradiction in the functioning of democratic politics: It raises spending but not equality. As shown by the political determinants of welfare spending, democratic procedures have the potential to redistribute income. At the same time, if democratically induced public benefits go to the middle-income groups rather than to the poor, they maintain levels of equality rather than increase them. Transfers across generations occur, but few involve shifts of income from the middle classes to the poor.

From this viewpoint, democracy does not necessarily offer a means to achieve socialism or transformation of the stratification system, although it certainly increases welfare spending. Seen as a competitive struggle for people's votes (Schumpeter, 1975), democracy may instead limit direct class competition. In order to obtain sufficient votes for election, compromises in socialist ideals (or any ideological position) must be made (Downs, 1957; Przeworski, 1980). Once in power, after having compromised to win an election, parties become further deradicalized, either unwilling or unable to implement tangible policy outcomes (Jackman, 1986). Rather than being a group based on some unifying principle or common class position, parties end up more as practical coalitions that act in concert to gain political power (Schumpeter, 1975). Rather than leading to truly redistributive policies, democratic politics and the struggle for votes lead to spending that favors the largest middle-income groups rather than the poor. Politics may have the potential to reshape the stratification system, but in practice, such redistribution has not occurred given the strong political base of the middle class in advanced industrial democracies.

Alternatively, parties may prove unimportant only for the post-World War II period we study. Perhaps all parties can favor welfare spending during periods of prosperity, but during periods of crisis, rightist parties more actively oppose spending, since it represents a drain on scarce profits. Partisanship has been more clearly defined in battles over initial welfare legislation before World War II. Although the major issues of contention between leftist and rightist parties, and the social composition of party support, have changed dramatically since then (Inglehart, 1977, 1987), partisanship may have emerged with renewed strength during the 1980s and may grow in the years to follow as it becomes increasingly difficult to expand the welfare system continually and to maintain economic growth. Indeed, some indication of the negative effects of rightist parties appeared in the late 1970s in our models. Estimation of models for later time periods would provide one means to confirm this possibility.

Additional investigation of the political influence of nonclass groups across a variety of nations could also add to the credibility of these arguments. We have focused on the aged here, while ethnic and linguistic politics may be more important in other arenas. Research on ethnic mobilization offers a profitable research strategy (e.g., Nielsen, 1985), as would research on political participation of the aged. We have not been able to measure their actual political participation here, or the activity of their representative organizations (e.g., Pratt, 1976), but the potential for such study exists.[3]

Issues of research design

One source of the differences between our findings and previous research is methodological in origin. We have explicitly considered longitudinal variation (whenever possible), along with cross-sectional variation across nations. One form of variation is not superior to the other, and it is not possible to use one type of model to make inferences about the other (Firebaugh, 1980). Both types of variation require explanation, and models relying on both types of data are necessary. We assume that variables that explain both changes over time within nations and differences across nations are superior to those that explain only one form of variation. For example, our data on welfare spending in 18 advanced industrial democracies cover a 30-year time span. The growth of percent aged within nations corresponds closely to the growth of welfare spending; also, the percent aged is highest in high-spending nations such as Sweden or Austria. In contrast, GNP explains the trend in spending within nations, but not the differences across nations; rightist government control explains differences across nations but not increases over time within nations. Because variables must explain both types of variation and show some generality in the scope of their relationship with spending, the pooled time-series cross-sectional design provides a more rigorous, stringent test of their influence.

The limited range of variation in the data used by many previous researchers may account for the divergence in findings from our own. The effects of political parties on welfare spending are strongest, and the effects of developmental variables weakest, in cross-sectional studies of high-income nations that limit the range of variation in the industrialism variables. The bias in this approach is shown when inclusion of additional variation in the form of time-series data reduces the effects of political parties and increases those of age structure. A similar example of bias occurs in our study of infant mortality in developed nations. Despite a weak cross-sectional relationship between development and infant mortality, the pooled data show a stronger relationship because of the important time-series relationship. Scholars need to be wary of cross-sectional results, particularly for a homogeneous group of high-income nations.

Other studies come close to the full use of longitudinal and cross-sectional data, but rely on a design that partly eliminates available variation. Several studies examine change over at least two time points for a cross section of nations by using a change score as a dependent variable or allowing a lagged dependent variable and lagged independent variables to predict a dependent variable some years later. Sometimes the period of change covers 10 years or more (Cameron, 1978; Hicks and Swank, 1984), and at other times only one year (Griffin et al., 1983). Although interest in change is fully appropriate for theoretical reasons, such models minimize the influence of developmental or long-term trend variables such as percent aged. The size of the aged population does not account for short-term fluctuations in spending, but it does explain the *levels* of spending that nations have reached. Change models tell us little about the long-term trends that the developmental models are meant to explain.[4] Even with time-series data, then, such statistical models may be less appropriate for testing the influence of developmental variables (Jennings, 1983).

Connected to the lack of variation in previous studies is the problem of small sample size. Even if cross-sectional variation among these nations was substantial, the small number of advanced industrial nations makes multivariate analysis difficult. Many studies base their claim that socialist parties dominate welfare spending on simple models without adequate controls for developmental variables. Some base their conclusions only on correlations (Castles, 1982); others add many variables but reduce the degrees of freedom and maximize the influence of random error. The same holds true for studies of infant mortality in developed nations, where analysis relies on bivariate associations without appropriate controls (Sidel and Sidel, 1983). Our own study of income inequality suffers from the same problem of limited degrees of freedom, since time-series data are not available. Otherwise, the pooled data increase the degrees of freedom and allow more complete and thorough multivariate analysis. The more complex and detailed models that result help to explain the contrast between our results and those of previous studies.

Even with appropriate data, it is still necessary to specify correctly the functional forms of the relationships between development and democracy, welfare spending, and equality. For instance, democracy fails to affect welfare spending when treated as an additive variable; we show instead that its effect is to facilitate other variables. Another example concerns the influence of national product on income inequality. Early studies claimed that dependency determined inequality and eliminated the effect of national product. Yet, these studies failed to specify the curvilinear form of the developmental effect; when treated as a quadratic, GNP dominates the level of inequality and dependency has no effect.

For these reasons, our results are neither startling nor idiosyncratic. When the range of variation is increased, when long-term trends rather than short-term fluctuations are studied, when the degrees of freedom are sufficient for multivariate analysis, and when proper specifications of the variables are made, the results may differ from what has been reported by previous researchers. In these ways, the present study represents a marked improvement over previous studies and yields findings with a sounder methodological basis.

Our methods are, of course, not without limitations. We explicitly rely on abstract measures and generalized propositions that apply to multiple nations and time points rather than on the concrete causal configurations unique to a single nation (see Ragin and Zaret, 1983, for a comparison of the two strategies). Comparative analysis of general patterns has advantages, but more detailed study of single nations may indicate how specific cases may deviate from the general pattern (Griffin et al., 1986; Rice, 1986). Mutliple methodological approaches to comparative research are necessary, and the framework we use can contribute, along with others, to an understanding of the welfare state.

Evaluation of the theories

Throughout this study, we have tied the analyses and results to broader theoretical perspectives on the welfare state. We identified five theories that make clear, divergent, and testable predictions. The classification of these theories, along with identification of how they may overlap and diverge, offers some clarity to the field and allows evaluation of some general perspectives on the welfare state. The demand-based theories address three questions: (1) What are the relative roles of class (e.g., union power, monopoly capital assets) and nonclass (e.g., economic development, age structure) factors in determining social welfare spending? (2) Does social welfare spending reduce or maintain inequality? (3) Does political democracy play an important independent role in a society's level of social welfare spending and equality? Most studies consider only the first question and fail to distinguish between quite different varieties of class or nonclass theories. For instance, monopoly capitalism theories and social democratic (or working-class strength) theories agree on the importance of class structure but differ on whether welfare increases inequality and on the importance of democratic political parties for welfare state growth. Industrialism and interest group politics theories likewise differ over the impact of welfare spending on equality and the influence of democratic politics on the welfare state. Equally important, the nonclass and class theories share important arguments. Only through the study of all three questions can the theories be fully distinguished and tested. Still another theory, the state-centered theory, proposes that the structure of the state, rather than that of groups making demands on the state, is fundamental for the growth of welfare spending and the decline in inequality.

A match of the predictions with the results, although necessarily simplifying complex findings, is straightforward. Generally, nonclass variables determine welfare spending, welfare spending has small and inconsistent effects on equality, and democratic politics influence welfare spending (regardless of the ideology of the party in power) but do not reduce equality. Although all theories find support (depending on the nations, programs, and variables studied), the results best fit the predictions of the interest group politics theory.

The industrialism theory correctly predicts that welfare spending is driven by economic development and demographic change. Yet, the theory does not completely specify the mechanism by which these changes translate into higher spending. Rather than being an economic process by which industrial change automatically leads to public spending for groups in need, growth of the welfare state is inherently political. More than need alone, political organization, mobilization, and power to pressure government bodies allow groups to obtain higher benefits. Perhaps the political aspects of the welfare state are consistent with industrialism arguments; yet, the limited attention to politics identifies a weakness of specification in the theory. In addition, the industrialism theory predicts stronger effects of welfare spending on equality than we find. Welfare spending is assumed to meet the needs of groups with the least income rather than those with the most political power. In fact, the benefits of the welfare state for the needy and for society in general may be overemphasized by the industrialism theory.

The monopoly capitalism version of class theories proves the most difficult to test in a study like this. Still, it fares well in the study of welfare spending in developing nations. Ties to core nations and the capitalist world system increase welfare spending, suggesting that the welfare state emerges most quickly as a form of state capitalism. Among advanced industrial democracies, evidence for state capitalism is weaker, showing only in the effects of unemployment. Otherwise, the monopoly capitalism theory correctly predicts the weak effects of welfare spending on equality, but fails to predict the role of democratic politics on welfare spending.

The social democratic theory, which emphasizes the role of leftist control of the government, fares best in explaining spending for means-tested public assistance programs. It does less well in accounting for variation in the bulk of social welfare spending for contributory-based social insurance spending. Further, the redistributive nature of welfare spending claimed by the theory finds support only in isolated instances. These conclusions may prove valid only for the post-World War II period of welfare expansion, and may apply only to spending levels rather than to the form and qualifying criteria for receipt of benefits, but nonetheless require the arguments of the social democratic theories to be qualified.

In general, both class theories overemphasize the division between labor and capital at the expense of age, religious, ethnic, occupational, and regional differences that define interest and status groups. Our results show that class variables have modest effects on welfare spending and equality: Labor and capital influence, but do not dominate, the welfare state. Class characteristics may be most important when they are based on more than the simple distinction between labor and capital and when they explicitly consider the middle class. We ourselves have referred continually to the importance of middle-income and middle-class groups.[5] Yet, until they can better integrate the importance of a variety of status and interest groups into their conceptions, the class theories provide only a truncated picture of the welfare state.

We are unable to measure and demonstrate important effects of state structure of welfare spending or social equality. Since our tests consist only of a preliminary investigation of diverse and isolated hypotheses, we are not able to evaluate fully the state-based theories, many of which address the historical emergence of welfare programs in specific countries. The explanatory value of state arguments has been shown in historical studies of individual nations rather than in quantitative studies of more recent expansion of the welfare state. The conceptual development of abstract hypotheses that generalize across many nations has proceeded more slowly, and, as some claim (Skocpol, 1985a), may be incapable of capturing important components of state characteristics. Even so, we investigated the influence of state centralization, federalism, corporatism, tax structure, administrative cost, cabinet formation, and electoral cycle – all with little success. Instead, the effects of state structure are shown indirectly, through legal and administrative influences on political participation and party turnout. Moreover, certain state structures, although themselves constant, may facilitate or inhibit the ways in which demands for spending translate into public policy.[6] Further specification of complex interactions, and continued search for relationships that generalize across nations, may yet verify state-centered theories.

The interest group politics theory correctly suggests that democratic processes offer the means for a variety of groups to influence public policy in their favor. Pressures for more spending are greatest where development changes age structure and diversifies interests, but they may also exist in the less developed democratic nations. The aged appear to be especially crucial in these political processes, partly because their size is more easily measured than that of other groups. But other less easily measured but still politically active groups are also important. That welfare spending is politically driven further suggests that it is not directed to those most in need, but rather reflects, in part, political strength. We find support for the interest group theory's prediction that welfare spending has minimal effects on equality. The theory rejects the clear functionalism of industrialism and traditional pluralist theories, as well as the emphasis on balanced competition, equilibrium, and the benefits of the welfare system; spending is not assumed to be functional for all of society, but rather benefits some groups more than others. At the same time, interest group theory avoids oversimplified reliance on the division between capital and labor. Consideration of groups that cut across class groupings thus extends conflict to a more complex, divisive structure. Further activity to develop this theory appears promising.

The theory would predict that forces leading to the growth of the welfare state from 1950 to 1980 remain and will continue to influence welfare spending in the future. Public support for the programs of the welfare state remains strong because, according to the theory, middle-income groups in advanced democracies receive their benefits. In representative democracies, it is difficult to stem the demands of such groups for continued benefits. In this sense, the battle over welfare spending was won long ago: The end of the welfare state, or even major reductions in its scope or benefits, is unlikely (Zald, 1985). In fact, pressures for expansion of the welfare state may grow. The political mobilization of ascriptive groups continues, and their organizational ability to influence policy can only grow (Fox, 1981). Expanded conceptions of social rights will likely bring even more groups into the political arena, lead to the development of more numerous and powerful interest groups (Olson, 1982), and increase demands for spending (Janowitz, 1976).

Notes

1. We note again that overlap exists between social insurance and means-tested programs to the extent that pensions or medical care programs are based on need rather than on universal rights or contributions. Such programs are the exception rather than the rule, and the ILO classification of pensions, medical, unemployment, occupational injury, and family allowance programs as social insurance applies well to the advanced industrial nations.

2. We correlated the 1980 percent aged figure with deficit spending figures reported by the ILO (1985) for the 18 advanced industrial democracies. The ILO measures the excess of social insurance expenditures over receipts from government, employer, and employee contributions. Taken as a percentage of GNP, the size of the deficit has a correlation of 0.6 with percent aged, indicating the potential influence of age structure in creating pressure for spending and difficulties in funding.

3. To explore the important mediating role of the political participation of the aged, scholars might analyze cross-national voting surveys. For instance, the 1975 Eurobarometer survey of a probability sample of adult aged populations in eight nations allows calculation of the percentage of voters over age 65. Denmark shows the highest percentage of the voting population over age 65 (26 percent), whereas Italy shows the lowest (20 percent). In either case, or for those in between, the aged make up a huge part of the active electorate. Further, when percent aged voters is correlated with pension expenditures in constant U.S. dollars per person aged 65 and over, the coefficient for these eight nations is 0.58. Although far from complete, results such as these are consistent with our aggregate-level results and suggest further avenues for research.

4. Change models bias downward the effects of developmental variables. The lagged dependent variable residualizes the dependent variable and the other independent variable of previous levels. Yet, the lagged dependent variable itself is a function of the developmental variables. The design thereby effectively eliminates much variation that may be explained by the developmental variables and exaggerates the importance of the lagged dependent variable.

5. Some use the term *middle class* to refer to a distinct group of workers subject to the hiring power of capital but superordinate over other workers. This contradictory class location thus defines the middle class by its relations to the means of production and to authority (Wright, 1985; Vanneman and Cannon, 1988). With a focus on the aged – a group that does not fit class definitions based on productive relations – we must use the term *middle class* or *middle income* more broadly to refer to a more vaguely defined segment of the population located between the poor and rich, between the workers and capital.

6. Tilton (1986:20) may be suggesting much the same when he argues that ''state structure in and of itself can never be a sufficient explanation of welfare state development, but is a necessary element in any explanation that strives for completeness.''

References

Aaron, Henry. 1967. "Social Security: International Comparisons," *in* Otto Eckstein (ed.), *Studies in the Economics of Income Maintenance*, pp. 13–48. Washington, D.C.: Brookings Institute.

Ahluwalia, Montek S. 1976. "Inequality, Poverty and Development," *Journal of Developmental Economics* 3:307–42.

Alford, Robert R., and Roger Friedland. 1975. "Political Participation and Public Policy," *Annual Review of Sociology* 1:429–79.

Allison, Paul D. 1978. "Measures of Inequality," *American Sociological Review* 43:865–80.

Anderson, James G. 1973. "Causal Models and Social Indicators: Toward the Development of Social Systems Models," *American Sociological Review* 38:285–301.

Atkinson, Anthony B. 1973. "On the Measurement of Inequality," *in* Anthony B. Atkinson (ed.), *Wealth, Income, and Inequality*, pp. 46–68. London: Penguin.

Banks, Arthur S., and William Overstreet (eds.). 1980. *Political Handbook of the World*. New York: McGraw-Hill.

Barfield, Richard E., and James Morgan. 1969. *Early Retirement: The Decision and the Experience*. Ann Arbor: Institute for Social Research, University of Michigan.

Barrett, Richard E., and Martin King Whyte. 1982. "Dependency Theory and Taiwan: Analysis of a Deviant Case," *American Journal of Sociology* 87:1064–89.

Becker, Gary S. 1983. "A Theory of Competition Among Pressure Groups for Political Influence," *The Quarterly Journal of Economics* 98:371–401.

Bell, Daniel. 1973. *The Coming of Post-Industrial Society*. New York: Basic Books.

    1976. *The Cultural Contradictions of Capitalism*. New York: Basic Books.

Belsley, David A., Edwin Kuh, and Roy E. Welsch. 1980. *Regression Diagnostics: Identifying Influential Data and Sources of Collinearity*. New York: John Wiley.

Berger, Peter L. 1986. *The Capitalist Revolution: Fifty Propositions About Prosperity, Equality, and Liberty*. New York: Basic Books.

Berk, Richard A., Donnie M. Hoffman, Judith E. Maki, David Rauma, and Herbert Wong. 1979. "Estimation Procedures for Pooled Cross-Sectional and Time Series Data," *Evaluation Quarterly* 3:385–410.

Berry, Jeffrey M. 1984. *The Interest Group Society*. Boston: Little, Brown.

Bird, Richard M. 1971. "Wagner's Law of Expanding State Activity," *Public Finances* 26:1–26.

Block, Fred. 1977. "The Ruling Class Does not Rule: Notes on the Marxist Theory of the State," *Socialist Revolution* 33:6–27.

Blumberg, Paul. 1980. *Inequality in an Age of Decline*. Oxford: Oxford University Press.

Bollen, Kenneth A. 1980. "Issues in the Comparative Measurement of Political Democracy," *American Sociological Review* 45:370–90.

    1983. "World System Position, Dependency, and Democracy: The Cross-National Evidence," *American Sociological Review* 48:468–79.

    and Burke Grandjean. 1981. "The Dimension(s) of Democracy: Further Issues in the Measurement and Effects of Political Democracy," *American Sociological Review* 46:651–9.

and Robert W. Jackman. 1985a. "Political Democracy and the Size Distribution of Income," *American Sociological Review* 50:438–57.

and Robert W. Jackman. 1985b. "Regression Diagnostics: An Expository Treatment of Outliers and Influential Cases," *Sociological Methods and Research* 13:510–42.

and Robert W. Jackman. 1988. "Democracies, Dichotomies, and Stability: Back to the Future." Unpublished paper, University of North Carolina.

Borcherding, Thomas E. 1985. "The Causes of Government Expenditure Growth: A Survey of the U.S. Evidence," *Journal of Public Economics* 28:359–82.

Bornschier, Volker. 1981. "Comment," *International Studies Quarterly* 25:283–8.

and Christopher Chase-Dunn. 1985. *Transnational Corporations and Underdevelopment.* New York: Praeger.

Christopher Chase-Dunn, and Richard Rubinson. 1978. "Cross-National Evidence of the Effects of Foreign Investment and Aid on Economic Growth and Inequality: A Survey of Findings and Reanalysis," *American Journal of Sociology* 84:651–83.

and Peter Heintz (eds.). 1979. *Compendium of Data for World-System Analysis.* Zurich: University of Zurich Press.

Boskin, Michael J. 1986. *Too Many Promises: The Uncertain Future of Social Security.* Homewood, Ill.: Dow-Jones-Irwin.

Boulier, Bryan L. 1977. "Population Policy and Income Distribution," *in* Charles R. Frank and Richard C. Webb (eds.), *Income Distribution and Growth in the Less-Developed Countries,* pp. 159–213. Washington, D.C.: The Brookings Institute.

Bowen, William G., and T. Aldrich Finegan. 1969. *The Economics of Labor Force Participation.* Princeton, N.J.: Princeton University Press.

Bradshaw, York. 1985. "Dependent Development in Black Africa: A Cross-National Study," *American Sociological Review* 50:195–206.

Brittan, Samuel 1975. "The Economic Contradictions of Democracy," *British Journal of Political Science* 5:129–59.

Browne, William P., and Laura Katz Olson (eds.). 1983. *Aging and Public Policy: The Politics of Growing Old in America.* Westport, Conn.: Greenwood Press.

Buchanan, James M., and Gordon Tullock (eds.). 1980. *Toward a Theory of the Rent-Seeking Society.* College Station: Texas A&M Press.

Burkhauser, Richard V., and Jennifer L. Warlick. 1981. "Disentangling the Annuity from the Redistributive Aspects of Social Security in the United States." *Review of Income and Wealth* 27:401–22.

Buroway, Michael. 1982. "Introduction: The Resurgence of Marxism in American Sociology," *American Journal of Sociology* 88(Suppl.):1–29.

Burstein, Paul. 1985. *Discrimination, Jobs, and Politics: The Struggle for Equal Opportunity in the United States Since the New Deal.* Chicago: University of Chicago Press.

Caldwell, J. C. 1979. "Education as a Factor in Mortality Decline – An Examination of Nigerian Data," *Population Studies* 33:395–413.

Cameron, David R. 1978. "The Expansion of the Public Economy: A Comparative Analysis," *American Political Science Review* 72:1243–61.

Castles, Francis G. 1982. "The Impact of Parties on Public Expenditures," *in* Francis G. Castles (ed.), *The Impact of Parties,* pp. 21–95. Beverly Hills, Calif.: Sage.

1985. *The Working Class and Welfare: Reflections on the Political Development of the Welfare State in Australia and New Zealand, 1890–1980.* London: Allen & Unwin.

and R. D. McKinlay. 1979. "Public Welfare Provision, and the Sheer Futility of the Sociological Approach to Politics," *British Journal of Political Science* 9:157–72.

Cates, Jerry R. 1983. *Insuring Inequality: Administrative Leadership in Social Security, 1935–54.* Ann Arbor: University of Michigan Press.

Cawson, Alan. 1985. "Introduction: Varieties of Corporatism: The Importance of the Meso-Level of Interest Intermediation.'' *in* Alan Cawson (ed.), *Organized Interests and the State*, pp. 1–22. London: Sage.

Chase-Dunn, Christopher. 1975. ''The Effects of International Economic Dependence on Development and Inequality: A Cross-National Study,'' *American Sociological Review* 40:720–38.

Chirot, Daniel. 1977. *Social Change in the Twentieth Century*. New York: Harcourt Brace Jovanovich.

1986. *Social Change in the Modern Era*. New York: Harcourt Brace Jovanovich.

Clark, Robert L., and John A. Menefee. 1981. ''Federal Expenditures for the Elderly: Past and Future,'' *The Gerontologist* 21:132–7.

and Joseph J. Spengler. 1980. *The Economics of Individual and Population Aging*. Cambridge: Cambridge University Press.

Cohen, Wilbur J., and Milton Friedman. 1972. *Social Security: Universal or Selective?* Washington D.C.: American Enterprise Institute for Public Policy Research.

Connor, Walter D. 1979. *Socialism, Politics, and Equality: Hierarchy and Change in Eastern Europe and the USSR*. New York: Columbia University Press.

Coughlin, Richard M. 1979. ''Social Policy and Ideology: Public Opinion in Eight Rich Nations,'' *Comparative Social Research* 2:3–40.

and Philip K. Armour. 1983. ''Sectorial Differentiation in Social Security Spending in the OECD Nations,'' *Comparative Social Research* 6:175–99.

Crystal, Stephen. 1982. *America's Old Age Crisis: Public Policy and the Two Worlds of Aging*. New York: Basic Books.

Cutler, Neal E. 1977. ''Demographic, Social-Psychological, and Political Factors in the Politics of Aging: A Foundation for Research in 'Political Gerontology,' '' *American Political Science Review* 71:1011–25.

1981. ''Political Characteristics of Elderly Cohorts in the Twenty-First Century,'' *in* Sara B. Kiesler, James N. Morgan, and Valerie Kincade Oppenheimer (eds.), *Aging: Social Change*, pp. 127–57. New York: Academic Press.

Cutright, Phillips. 1965. ''Political Structure, Economic Development and National Social Security Programs,'' *American Journal of Sociology* 70:539–55.

1967. ''Income Redistribution: A Cross-National Analysis,'' *Social Forces* 46:180–90.

Dahl, Robert A. 1956. *A Preface to Democratic Theory*. Chicago: University of Chicago Press.

Danziger, Sheldon, Robert H. Haverman, and Robert Plotnick. 1981. ''How Income Transfer Programs Affect Work, Savings, and the Income Distribution: A Critical Review,'' *Journal of Economic Literature* 19:975–1028.

Jacques van der Gaag, Eugene Smolensky, and Michael K. Taussig. 1984. ''Implications of the Relative Economic Status of the Elderly for Transfer Policy,'' *in* Henry J. Aaron and Gary Burtless (eds.), *Retirement and Economic Behavior*, pp. 175–96. Washington, D.C.: Brookings Institute.

and Peter Gottschalk. 1986. ''Do Rising Tides Lift All Boats? The Impact of Secular and Cyclical Changes in Poverty,'' *American Economic Review* 76:405–10.

and Daniel H. Weinberg (eds.). 1986. *Fighting Poverty: What Works and What Doesn't*. Cambridge, Mass.: Harvard University Press.

Davis, Christopher, and Murray Feshbach. 1980. *Rising Infant Mortality in the USSR in the 1970s*. U.S. Bureau of the Census, Series P-95, No. 74. Washington, D.C.: U.S. Government Printing Office.

Davis, Kingsley, and Pietronella van den Oever. 1981. ''Age Relations and Public Policy in Advanced Industrial Societies,'' *Population and Development Review* 7:1–18.

Delacroix, Jacques, and Charles C. Ragin, 1981. ''Structural Blockage: A Cross-National Study of Economic Dependency, State Efficacy, and Underdevelopment,'' *American Journal of Sociology* 86:1311–47.

de Tocqueville, Alexis. 1945. *Democracy in America*. New York: Vintage Books.

Devine, Joel A. 1983. "Fiscal Policy and Class Income Inequality: The Distributional Consequences of Government Revenues and Expenditures in the United States, 1949–1976," *American Sociological Review* 48:606–22.

1985. "State and State Expenditures: Determinants of Social Investment and Social Consumption Spending in the Postwar United States," *American Sociological Review* 50:150–65.

and William L. Canak. 1986. "Redistribution in a Bifurcated Welfare State: Quintile Shares and the U.S. Case," *Social Problems* 33:391–406.

DeViney, Stanley. 1983. "Characteristics of the State and the Expansion of Public Social Expenditures," *Comparative Social Research* 6:151–73.

1984. "The Political Economy of Public Pensions: A Cross-National Analysis," *Journal of Political and Military Sociology* 12:295–310.

1987. "Public Pensions and Income Inequality: A Cross-National Analysis." Presented at the Annual Meetings of the American Sociological Association, Chicago.

and Robert Nash Parker. 1984. "Democracy, Political Struggle, State Policy, and Income Distribution: A Comparative Analysis." Presented at the Annual Meetings of the American Sociological Association, San Antonio.

Dixon, John. 1986. *Social Security Traditions and Their Global Applications*. Belconnen, Australia: International Fellowship for Social and Economic Development.

Downs, Anthony. 1957. *An Economic Theory of Democracy*. New York: Harper & Row.

Dryzek, John. 1978. "Politics, Economics, and Inequality: A Cross-National Analysis," *European Journal of Political Research* 6:399–410.

Dubos, Rene. 1959. *Mirage of Health: Utopias, Progress, and Biological Change*. New York: Harper & Row.

Duncan, Greg J., Martha Hill, and Willard Rodgers. 1986. "The Changing Fortunes of Young and Old," *American Demographics* 8(8):26–33.

Eberstadt, Nick. 1981. "The Health Crisis in the USSR," *New York Review of Books* 28(2):23–31.

Eisenstadt, S. N., and Ora Ahimeir (eds.). 1985. *The Welfare State and Its Aftermath*. London: Croom Helm.

Ellwood, David T., and Lawrence Summers. 1986. "Poverty in America: Is Welfare the Answer or the Problem?", *in* Sheldon H. Danziger and Daniel H. Weinberg (eds.), *Fighting Poverty: What Works and What Doesn't*, pp. 78–105. Cambridge, Mass.: Harvard University Press.

Entwisle, Barbara, and C. K. Winegarden. 1984. "Fertility and Pension Programs in LDCs: A Model of Mutual Reinforcement," *Economic Development and Cultural Change* 32:331–54.

Esping-Andersen, Gosta. 1981. "Politics Against Markets: De-Commodification in Social Policy." Paper Presented at the Arne Ryde Symposium, Lund University, Lund, Sweden.

1985a. *Politics Against Markets: The Social Democratic Road to Power*. Princeton, N.J.: Princeton University Press.

1985b. "Power and Distributional Regimes," *Politics and Society* 14:223–56.

Estes, Carroll L. 1979. *The Aging Enterprise*. San Francisco: Jossey-Bass.

Estes, Richard J. 1984. *The Social Progress of Nations*. New York: Praeger.

Evans, Peter. 1979. *Dependent Development: The Alliance of Multinational, State and Local Capital in Brazil*. Princeton, N.J.: Princeton University Press.

Firebaugh, Glenn. 1980. "Cross-National versus Historical Regression Models: Conditions of Equivalence in Comparative Research," *Comparative Social Research* 3:333–44.

Fischer, Paul. 1978. "The Social Security Crisis: An International Dilemma," *Aging and Work* 1:1–14.

Flegg, A. T. 1982. "Inequality of Income, Illiteracy, and Medical Care as Determinants of Infant Mortality in Underdeveloped Countries," *Population Studies* 36:441–58.

Foner, Anne. 1974. "Age Stratification and Age Conflict in Political Life," *American Sociological Review* 39:187–96.

Form, William. 1976. *Blue-Collar Stratification: Autoworkers in Four Countries*. Princeton, N.J.: Princeton University Press.

——— 1979. "Comparative Industrial Sociology and the Convergence Hypothesis," *Annual Review of Sociology* 5:1–25.

——— 1982. "Self-Employed Manual Workers: Petty Bourgeois or Working Class?", *Social Forces* 60:1050–69.

——— 1985. *Divided We Stand: Working Class Stratification in America*. Urbana: University of Illinois Press.

Fox, Richard G. 1981. "The Welfare State and the Political Mobilization of the Elderly," *in* Sara B. Kiesler, James N. Morgan, and Valerie Oppenheimer (eds.), *Aging: Social Change*, pp. 159–82. New York: Academic Press.

Friedland, Roger, and Jimy Sanders. 1985. "The Public Economy and Economic Growth in Western Market Economies," *American Sociological Review* 50:421–37.

——— 1986. "Private and Social Wage Expansion in the Advanced Market Economies," *Theory and Society* 15:193–222.

Fuchs, Victor R. 1974. *Who Shall Live? Health, Economics, and Social Choice*. New York: Basic Books.

Fuller, Wayne A., and George E. Battese. 1974. "Estimatio of Linear Models with Crossed-Error Structure," *Journal of Econometrics* 2:67–78.

Furniss, Norman. 1986. "The Welfare State between 'State' and 'Civil Society,'" *in* Norman Furniss (ed.), *Futures for the Welfare State*, pp. 307–403. Bloomington: Indiana University Press.

Gagliani, Giorgio. 1987. "Income Inequality and Economic Development," *Annual Review of Sociology* 13:313–34.

Galtung, Johan. 1971. "A Structural Theory of Imperialism," *Journal of Peace Research* 8:102–16.

Geronimus, Arline T. 1986. "The Effects of Race, Residence, and Prenatal Care on the Relationship of Maternal Age to Neonatal Mortality," *American Journal of Public Health* 76:1416–21.

Gilder, George. 1981. *Wealth and Poverty*. New York: Bantam Books.

Gist, John R. (ed.) 1988. *Social Security and Economic Well-Being Across Generations*. Washington, D.C.: Public Policy Institute, American Association of Retired Persons.

Gold, David A., Clarence Y. H. Lo, and Erik Olin Wright. 1975. "Recent Developments in Marxist Theories of the Capitalist State," *Monthly Review* 2:29–43.

Goldthorpe, John J. 1969. "Social Stratification in Industrial Society," *in* Celia S. Heller (ed.), *Structured Social Inequality: A Reader in Comparative Social Stratification*, pp. 452–65. London: Macmillan.

Gortmaker, Steven L. 1979. "Poverty and Infant Mortality in the United States," *American Sociological Review* 44:280–97.

Gough, Ian. 1979. *The Political Economy of the Welfare State*. London: Macmillan.

Griffin, Larry J., Joel A. Devine, and Michael Wallace. 1983. "On the Economic and Political Determinants of Welfare Spending in the Post–World War II Era," *Politics and Society* 12:331–72.

——— and Kevin Leicht. 1986. "Politicizing Welfare Expenditures in the United States," *in* Norman Furniss (ed.), *Futures for the Welfare State*, pp. 320–56. Bloomington: Indiana University Press.

——— Pamela Barnhouse Walters, Philip O'Connell, and Edward Moor. 1986. "Methodological Innovations in the Analysis of Welfare-State Development: Pooling Cross Sections and Time Series," *in* Norman Furniss (ed.), *Futures for the Welfare State*, pp. 101–38. Bloomington: Indiana University Press.

Gronbjerg, Kirsten A. 1977. *Mass Society and the Extension of Welfare, 1960–1970*. Chicago: University of Chicago Press.

Grossman, Michael, and Steven Jacobowitz. 1981. "Variations in Infant Mortality Rates Among Counties of the United States: The Roles of Public Policies and Programs," *Demography* 18:695–713.

Hannan, Michael T., and Alice A. Young. 1977. "Estimation in Panel Models: Results on Pooling Cross-Sections and Time-Series," *in* David Heise (ed.), *Sociological Methodology 1977*, pp. 52–83. San Francisco: Jossey-Bass.

Hasenfield, Yeheskel, Jane A. Rafferty, and Mayer N. Zald. 1987. "The Welfare State, Citizenship, and Bureaucratic Encounters," *Annual Review of Sociology* 13:387–415.

Hechter, Michael (ed.). 1983. *The Micro Foundations of Macro-Sociology.* Philadelphia: Temple University Press.

Hedstrom, Peter, and Stein Ringen. 1987. "Age and Income in Contemporary Society," *Journal of Social Policy* 16:227–40.

Hewitt, Christopher. 1977. "The Effect of Political Democracy and Social Democracy on Equality in Industrial Societies: A Cross-National Comparison," *American Sociological Review* 42:450–64.

Hibbs, Douglas A., Jr. 1978. "On the Political Economy of Long-Run Trends in Strike Activity," *British Journal of Political Science* 8:153–75.

Hicks, Alexander, and Duane Swank. 1984. "On the Political Economy of Welfare Expansion: A Comparative Analysis of 18 Advanced Capitalist Democracies, 1960–1971," *Comparative Political Studies* 17:81–120.

and Duane Swank. 1985. "The Determinants and Redistributive Impacts of State Welfare Spending in the Advanced Capitalist Democracies, 1960–1980," *in* Norman J. Vig and Steven E. Schier (eds.), *Political Economy in Western Democracies*, pp. 115–39. New York: Holmes & Meier.

Duane H. Swank, and Martin Ambuhl. 1989. "Welfare Expansion Revisited: Policy Routines and the Mediation by Party, Class, and Crisis, 1957–1982." Forthcoming, *European Journal of Political Research.*

Hobcraft, J. N., J. W. McDonald, and S. O. Rutstein. 1984. "Socio-Economic Factors in Infant and Child Mortality: A Cross-National Comparison," *Population Studies* 38:193–223.

Hodson, Randy, Paul Schervish, and Robin Stryker. 1988. "Class Interests and Class Fractions in the Late Twentieth Century," *Research in Politics and Society* 3:191–220.

Hollingsworth, J. Rogers, and Robert A. Hanneman. 1982. "Working-Class Power and the Political Economy of Western Capitalist Societies," *Comparative Social Research* 5:61–80.

Hudson, Robert B. 1978. "The 'Graying' of the Federal Budget and the Consequences for Old Age Policy," *The Gerontologist* 18:428–40.

and John Strate. 1985. "Aging and Political Systems," *in* Robert H. Binstock and Ethel Shanas (eds.), *Handbook of Aging and the Social Sciences*, pp. 554–85. New York: Van Nostrand Reinhold.

Inglehart, Ronald. 1977. *The Silent Revolution: Changing Values and Political Styles Among Western Publics.* Princeton, N.J.: Princeton University Press.

1987. "Value Change in Industrial Societies," *American Political Science Review* 81:1289–1303.

Inkeles, Alex. 1981. "Convergence and Divergence in Industrial Societies," *in* Mustafa O. Attir, Burkhart Holzner, and Zdenek Suda (eds.), *Directions of Change: Modernization Theory, Research, and Realities*, pp. 3–38. New York: Westview Press.

and Larry Sirowy. 1983. "Convergent and Divergent Trends in National Educational Systems," *Social Forces* 62:303–33.

International Labour Office. 1985. *The Cost of Social Security.* Geneva: International Labour Organization.

Isaac, Larry, and William R. Kelly. 1981. "Racial Insurgency, the State, and Welfare Expansion:

Local and National Evidence from the Postwar United States," *American Journal of Sociology* 86:1348–86.

Jackman, Robert W. 1975. *Politics and Social Equality: A Comparative Analysis.* New York: John Wiley.

1980. "Socialist Parties and Income Inequality in Western Industrial Societies," *The Journal of Politics* 42:135–49.

1986. "Elections and the Democratic Class Struggle," *World Politics* 39:123–46.

1987. "Political Institutions and Voter Turnout in the Industrial Democracies," *American Political Science Review* 81:405–23.

Janowitz, Morris. 1976. *Social Control of the Welfare State.* Chicago: University of Chicago Press.

1985. "Youth and the Welfare State in the United States," *in* S. N. Eisenstadt and Ora Ahimeir (eds.), *The Welfare State and Its Aftermath,* pp. 93–108. London: Croom Helm.

Jencks, Christopher. 1985. "Methodological Problems in Studying 'Military Keynesianism,' " *American Journal of Sociology* 91:373–9.

Jennings, Edward T., Jr. 1983. "Racial Insurgency, the State, and Welfare Expansion: A Critical Comment and Reanalysis," *American Journal of Sociology* 88:1220–36.

Jones, Catherine. 1985. "Types of Welfare Capitalism," *Government and Opposition,* 20:328–42.

Judge, George G., William E. Griffiths, R. Carter Hill, and Tsoung-Chao Lee. 1980. *The Theory and Practice of Econometrics.* New York: John Wiley.

Kelley, Johnathon, Ian McAllister, and Anthony Mughan. 1985. "The Decline of Class Revisited: Class and Party in England, 1964–1979," *American Political Science Review* 79:719–36.

Kerr, Clark. 1983. *The Future of Industrial Societies: Convergence or Continuing Diversity?* Cambridge, Mass.: Harvard University Press.

J. T. Dunlop, Frederick Harbison, and Charles Myers. 1964. *Industrialism and Industrial Man.* New York: Oxford University Press.

Khoury, Muin J., J. David Erikson, and Myron J. Adams. 1984. "Trends in Postneonatal Mortality in the United States: 1962 Through 1978," *Journal of the American Medical Association* 252: 367–72.

Kmenta, Jan. 1971. *Elements of Econometrics.* New York: Macmillan.

Korpi, Walter. 1983. *The Democratic Class Struggle.* London: Routledge & Kegan Paul.

Kristol, Irving. 1978. *Two Cheers for Capitalism.* New York: Basic Books.

Kuznets, Simon, 1955. "Economic Growth and Income Inequality," *American Economic Review* 45:1–28.

1963. "Quantitative Aspects of the Economic Growth of Nations: VIII. Distribution of Income by Size," *Economic Development and Cultural Change* 11:1–80.

Larkey, Patrick D., Chandler Stolp, and Mark Winer. 1981. "Theorizing About Growth of Government: A Research Assessment," *Journal of Public Policy* 1:157–220.

Lee, Kuang Sun, Nigel Paneth, Lawrence M. Carter, and Mark Pearlman. 1980. "The Very Low-Birthweight Rate: Principal Predictor of Neonatal Mortality Rates in Industrial Populations," *Journal of Pediatrics* 97:759–64.

Le Grand, Julian. 1982. *The Strategy of Equality.* London: George Allen & Unwin.

Lehner, Franz, and Ulrich Widmaier. 1983. "Market Failure and Growth of Government: A Sociological Explanation," *in* Charles Lewis Taylor (ed.), *Why Governments Grow,* pp. 240–60. Beverly Hills, Calif.: Sage.

Lenski, Gerhard. 1966. *Power and Privilege.* Toronto: McGraw-Hill.

Levy, Frank. 1987. *Dollars and Dreams: The Changing American Income Distribution.* New York: Russell Sage.

Lijphart, Arend. 1980. "Language, Religion, Class, and Party Choice: Belgium, Canada, Switzerland, and South Africa Compared," *in* Richard Rose (ed.), *Electoral Participation: A Comparative Analysis,* pp. 283–328. Beverly Hills, Calif.: Sage.

1984. *Democracies: Patterns of Majoritarian and Consensus Government in Twenty-One Countries*. New Haven, Conn.: Yale University Press.

Lindbolm, Charles E. 1977. *Politics and Markets: The World's Political-Economic Systems*. New York: Basic Books.

Lindert, Peter H. 1986. "Unequal English Wealth Since 1670," *Journal of Political Economy* 94:1127–62.

Lipset, Seymour Martin. 1964. *Political Man: The Social Bases of Politics*. Garden City, N.Y.: Anchor Books.

   1981. *Political Man* (expanded and updated edition). Baltimore: Johns Hopkins University Press.

Lipton, Michael. 1977. *Why Poor People Stay Poor: A Study of Urban Bias in World Development*. Cambridge, Mass.: Harvard University Press.

Lowi, Theodore J. 1979. *The End of Liberalism: The Second Republic in the United States*. New York: Norton.

Marshall, T. H. 1964. *Class, Citizenship, and Social Development*. Chicago: University of Chicago Press.

McFarland, Andrew S. 1987. "Interest Groups and Theories of Power in America," *British Journal of Political Science* 17:129–47.

Meltzer, Allan H., and Scott F. Richard. 1981. "A Rational Theory of the Size of Government," *Journal of Political Economy* 89:914–27.

Midgley, James. 1984. *Social Security, Inequality, and the Third World*. New York: John Wiley.

Miliband, Ralph. 1969. *The State in Capitalist Society*. New York: Basic Books.

Miller, Michael K., and C. Shannon Stokes. 1978. "Health Status, Health Resources, and Consolidated Structural Parameters: Implications for Public Health Care Policy," *Journal of Health and Social Behavior* 19:263–79.

Mishra, Ramesh. 1984. *The Welfare State in Crisis: Social Thought and Social Change*. New York: St. Martin's Press.

Moon, Bruce E., and William J. Dixon. 1985. "Politics, the State, and Basic Human Needs: A Cross-National Study," *American Journal of Political Science* 29:661–95.

Moon, Marilyn. 1986. "Impact of the Reagan Years on the Distribution of Income of the Elderly," *The Gerontologist* 26(1):32–7.

Morris, Morris David. 1979. *Measuring the Condition of the World's Poor: The Physical Quality of Life Index*. New York: Pergamon Press.

Mosteller, Frederick, and John W. Tukey. 1977. *Data Analysis and Regression*. Reading, Mass.: Addison-Wesley.

Mueller, Dennis C. 1979. *Public Choice*. Cambridge: Cambridge University Press.

   and Peter Murrell. 1985. "Interest Groups and the Political Economy of Government Size," *in* Francesco Forte and Alan Peacock (eds.), *Public Expenditures and Government Growth*, pp. 13–36. Oxford: Blackwell.

Muller, Edward N. 1988. "Democracy, Economic Development, and Income Inequality," *American Sociological Review* 53:50–68.

Murray, Charles. 1984. *Losing Ground: American Social Policy 1950–1980*. New York: Basic Books.

Murrell, Peter. 1984. "An Examination of the Factors Affecting the Formation of Interest Groups in OECD Countries," *Public Choice* 43:151–71.

Myles, John. 1984. *Old Age in the Welfare State: The Political Economy of Public Pensions*. Boston: Little, Brown.

Nagel, Joane, and Susan Olzak. 1982. "Ethnic Mobilization in New and Old States: An Extension of the Competition Model," *Social Problems* 30:127–43.

Nelson, Gary. 1983. "Tax Expenditures for the Elderly," *The Gerontologist* 23:471–8.

Neugarten, Bernice L. 1974. "Age Groups in American Society and the Rise of the Young-Old," *Annals of the American Academy of Political and Social Science* 415:187–98.

(ed.). 1982. *Age or Need: Public Policies for Older People.* Beverly Hills, Calif.: Sage.

Nielsen, Francois. 1980. "The Flemish Movement in Belgium after World War II: A Dynamic Analysis," *American Sociological Review* 45:76–94.

——— 1985. "Toward a Theory of Ethnic Solidarity in Modern Societies," *American Sociological Review* 50:133–49.

——— 1987. "Subnationalism and Collective Action," *Contemporary Sociology* 16:57–9.

Niskanen, William A. 1971. *Bureaucracy and Representative Government.* Chicago: Aldine.

North, Douglas C. 1985. "The Growth of Government in the United States: An Economic Historian's Perspective," *Journal of Public Economics* 28:383–99.

O'Connor, James. 1973. *The Fiscal Crisis of the State.* New York: St. Martin's Press.

Offe, Claus. 1972. "Advanced Capitalism in the Welfare State," *Politics and Society* 7:479–88.

——— 1984. *Contradictions of the Welfare State.* Cambridge: Massachusetts Institute of Technology Press.

O'Hare, William P. 1985. *Poverty in America: Trends and New Patterns.* Washington, D.C.: Population Reference Bureau.

Olson, Laura Katz. 1982. *The Political Economy of Aging: The State, Private Power, and Social Welfare.* New York: Columbia University Press.

Olson, Mancur. 1963. "Rapid Growth as a Destabilizing Force," *Journal of Economic History* 23:529–52.

——— 1965. *The Logic of Collective Action: Public Goods and the Theory of Groups.* Cambridge, Mass.: Harvard University Press.

——— 1982. *The Rise and Decline of Nations: Economic Growth, Stagflation, and Social Rigidities.* New Haven, Conn.: Yale University Press.

Olzak, Susan. 1982. "Ethnic Mobilization in Quebec," *Ethnic and Racial Studies* 5:253–75.

Orloff, Ann Shola, and Theda Skocpol. 1984. "Why Not Equal Protection? Explaining the Politics of Public Social Spending in Britain, 1900–1911, and the United States, 1890s–1920," *American Sociological Review* 49:726–50.

Page, Benjamin I. 1983. *Who Gets What from Government.* Berkeley: University of California Press.

Pampel, Fred C. 1981. *Social Change and the Aged: Recent Trends in the United States.* Lexington, Mass.: Lexington Books.

——— and Vijayan Pillai. 1986. "Patterns and Determinants of Infant Mortality in Developed Nations, 1950–1975," *Demography* 23:525–42.

——— and Robin Stryker. 1989. "Age Structure, the State, and Social Welfare Spending: A Reanalysis." Forthcoming, *British Journal of Sociology.*

——— and John B. Williamson. 1985. "Age Structure, Politics, and Cross-National Patterns of Public Pension Expenditures," *American Sociological Review* 50:782–98.

Pamuk, E. R. 1985. "Social Class Inequality in Mortality from 1921 to 1972 in England and Wales," *Population Studies* 39:17–31.

Parkin, Frank. 1971. *Class Inequality and Political Order: Social Stratification in Capitalist and Communist Societies.* New York: Praeger Press.

——— 1979. *Marxism and Class Theory: A Bourgeois Critique.* New York: Columbia University Press.

Peltzman, Sam. 1980. "The Growth of Government," *The Journal of Law and Economics* 23:209–88.

Pindyck, Robert S., and Daniel L. Rubinfeld. 1976. *Economic Models and Econometric Forecasts.* New York: McGraw-Hill.

Piven, Francis Fox, and Richard A. Cloward. 1971. *Regulating the Poor: The Functions of Social Welfare.* New York: Vintage Books.

——— 1982. *The New Class War.* New York: Pantheon Press.

Plotnick, Robert. 1984. "The Redistributive Impact of Cash Transfers," *Public Finance Quarterly* 12:27–50.

190

References

Poulantzas, Nicos. 1973. *Political Power and Social Classes*. London: NLB.

    1978. *State, Power, Socialism*. London: NLB.

Powell, G. Bingham, Jr. 1986. "American Voter Turnout in Comparative Perspective," *American Political Science Review* 80:17–43.

Pratt, Henry J. 1976. *The Grey Lobby*. Chicago: University of Chicago Press.

Preston, Samuel H. 1975. "The Changing Relationship between Mortality and Level of Economic Development," *Population Studies* 29:231–48.

    1977. "Mortality Trends," *Annual Review of Sociology* 3:163–78.

    1984. "Children and the Elderly: Divergent Paths for America's Dependents," *Demography* 21:435–57.

Pryor, Frederic. 1968. *Public Expenditures in Communist and Capitalist Nations*. Homewood, Ill.: Irwin.

Przeworski, Adam. 1980. "Social Democracy as an Historical Phenomena," *New Left Review* 122:27–58.

    1985. *Capitalism and Social Democracy*. Cambridge: Cambridge University Press.

    and Michael Wallerstein. 1988. "Structural Dependence of the State on Capital," *American Political Science Review* 82:11–29.

Quadagno, Jill S. 1984. "Welfare Capitalism and the Social Security Act of 1935," *American Sociological Review* 49:632–47.

Quinn, Joseph F. 1987. "The Economic Status of the Elderly: Beware of the Mean," *Review of Income and Wealth* 33:63–82.

Ragin, Charles D. 1979. "Ethnic Political Mobilization: The Welsh Case," *American Sociological Review* 44:619–35.

    and David Zaret. 1983. "Theory and Method in Comparative Sociology: Two Research Strategies," *Social Forces* 61:731–54.

Rainwater, Lee, Martin Rein, and Joseph Schwartz. 1986. *Income Packaging in the Welfare State: A Comparative Study of Family Income*. Oxford: Clarendon Press.

Rein, Martin, and Lee Rainwater. 1986. *Public/Private Interplay in Social Protection: A Comparative Study*. Armonk, N.Y.: M. E. Sharpe.

Reynolds, Morgan, and Eugene Smolensky. 1977. *Public Expenditures, Taxes, and the Distribution of Income: The United States, 1950, 1961, 1970*. New York: Academic Press.

Rice, Tom W. 1986. "The Determinants of Western European Government Growth, 1950–1980," *Comparative Political Studies* 19:233–57.

Rodgers, G. B. 1979. "Income and Inequality as Determinants of Mortality: An International Cross-Sectional Analysis," *Population Studies* 33:343–51.

Rosa, Jean-Jacques. 1982. "Social Security and the Future," *in* Jean-Jacques Rosa (ed.), *The World Crisis in Social Security*, p. 1–8. San Francisco: Institute for Contemporary Studies.

Rose, Richard. 1984a. "The Programme Approach to the Growth of Government," *British Journal of Political Science* 15:1–28.

    1986b. *Understanding Big Government: The Programme Approach*. London: Sage.

Rubinson, Richard. 1976. "The World-Economy and the Distribution of Income within States: A Cross-National Study," *American Sociological Review* 41:638–59.

    and Dan Quinlan. 1977. "Democracy and Social Inequality: A Reanalysis," *American Sociological Review* 42:611–23.

Sawyer, Malcolm. 1976. "Income Distribution in OECD Countries," *OECD Occasional Papers*, July.

Schlesinger, Joseph A. 1984. "On the Theory of Party Organization," *The Journal of Politics* 46:369–400.

Schmitter, Philippe C. 1982. "Reflections on Where the Theory of Neo-Corporatism Has Gone and Where the Praxis of Neo-Corporatism May Be Going," *in* G. Lehmbruch and Philippe G.

Schmitter (eds.), *Patterns of Corporatist Policy-Making*, pp. 259–79. Beverly Hills, Calif.: Sage.

Schulz, James H. 1980. *The Economics of Aging*, 2nd ed. Belmont, Calif.: Wadsworth.

Schumpeter, Joseph A. 1975 [1942]. *Capitalism, Socialism, and Democracy*. New York: Harper & Row.

Shalev, Michael. 1983. "The Social Democratic Model and Beyond: Two Generations of Comparative Research on the Welfare State," *Comparative Social Research* 6:315–52.

Shin, Eui Hang. 1975. "Economic and Social Correlates of Infant Mortality: A Cross-National and Longitudinal Analysis of 63 Countries," *Social Biology* 22:315–25.

Sidel, Victor W., and Ruth Sidel. 1983. *A Healthy State: An International Perspective on the Crisis in United States Medical Care*. New York: Pantheon.

Skocpol, Theda. 1980. "Political Response to Capitalist Crisis: Neo-Marxist Theories of the State and the Case of the New Deal," *Politics and Society* 10:155–201.

1985a. "What Is Happening to Western Welfare States," *Contemporary Sociology* 14:307–11.

1985b. "Bringing the State Back In: Strategies of Analysis in Current Research," in Peter B. Evans, Dietrich Rueschemeyer, and Theda Skocpol (eds.), *Bringing the State Back In*, pp. 3–37. New York: Cambridge University Press.

and Edwin Amenta. 1986. "States and Social Policies," *Annual Review of Sociology* 12:131–57.

and John Ikenberry. 1983. "The Political Formation of the American Welfare State in Historical and Comparative Perspective," *Comparative Social Research* 6:87–148.

Smeeding, Timothy, and Barbara Boyle Torrey. 1986. "An International Perspective on the Income and Poverty Status of the U.S. Aged: Lessons from the Luxembourg Income Study," *Luxembourg Income Study Working Paper 9*, Luxembourg.

Snyder, David, and Edward L. Kick. 1979. "Structural Position in the World System and Economic Growth, 1955–1970: Mutliple-Network Analysis of Transnational Interactions," *American Journal of Sociology* 84:1096–1126.

Stack, Steven. 1978. "The Effects of Political Participation and Socialist Party Strength on the Degree of Income Inequality," *American Sociological Review* 44:168–71.

Statistics Sweden. 1986. *Statistical Abstract of Sweden*. Stockholm: Statistics Sweden.

Statistiches Bundesant. 1986. *Statistiches Jahrbuch*. Weisbaden: Statistiches Bundesant.

Stephens, John D. 1979. *The Transition from Capitalism to Socialism*. London: Macmillan.

1984. "Class, Power, and Pensions," *Contemporary Sociology* 14:29–32.

Stigler, George J. 1970. "Director's Law of Public Income Redistribution," *Journal of Law and Economics* 13:1–10.

Stimson, James A. 1985. "Regression in Space and Time: A Statistical Essay," *American Journal of Political Science* 29:914–47.

Stinchcombe, Arthur L. 1968. *Constructing Social Theories*. New York: Harcourt Brace and World.

1985. "The Functional Theory of Social Insurance," *Politics and Society* 14:411–30.

Stockwell, E. G., J. W. Wicks, and D. J. Adamchak. 1978. "Research Needed on Socioeconomic Differentials in U.S. Mortality," *Public Health Reports* 93:666–72.

Storey, James R. 1983. "Older Americans in the Reagan Era: Impacts of Federal Policy Changes." Washington, D.C.: Urban Institute.

Summers, Robert, and Alan Heston. 1984. "Improved International Comparisons of Real Product and Its Composition: 1950–1980," *Review of Income and Wealth* 30:207–62.

Szymanski, Albert. 1978. *The Capitalist State and the Politics of Class*. Cambridge, Mass.: Winthrop.

Taylor, Charles Lewis (ed.). 1983. *Why Governments Grow*. Beverly Hills, Calif.: Sage.

and David A. Jodice (eds.). 1983. *World Handbook of Political and Social Indicators III: 1948–77*. Ann Arbor: Inter-American University Consortium for Political and Social Research.

Thurow, Lester C. 1981. *The Zero-Sum Society*. New York: Penguin Books.

Tilton, Timothy. 1986. "Perspectives on the Welfare State," *in* Norman Furniss (ed.), *Futures of the Welfare State*, pp. 13–40. Bloomington: Indiana University Press.

Tomasson, Richard F. 1984. "Government Old Age Pensions Under Affluence and Austerity: West Germany, Sweden, the Netherlands, and the United States," *Research in Social Problems and Public Policy* 3:217–72.

Torrey, Barbara Boyle. 1982. "Guns vs. Canes: The Fiscal Implications of An Aging Population," *American Economic Review* 72:309–13.

Treas, Judith. 1983. "Trickle Down or Transfers? Postwar Determinants of Family Income Inequality," *American Sociological Review* 48:546–59.

    and Robin Jane Walther. 1978. "Family Structure and the Distribution of Family Income," *Social Forces* 56:866–80.

Trussell, James, and Anne R. Pebley. 1984. "The Potential Impact of Changes in Fertility on Infant, Child, and Maternal Mortality," *Studies in Family Planning* 15:267–80.

Tufte, Edward R. 1978. *Political Control of the Economy*. Princeton, N.J.: Princeton University Press.

U.S. Bureau of the Census. 1975. *Historical Statistics of the United States, Colonial Times to 1970*. Washington, D.C.: U.S. Government Printing Office.

U.S. Social Security Administration. 1981. *Social Security Throughout the World*. Washington, D.C.: U.S. Government Printing Office.

Vanneman, Reeve, and Lynn Weber Cannon. 1988. *The American Perception of Class*. Philadelphia: Temple University Press.

Wagner, Adolf. 1983 [1883]. "The Nature of the Fiscal Economy," *in* Richard A. Musgrove and Alan R. Peacock (eds.), *Classics in the Theory of Public Finance*, pp. 1–8. London: Macmillan.

Wagner, Richard E., and Warren E. Weber. 1977. "Wagner's Law, Fiscal Institutions, and the Growth of Government," *National Tax Journal* 30:59–68.

Wall Street Journal. 1985. "Senior Citizens Mobilize to Block Plan to Curb Social Security Benefits," April 17:1.

Wallerstein, Immanuel. 1974. "The Rise and Future Demise of the World Capitalist System: Concepts for Comparative Analysis," *Comparative Studies in Society and History* 16:387–415.

Walton, John. 1986. *Sociology and Critical Inquiry: The Work, Tradition, and Purpose*. Chicago: Dorsey.

Weatherby, Norman L., Charles B. Nam, and Larry W. Isaac. 1983. "Development, Inequality, Health Care, and Mortality at the Older Ages: A Cross-National Analysis," *Demography* 20:27–43.

Weede, Erich. 1980. "Beyond Misspecification in Sociological Analyses of Income Inequality," *American Sociological Review* 45:497–501.

    1982. "The Effects of Democracy and Socialist Strength on the Size of Distribution of Income: Some More Evidence," *International Journal of Comparative Sociology* 23:151–65.

    and Horst Tiefenbach. 1981. "Some Recent Explanations of Income Inequality: An Evaluation and Critique," *International Studies Quarterly* 25:255–82.

Weir, Margaret, and Theda Skocpol. 1985. "State Structures and the Possibilities for 'Keynesian' Responses to the Great Depression in Sweden, Britain, and the United States," *in* Peter B. Evans, Dietrich Rueschemeyer, and Theda Skocpol (eds.), *Bringing the State Back In*, pp. 107–63. Cambridge: Cambridge University Press.

Wildavsky, Aaron. 1985. "The Logic of Public Sector Growth," *in* Jan-Erik Lane (ed.), *State and Market: The Politics of the Public and Private*, pp. 231–70. London: Sage.

Wilensky, Harold L. 1968. "Women's Work: Economic Growth, Ideology, and Social Structure," *Industrial Relations* 7:235–48.

1975. *The Welfare State and Equality: Structural and Ideological Roots of Public Expenditures.* Berkeley: University of California Press.

1976. *The "New Corporatism," Centralization, and the Welfare State.* Beverley Hills, Calif.: Sage.

1981. "Leftism, Catholicism, and Democratic Corporatism: The Role of Political Parties in Recent Welfare State Development," in Peter Flora and Arnold J. Heidenheimer (eds.), *The Development of Welfare States in Europe and America,* pp. 345–82. New Brunswick, N.J.: Transaction Books.

and Charles N. Lebeaux. 1958. *Industrial Society and Social Welfare.* New York: Russell Sage.

Williamson, Jeffrey G. 1985. *Did British Capitalism Breed Inequality?* Boston: Allen & Unwin.

and Peter H. Lindert. 1980. *American Inequality: A Macroeconomic History.* New York: Academic Press.

Williamson, John B. 1987. "Social Security and Physical Quality of Life in Developing Nations: A Cross-National Analysis," *Social Indicators Research* 19:205–28.

Linda Evans, and Lawrence A. Powell. 1982. *The Politics of Aging: Power and Policy.* Springfield, Ill.: Charles C. Thomas.

and Fred C. Pampel. 1986. "Social Security and the Welfare State: A Cross-National Analysis," *International Journal of Comparative Sociology* 27:15–30.

and Joseph W. Weiss. 1979. "Egalitarian Political Movements, Social Welfare Effort and Convergence Theory: A Cross-National Analysis," *Comparative Social Research* 2:289–302.

Wolfinger, Raymond E., and Stephen J. Rosenstone. 1980. *Who Votes?* New Haven, Conn.: Yale University Press.

World Bank. 1983. *World Tables,* 3rd ed., Volumes I and II. Baltimore: Johns Hopkins University Press.

World Health Organization. 1982. *Infant Mortality in Eastern Europe, 1950–1980.* Budapest: Statistical Publishing House.

Wright, Erik Olin. 1985. *Classes.* London: Verso.

and Bill Martin. 1987. "The Transformation of the American Class Structure, 1960–1980," *American Journal of Sociology* 93:1–29.

Zald, Mayer N. 1985. "Political Change, Citizenship Rights, and the Welfare State," *Annals, American Academy of Political and Social Science* 479:48–66.

Index

Other books in the series

J. Milton Yinger, Kiyoshi Ikeda, Frank Laycock, and Stephen J. Cutler: *Middle Start: An Experiment in the Educational Enrichment of Young Adolescents*

James A. Geschwender: *Class, Race, and Worker Insurgency: The League of Revolutionary Black Workers*

Paul Ritterband: *Education, Employment, and Migration: Israel in Comparative Perspective*

John Low-Beer: *Protest and Participation: The New Working Class in Italy*

Orin E. Klapp: *Opening and Closing: Strategies of Information Adaptation in Society*

Rita James Simon: *Continuity and Change: A Study of Two Ethnic Communities in Israel*

Marshall B. Clinard: *Cities with Little Crime: The Case of Switzerland**

Steven T. Bossert: *Tasks and Social Relationships in Classrooms: A Study of Instructional Organization and Its Consequences**

Richard E. Johnson: *Juvenile Delinquency and Its Origins: An Integrated Theoretical Approach**

David R. Heise: *Understanding Events: Affect and the Construction of Social Action*

Ida Harper Simpson: *From Student to Nurse: A Longitudinal Study of Socialization*

Stephen P. Turner: *Sociological Explanation as Translation*

Janet W. Salaff: *Working Daughters of Hong Kong: Filial Piety or Power in the Family?*

Joseph Chamie: *Religion and Fertility: Arab Christian–Muslim Differentials*

William Friedland, Amy Barton, Robert Thomas: *Manufacturing Green Gold: Capital, Labor, and Technology in the Lettuce Industry*

Richard N. Adams: *Paradoxical Harvest: Energy and Explanation in British History, 1870–1914*

Mary F. Rogers: *Sociology, Ethnomethodology, and Experience: A Phenomenological Critique*

James R. Beniger: *Trafficking in Drug Users: Professional Exchange Networks in the Control of Deviance*

Andrew J. Weigert, J. Smith Teitge, and Dennis W. Teitge: *Society and Identity: Toward a Sociological Psychology*

Jon Miller: *Pathways in the Workplace: The Effects of Race and Gender on Access to Organizational Resources*

Michael A. Faia: *Dynamic Functionalism: Strategy and Tactics*

Joyce Rothschild and J. Allen Whitt: *The Co-operative Workplace: Potentials and Dilemmas of Organizational Democracy*

Russell Thornton: *We Shall Live Again: The 1870 and 1890 Ghost Dance Movements as Demographic Revitalization*

Severyn T. Bruyn: *The Field of Social Investment*

Guy E. Swanson: *Ego Defenses and the Legitimation of Behaviour*

Liah Greenfeld: *Different Worlds: A Sociological Study of Taste, Choice and Success in Art*

Thomas K. Rudel: *Situations and Strategies in American Land-Use Planning*

Percy C. Hintzen: *The Costs of Regime Survival: Racial Mobilization, Elite Domination and Control of the State in Guyana and Trinidad*

John T. Flint: *Historical Role Analysis in the Study of Religious Change: Mass Educational Development in Norway, 1740–1891*

Judith R. Blau: *The Shape of Culture: A Study of Cultural Patterns in the United States*

*Available from the American Sociological Association, 1722 N Street, N.W., Washington, DC 20036.